Rossica 17

INTERNATIONAL REVIEW OF RUSSIAN CULTURE

FOUND in TRANSLATION

I RECEIVED
WHAT
PASSED FOR
A NORMAL
LITERARY
EDUCATION.
MY MOTHER
TOLD ME
THE TALES
OF HANS
CHRISTIAN
ANDERSEN,
LAFONTAINE

AND
PERRAULT;
MY FATHER,
WHO HAD
HAD A
CLASSICAL
FORMATION,
RECITED
AESOP AND
HOMER.
I SPENT
HOLIDAYS IN
FRANCE IN

COMPANY WITH ASTERIX AND TINTIN; IN AUSTRIA WITH THE BROTHERS GRIMM; IN ITALY WITH PINOCCHIO. I FELL IN LOVE WITH YOUNG WERTHER AND THE POEMS OF SEFERIS

FOUND IN TRANSLATION

М. В. Ломоносов (с портрета худ. Л. С. Миропольского, 1787 года)

This special issue is devoted to the Rossica Translation Prize, awarded this year for the second time.

Illustrations by Alexander Florensky who lives and works in St Petersburg.

Rossica – a word coined in 18th-century Europe, denoting all that relates to Russia.

Russian culture has always been inextricably linked to wider traditions, in a constant exchange of ideas, literature, music and art. ROSSICA journal seeks to foster such links and contacts today, providing a window on Russian culture for audiences across the world, keeping them informed of the most interesting Russian cultural events in Russia, Britain and further afield.

ROSSICA is published by ACADEMIA ROSSICA, a non-profit organisation (UK Registered Charity no 1091022) created in 2000 with the aim of promoting a deeper international understanding of Russian culture and of assisting in Russia's further integration into the world community.

Subscribe to the Rossica journal and ACADEMIA ROSSICA E-NEWS on www.academia-rossica.org

CONTENTS

письменный прибор

WRITING SET

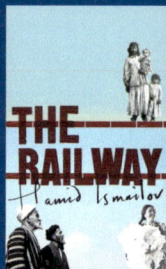

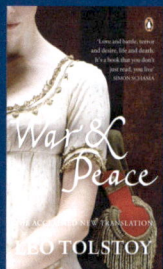

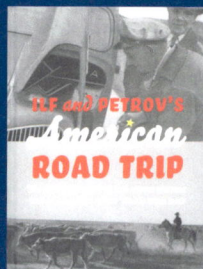

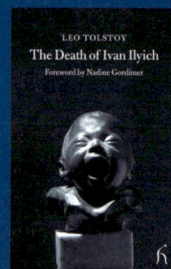

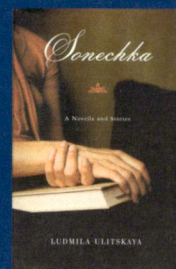

THE ROSSICA PRIZE

2007

The only award in the world for literary translation from Russian into English, the Rossica Prize was established in 2004. It is a biennial award, made to both the translator and publisher of the work that the panel of judges considers to be the best translation of the past two years.

The discovery of Russian literature in the late 19th and early 20th century, it has been remarked, was an event as important to British culture as the impact of renaissance Italy on the England of Shakespeare and Marlowe. It is hardly surprising, therefore, how constant the curiosity of the English-speaking world in Russian literature has been ever since. The Rossica Prize for Literary Translation was established to encourage, promote and support the efforts both of translators who are indispensable in this work, and of the publishers who appreciate the value of their efforts.

гусиное перо
GOOSE - QUILL

Because the prize is awarded for a translation, and not the original work, the range of submitted titles is extraordinarily wide and rich. From the great and universally familiar classics of the 19th century to the latest novels of the early 21st century, from travelogue to poetry. As each new panel of judges has remarked, alongside the familiar and predictable there are always surprises: new authors, forgotten works, novel genres – as indeed there should be, when the Rossica Prize reflects the rich traditions and living growth of Russian literature.

Since the Rossica prize was first awarded in 2005 other awards have followed its lead – in France where Russophonie rewards translations into French and, soon, in Spain where a similar prize is being established. In its turn, British Council established The Lion and Unicorn Prizes in Moscow which are awarded for translation of prose and poetry from English into Russian language.

WINNER

Joanne Turnbull and Glas / New Russian Writing (Moscow 2006)
for Sigizmund Krzhizhanovsky, *7 Stories*
A wonderfully bizarre set of fables by a recently discovered writer of the Soviet
1920s, rendered into an assured and atmospheric translation that in English takes
on a convincing life of its own.

SPECIAL COMMENDATION

Robert Chandler and Harvill Secker (London 2006)
for Hamid Izmailov, *The Railway*
In recognition both of the merits of this particular rendition, and of the excellent work
that Robert Chandler has done over the years in bringing Russian literature to the
English reader

SHORTLISTED

Hugh Aplin and Hesperus Press (London 2005)
for Leo Tolstoy, *The Death of Ivan Ilyich*

Anthony Briggs and Penguin Books (London 2005)
for Leo Tolstoy, *War and Peace*

Anne O. Fisher and Princeton Architectural Press (New York 2006)
for *Ilya Ilf and Evgeny Petrov, Ilf & Petrov's American Road-Trip:
The 1935 Travelogue of Two Soviet Writers*

Arch Tait and Schocken Books (New York 2005)
for *Ludmila Ulitskaya, Sonechka, a Novella and Stories*

AR PARTNERS

The Foundation of the First President of Russia, Boris Yeltsin

The Foundation was established in Moscow
in 2000 as an independent charitable
organisation. Its primary aim is to create an
environment which will help the younger
generation to fulfil its creative potential. The
Foundation strives to promote humanitarian
and cultural cooperation and an open
exchange of ideas and information between
Russia and the West.

London Review of Books

'The London Review of Books is the liveliest,
the most serious and also the most radical
literary magazine we have,' Alan Bennett.
Since its establishment in 1979, the LRB has
provided leading writers, critics and thinkers
with a platform to develop and express their
ideas at length and in depth.

British Council

The British Council promotes cultural
links across the globe, building mutually
beneficial relationships and understanding
between people in the UK and other
countries. The British Council's Literature
Department has made literature in
translation a priopity: 'translation of
literatures into and from English is one of
the most successful and straightforward
ways of encouraging an understanding
and appreciation of other cultures.'

Apostolic Saints Kirill and Methodios
The Source of Russian Literacy

The Rossica Prize is awarded on 24 May the Day of Apostolic Saints Kirill and Methodios, the creators of Slavic alphabet.

The creation of an alphabet suited to the languages of the Slav family of nations is one of Byzantium's greatest contributions to Russian culture. Two Greek brothers, the Apostolic Saints Kyrill and Methodios, were responsible for this enormously significant achievement. Never in their lives did they set foot in the lands of early mediaeval Russia and they lived and died a century before Grand Prince Vladimir of Kiev had his people formally admitted to the Christian faith. Yet by creating the Slavic alphabet they laid the foundations for Russian literature and opened Christian and Hellenic cultures to Slavic peoples.

Born in Salonika, Kyrill was the youngest and Methodios, the eldest of the eight sons of a noble military leader. Methodios (820-885 AD) served in the Imperial army and for ten years was governor of one of Byzantium's Slavic provinces. He then retreated to a monastery in Asia Minor. Kyrill (c. 827-869), a gifted but sickly boy, was adopted by the court of Michael III as a schoolmate for the prince. Taught by the best instructors of the day, Kyrill studied Classical literature, rhetoric and the full panoply of traditional learning as well as Greek, Latin, Hebrew, Arabic and the Slavic languages he and his brother Methodios had known from childhood. Among his teachers was Photios, the famed future Patriarch of Constantinople. Subsequently Kyrill was appointed librarian of Hagia Sophia and would teach Greek and Christian philosophy in the most advanced school of the Empire.

In about 860 AD the brothers left on a mission to convert the Khazars to Christianity. Passing through Chersoneses of Tauride Kyrill and Methodios discovered the relics of St Clement, the early Bishop (Pope) of Rome. Having baptised some two hundred Khazars and taken with them the Greek slaves released into their charge, they returned to Byzantium. With them they also carried the remains of St Clement. In a secluded monastery within the capital the brothers then set about devising an alphabet for the Slavs.

No universal opinion exists among scholars as to which alphabet Kyrill and Methodios created. Was it Cyrillic, named in honour of the younger brother, the alphabet familiar today in Russia, Bulgaria, Serbia, the Ukraine, Belorussia and among a further sixty nations across the world? Or was it the earlier Glagolitic script with its more complex forms that were derived, it is thought, from Hebrew and Aramaic? Until the 10-11th centuries the two alphabets were equally in use. Thereafter Cyrillic completely displaced Glagolitic. Twenty-five of the letters, used then as now in Cyrillic script, were borrowed from Greek while a further 18 were added to convey sounds only found in the early Slavonic languages.

With the help of his brother Methodios, Kyrill first translated the Gospels, Epistles and Psalter into Slavonic – the texts essential for the liturgy. In 863 the emperor sent the brothers to the aid of Prince Rostislav of Moravia (today part of the Czech republic). The Bishop of Bavaria was claiming jurisdiction over the territory while the German princes, led by Ludwig, wished to conquer and annex the Moravian lands. War broke out and, forced out by the hostility of the Latinate German clergy, Kyrill and Methodios decided to return to Constantinople with their Moravian converts. On arrival in Venice a council of the local bishopric was summoned and the brothers were accused of violating the rule whereby services might only be conducted in one of three languages: Greek, Latin and Hebrew.

Since the 9th century it had been permitted to preach in the local language but Kyrill and Methodios had also conducted services in what would become Church Slavonic. Faced by this apparent failure the brothers clutched at any straw of hope and turned to Pope Adrian III. He welcomed them in grand style at his palace, in part perhaps because they brought with them the remains of his canonised predecessor Clement. Strange to relate, Adrian gave approval to their translation of biblical and liturgical texts into Slavonic, consecrated several of their followers as priests and even permitted the Slavonic liturgy to be performed in St Peter's. It was then that Kyrill, who had never been in good health, departed this life. At first his body was laid to rest in the vault where deceased Popes were buried. Later, at the request of Methodios, his remains were transferred to the church of St Clements in Rome.

It was 869 AD. Kyrill died on 14 February and towards the end of that year Adrian elevated Methodios to the bishopric of Moravia and Pannonia. Services might be held in Slavonic in the new bishop's eparchate on condition that the Gospel and Epistle were first read in Latin and then in Church Slavonic. This accommodating arrangement was given no chance to get established, however.

In 870 Methodios returned to Pannonia but that same year he was called before Adelwine, the Archbishop of Salzburg, and accused of encroaching on the latter's preserve. Three harsh years of imprisonment followed and it was only after the accession of a new Pope, John VIII, that Methodios was released and able to return to Moravia to resume conducting the liturgy in the Slavic language.

After the Great Schism of 1054 began to separate the church in East and West the Christians of Moravia and of other parts of the future Czechoslovakia and Croatia became part of Western Christendom. Yet the great work of spiritual education and enlightenment begun by Kyrill and Methodios did not fail and in time bore great fruit.

Кирилл и Мефодий
CYRIL & METHODIUS

Elaine Feinstein was educated at Newham College, Cambridge and was made a Fellow of the Royal Society of Literature in 1980. She has written fourteen novels, radio plays, television dramas, and five biographies. In 1990, she received a Cholmondeley Award for Poetry, and was given an Honorary D.Litt from the University of Leicester. She has been invited to read her work at international festivals across the world. She has been a Writer in Residence for the British Council in Singapore, and Tromso, Norway, and a Rockefeller Foundation Fellow at Bellagio in 1998. Her *Collected Poems and Translations* (2002) was a Poetry Book Society Special Commendation. Her biography of Anna Akhmatova, *Anna of All the Russias* was published in July 2005.

Peter France is Professor Emeritus of the University of Edinburgh. He has published widely on French, Russian and Comparative Literature, including *Poets of Modern Russia* (1982) and is the editor of the *Oxford Guide to Literature in English Translation* and the five-volume *Oxford History of Literary Translation in English* (2005-). His translations from Russian include collections of poetry by Aleksandr Blok and Boris Pasternak (both with Jon Stallworthy) and several volumes of the poetry of Gennady Aygi.

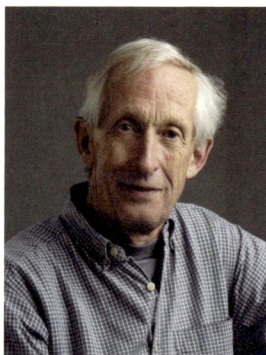

Catriona Kelly is Professor of Russian at the University of Oxford, and a Fellow of New College. She has published widely on Russian literature and cultural history, including *Russian Literature: A Very Short Introduction* (OUP 2001), and *Comrade Pavlik: The Rise and Fall of a Soviet Boy Hero* (Granta 2005). She is the editor of *Utopias: Russian Modernist Texts*, 1905-1940 (Penguin, 1999), and of *An Anthology of Russian Women's Writing*, 1777-1992 (OUP 1994). Both these collections included works that she had translated herself, and she has published numerous other translations of Russian poetry and prose, by Mayakovsky, Elena Shvarts, Olga Sedakova, Sergei Kaledin, Leonid Borodin, among others.

Judges' Statement

The Judges assessed a total of 29 books published in 2005 and 2006 (as against 37 for the four-year time-span covered by the 2005 Prize). The majority were submitted by publishers, but a small number were added at the Judges' request (see paragraph 4 of the Rules). It was decided that the expression 'literary translation' should be interpreted in a reasonably broad sense to include such texts as memoirs, letters and diaries.

The entries included books of many different kinds. Nearly half were translations of texts by classic authors: Pushkin (3), Dostoevsky (3), Tolstoy (2), Lermontov, Goncharov, Chekhov, and the modern classics Mayakovsky, Bulgakov, Ilf and Petrov. The other twentieth-century titles covered a wide range: memoirs and similar texts (4), recent poetry (4) and fiction (7). Fiction ranged from experimental writing to recent commercial successes, though we were disappointed by the small number of outstanding entries in the field of the contemporary novel. Several of the translators were established professionals, one being responsible for as many as 5 separate entries (it might be desirable in future to place a limit on the number of translations to be submitted by any one translator). In the case of texts which had been partially published in earlier years, the assessment of the translation was based only on newly published material.

The disparate nature of the entries gave rise to some discussion about criteria — how was one to compare a new translation of *War and Peace* with a popular detective story or with a slim bilingual collection of verse? We agreed that the primary consideration must be the quality of the translation. To reach the short list it was necessary for the translation to stand up in its own right as a rewarding piece of writing, while at the same time doing justice to the (in these cases very varied) qualities of the original. Our usual practice was therefore to begin by reading the English text and only then to compare it to the Russian in terms of accuracy, tone and style.

It was not easy to pick an overall winner. We were impressed by the quality of all the entries placed on the short list and several others besides. Judging the competition was for all of us a demanding but rewarding business, which impressed on us the value of the work being done by a relatively small number of publishers and translators in keeping Russian literature, both new and old, at the forefront of the literary scene in the English-speaking world. Academia Rossica is to be applauded on encouraging this important work, and it is to be hoped that the Prize will stimulate further translations, particularly in the field of contemporary fiction.

THE ROSSICA PRIZE COMMITTEE

Балалайка
BALALAIKA

Шекспир
SHAKESPEAR

Балалайка
BALALAIKA

Шекспир
SHAKESPEAR

валенки
VALENKI

The committee is an invaluable part of the Rossica Prize project. Its members' professionalism and longstanding expertise in various areas of the production and promotion of literature in translation enables Academia Rossica to conduct this, the only prize of its kind worldwide. The committee's unfailing support contributes greatly to the Prize's continuing success, as well as its growing reputation. The members of the committee are:

Prof. John Elsworth, academic and translator, Professor Emeritus of the University of Manchester, John specialises in Russian literature, principally the early twentieth century with a particular interest in the life and works of Andrey Bely (1880-1934).

Amanda Hopkinson, Director of the British Centre for Literary Translation, Amanda translates from Spanish, Portuguese, and French, most recently *Dead Horsemeat* by Dominique Manotti and *Money to Burn* by Ricardo Piglia. She is the Chair of the Writers in Translation Committee of English PEN.

Christopher MacLehose, publisher. Christopher was successively Literary Editor of The Scotsman, Editorial Director of Chatto & Windus and William Collins / HarperCollins and Publisher-at-Large of Harvill Press and Harvill Secker. In 2006 he was awarded the London Book Fair Lifetime Achievement Award in International Publishing.

Susanna Nicklin, Director of Literature at the British Council. Susanna became Director of English PEN in 2002 and joined the British Council as Director of Literature in October 2005. While at PEN, she initiated the Writers in Translation programme. At the British Council, literature in the Russian Federation will be one of her areas of concern.

Dr Alastair Niven OBE, President and Chair of the Executive Committee of English PEN and Principal of the King George VI and Queen Elizabeth Foundation of St. Catharine's at Cumberland Lodge in Windsor.

Boyd Tonkin, Literary Editor of *The Independent* since 1996 and founder of The Independent Foreign Fiction Prize. Before that Boyd worked for *New Statesman* as social policy editor and became Literary Editor at the *New Statesman* in 1991.

Alexander Drozdov, journalist, Executive Director of the Foundation of the First President of Russia, Boris Yeltsin.

Svetlana Adjoubei, art historian, Founding Director of ACADEMIA ROSSICA and Editor-in-Chief of ROSSICA.

TRIBUTE TO THE FIRST PRESIDENT OF RUSSIA, BORIS YELTSIN

Since its inception the Rossica Prize has been supported by the Boris Yeltsin Foundation.

'The end of an era.' In the days following the death of Boris Yeltsin on 23 April 2007 this phrase was on the lips of many. It is a banal and misleading assertion. Thankfully, the achievements of the first President of Russia have not vanished into thin air, they today remained embodied in the civil rights and liberties of our country's citizens, Russia's market economy, its political system and all the other institutions established since 1991.

The true value of the legacy, bequeathed to his country by Boris Yeltsin, lies precisely in the open view he took of the world, and the totality and modern nature of his outlook. Our task is to recognise this legacy as part of our common attainment as a society and prove ourselves capable of managing it properly. At the very least we follow Yeltsin's own example and make of our lives a model of that civil society towards which Russia is striving. No one can command this to happen. It can only arise when we feel a profound awareness of our personal responsibility, to our country and our fellow citizens. Yeltsin's life as a political leader was an unbroken succession of such acts of civic courage.

Today it is easy to question the decisions made in the 1990s. The first President of a free Russia can no longer answer for himself. Even in his lifetime Yeltsin was not over fond of discussing his time in office. He preferred to leave the comments to his compatriots and the verdict, to history. Especially since it was from his hands that the citizens of Russia received an unlimited freedom to openly express their own opinions for the first time in many decades. Freedom of speech and the free exchange of ideas were sacred principles for Boris Yeltsin.

It is the goal of the Yeltsin Foundation to preserve and expand his legacy. The experience of the Rossica Prize in the English-speaking world, and those that have followed – the Russian Prize in the CIS, the Russophonie award in France and the forthcoming prize for the Hispanophone countries – are thus of great importance to our foundation, for they embody Boris Yeltsin's love of his native tongue and his conviction that literature, culture and the arts transcend all national borders.

A man of unmistakable, original and colourfully Russian character, Yeltsin was at the same time wholly open to the world. Having led the breakthrough to freedom, he proved that Russia could become a different country. He believed that Russia would never return to the past: it is now up to us to show the same conviction and determination.

Alexander Drozdov
Executive Director of the First President of Russia Boris Yeltsin Foundation

{As Judged By}

почтовые лошади

Elaine Feinstein

My role in this judging process has been that of a writer in the English language, rather than an expert on the accuracy of translation from the Russian. I have had a good deal of experience in translating poetry from Russian, usually, though not always, with the assistance of a Russianist, and most notably working on the poems of Marina Tsvetaeva. The skills I brought to that enterprise were those of a poet rather than a linguist. I have never translated prose, though I have written many novels.

The books we had to consider for the Rossica Prize were widely disparate in period, size and ambition. There were translations from major works of Pushkin, Tolstoy, Dostoevsky, Goncharov, and Chekhov, alongside twentieth century fables such as Bulgakov's *The Heart of a Dog*, Boris Akunin's ingenious detective stories, travel writing, and the history of unfamiliar areas of the Soviet Union. There were also several contemporary writers whose names were altogether unfamiliar to me, and I am hoping this prize may encourage more publishers to risk editions of such worthwhile recent writings.

Among these submissions were books of Hamid Ismailov, Sigizmund Krzhizhanovsky, and Ludmila Ulitskaya. Ismailov's *Railway*, in Robert Chandler's lucid translation, uncovers a little-known world of a small town in Uzbekistan, and brings to life a whole cast of exotic characters whose stories have surprising contemporary resonance. Joanne Turnbull has a harder task in translating Krzhizhanovsky's strange stories. He is

a writer who trusts a bizarre logic – akin to that of Borges – which takes the reader to the very edge of sanity. What is astonishing is not that he was 'known for being unknown', but that his genius survived Soviet disapproval to be rediscovered long after his death. Ludmila Ulitskaya's novella, *Sonechka*, on the other hand, opens a book of short stories – quiet, poignant tales, all translated by Arch Tait with seeming transparency.

Discussion among the panel of judges was amicable, though we did not find it easy to arrive at a short list. For myself, I was particularly taken by Anthony Briggs amazingly fresh version of Tolstoy's *War and Peace*, which will make it possible for a whole generation of new readers to find themselves caught up in that great novel. However, Hugh Aplin's version of Tolstoy's *The Death of Ivan Ilyich*, a much blacker and briefer tale, was equally striking, and I should have been unhappy to see either of them fall off the list in order to avoid Tolstoy appearing twice. Our last choice for the shortlist was Ilf and Petrov: writers of great charm, although it has to be said that their description of travels across America, would not have discomfited a Soviet reader with any iconoclastic observations.

Those who share my respect for Antony Wood's dedication to the translation of the works of Alexander Pushkin will be disappointed not to find him included here. I think it fair to say he was the most contentious of our exclusions. But it is the nature of any prize which commands some of the greatest names in world literature to present peculiarly hard choices.

меч

весы

Фемида

Peter France

I was one of the lucky 5,000 who learned Russian by way of military service – in Bloomsbury and on Bodmin Moor. Studying all day and every day for 18 months gave us a pretty good knowledge of the language, including how to say things like 'axial-flow compressor', but a cold-war course of this kind didn't set out to instil a love of Russia and its culture. If we read Russian literature (such things as Polevoy's worthy *Story about a Real Man*), it was so as to learn as many words as possible. Luckily, however, some of our teachers were émigré Russians who loved their writers, so that when I went on to study Russian at Oxford, I was ready to lose myself in the world of Pushkin and Dostoevsky.

On graduating, I specialised in French literature. But Russian did not go away, indeed it was given a new lease of life for me by Jon Stallworthy's suggestion that he and I work together on translations of Blok and Pasternak. So it was as a translator, not an academic, that I continued to explore Russian literature, translating some prose and a great deal of poetry. In particular I became a friend of the Chuvash and Russian poet Gennady Aygi, translated several books of his poetry, and had many visits to him in Russia and Chuvashia.

Subsequently I acquired a Russian son-in-law, the painter Gennady Gogoliuk, some of my grandchildren are baptised in the Orthodox Church, and all of this has kept me close to Russia, even if I have never been a professional Slavist. It was therefore a great pleasure to be asked to judge this year's Rossica Prize. It has been fascinating to watch some excellent translators at work, to see how they face the formidable challenges of the best Russian writing. Pushkin's poetry is often declared 'untranslatable' (though isn't this true of all writing, if one sets the bar too high?), but I have admired the dedicated work in this field of two translators who for different reasons did not make the shortlist, Antony Wood and Roger Clarke. Modern prose can be almost equally fraught with challenges of tone and register, and several of our short-listed translators rose to them splendidly. And since we have been comparing translations with originals, I have found myself reading or rereading a variety of Russian texts in their own right; spurred on by Anthony Briggs's popular translation, I have started on another hike through the Russian *War and Peace* – as I write I am excitedly approaching the battle of Borodino.

Quite a lot of the entries were old acquaintances in a new guise, but there have also been some fascinating discoveries in the writing of the last 80 years, from contemporary poetry to the 1935 American journey of Ilf and Petrov, from the remarkable and unpronounceable Sigizmund Krzhizhanovsky – a writer of the twenties and thirties who has only just burst upon the Russian literary scene – to Hamid Ismailov, author of a wry yet poetic epic of Uzbek life. Not the least interesting were autobiographical writings such as Vasily Grossman's war diaries and *The Silent Steppe*, Mukhamet Shayakhmetov's moving story of his long and difficult life in Kazakhstan. My only regret is that there were only one or two really distinguished representatives of contemporary Russian literature; I hope the Rossica prize will encourage publishers to give us more of the excellent work that is being written today.

SIGIZMUND KRZHIZHANOVSKY

TRANSLATED BY JOANNE TURNBULL

7 STORIES

WINNER

Joanne Turnbull and Glas / New Russian
Writing for Sigizmund Krzhizhanovsky, *Seven Stories*. A
wonderfully bizarre set of fables by a recently rediscovered
writer of the Soviet 1920s, rendered into an assured
and atmospheric translation that in English takes on a
convincing life of its own.

Sigizmund Krzhizhanovsky (1887-1950) was born in Kiev to Polish Catholic parents, their only son, highly musical. As an adolescent, he read Kant's *Critique of Pure Reason*, a deeply unsettling experience: 'Before it had all seemed so simple: things cast shadows, but now it turned out that shadows cast things, or perhaps things did not exist at all.' Soon after, he encountered Shakespeare: 'The translation was rough and inexact, but suddenly I felt that I had a friend who could protect me from the metaphysical delusion.' Krzhizhanovsky took a degree in law while mastering six languages and exploring Europe. After the Revolution and a brief stint in the Red Army, he began lecturing in Kiev on the psychology of creativity, the history and theory of the theater, literature and music. But it was his move to Moscow (a quasi-character in many of his stories) in 1922 that galvanized his fiction: philosophical 'novellas', as he called them, with fantastical plots. Many of Krzhizhanovksy's heroes have lost their moorings in an illogical world whose margins they inhabit: 'I don't understand,' says one. 'Understanding,' comes the reply, 'is strictly forbidden.' 'Instead of inventing all those patent medicines for toothache and the common cold,' says another, 'science ought to come up with something for remorse.' Steady rejections by Soviet editors and eventually Gorky himself forced this Swiftian satirist to resort to other forms in order to eat: dramatizations of Chesterton's *The Man Who Was Thursday* and Pushkin's *Eugene Onegin*; articles on 'Laconism and the Psychological Novel' for the *Great Soviet Encyclopedia*; essays on the dramaturgy of the chessboard and the art of the epigraph, on Shaw and Shakespeare. The censors still found fault. Krzhizhanovsky's belated acceptance, in 1939, into the Writers' Union did not help him, but did afford his writings a berth in the State Archive of Literature and Arts, where they were unearthed a quarter of a century after his death. A quarter of a century after that, the publication of Krzhizhanovsky's collected works in Russian began – bearing out his belief that his reader would come in fifty years' time.

Joanne Turnbull has translated a number of books from Russian, including *The Grassy Street* by Asar Eppel, *Stamp Album* by Andrei Sergeev, *Here I Am* by Lev Rubinstein, *The Diary of a Soviet Schoolgirl: 1932-1937* by Nina Lugovskaya, and *Ivan the Fool: Russian Folk Belief* by Andrei Sinyavsky – all published by GLAS/New Russian Writing. She is currently at work on another selection of Krzhizhanovsky, this time for NYRB Classics. She has lived in Moscow since 1987.

Seven Stories

Written between 1922 and 1939, these remarkable stories attest to Krzhizhanovsky's boundless imagination, black humor and breathtaking irony. A man loses his way in the vast black waste of his own small room. A woman's former lovers wind up confined to the recesses of her pupil. The rebellious hand of a famous pianist flees a concert hall in mid-performance. Another man lives to try and bite his own elbow. A bibliophile finds that he has lost his 'I' in the new Soviet order. A scientist solves the energy crisis by converting human spite. The Eiffel Tower goes mad and drowns itself in Lake Constance...

Moscow: GLAS/New Russian Writing, 2006 ISBN 5-7172-0073-0

Joanne Turnbull   ON 'AUTOBIOGRAPHY OF A CORPSE' FROM SEVEN STORIES BY ....

In his famous essay denouncing socialist realism (1959), Andrei Sinyavsky wished for 'a phantasmagoric art with hypotheses instead of an aim and grotesque instead of descriptions of everyday life.' One must learn, he said, 'to be truthful with the help of absurd fantasy.'

Little did Sinyavsky know that a writer from Kiev (not Bulgakov) had done just that. Sigizmund Krzhizhanovsky (1887-1950) – whose 'experimental realism' features hyperbole, irony, paradox, and phantasms – was long dead and his writings (novels, stories, plays, essays – mostly unpublished) buried in the State Archive. Among them, 'Autobiography of a Corpse'.

It is hard to resist a story with a title like that. And Krzhizhanovsky took his titles very seriously. He considered their composition an art. In a 34-page monograph on the subject, *A Poetics of Titles* (Poetika zaglavii, 1931), he chides writers for clamping titles on texts 'pell-mell and in haste, like the hat on one's head'. Just as a book is a distillation of 'life's phraseology', so its title should be a distillation of the book.

'Autobiography of a Corpse' opens with the arrival in 1920s Moscow of a provincial journalist named Shtamm. Shtamm is determined 'to swap drops of ink for rubles' – despite the capital's appalling dearth of living space. Sheer luck leads him to a somewhat lugubrious room with a view, but no key. The key is lost. Unfazed, Shtamm buys a padlock and sets about looking for work. Days go by and then, late one night, he returns to his room to find a manuscript wedged in the door. Its author turns out to be the room's previous tenant, a suicide, who took the trouble to write his autobiography before taking his life. From this point on, the corpse does all the talking.

In a marvellously entitled essay, *Countries That Don't Exist* (Strany, kotorykh net), on man's imaginative attempts to expand 'the walls of the world', Krzhizhanovsky refers at one point to *Gulliver's Travels*: 'It is interesting that in both the first and second part,

Swift, as a genuine artist, allows himself to violate the true dimensions only once – to shrink or to enlarge the bodies of the people amongst whom his hero lives. Otherwise, he is exceedingly precise and nowhere does he deviate from a realistic manner of writing.' Here we have in a nutshell Krzhizhanovsky's own creative method, what he called 'experimental realism'.

Like Shtamm, Krzhizhanovsky arrived in Soviet Moscow already a writer and hoping to conquer the city. The year was 1922. Through a friend of a friend, he found a cell-like room on the Arbat (No. 44, Apt. 5). The apartment was home to an elderly count. Krzhizhanovsky's room, like Shtamm's, had been previously occupied by a dead man. Alexander Naryshkin, a regional vice-governor before the Revolution, had been living in the count's apartment when he was arrested one night in 1919. He died in prison two years later.

'Autobiography of a Corpse' is the story of an erudite bibliophile who, having come of age before the Revolution, now finds himself at sea in the illogical Soviet order. He cannot get outside himself to engage with another person's 'I'; then again, he can't even find his own 'I'. To describe his predicament, he calls on 'symbols of mathematical logic': 'A point in space may be found, they say, only by means of intersecting coordinates. But if those coordinates come apart then... space is vast, while a point has no size at all. Evidently, my coordinates had come apart, and to find me, a psychic point in infinity, turned out to be impossible.'

This stunning mathematical metaphor is emblematic of Krzhizhanovsky's style. On the one hand, we see his logic, his originality, his simplicity, his brilliance. On the other hand, there is his casual reference to extra-literary disciplines. Like the narrator of 'Autobiography of a Corpse', Krzhizhanovsky was a bibliophile, enormously erudite, multilingual. And like Swift, he is exceedingly precise in his use of terms – be they mathematical, musical, geographical, historical, philosophical, physical, astronomical, or anatomical. When, for instance, he mentions (in another story) 'the chaos of sounds given

Sigizmund Krzhizhanovsky

to the *kortievym spiraliam*', he is referring to the 'spiral organ of Corti' – that particular part of the inner ear by which sound is directly perceived.

Another consideration for translators is Krzhizhanovsky's fondness for neologisms – for instance, in 'Autobiography', *razbezdushit*'. To Russian readers, the meaning is crystal clear; this invented verb, with its fresh yet natural sound, doesn't make them trip. The translator trips right away – and must disassemble the word in Russian before attempting to reassemble it in English: dushit' ('to choke, stifle, suffocate'), which derives from dusha ('soul'); bez- ('-less, -free, -non, un-'); raz- (a second prefix which here denotes 'completion of action'). My eventual English equivalent: 'to desoulerate' – a word I don't entirely like because it's not as vivid as the Russian and because it sticks out.

One comes across these made-up words often. In Russian, Krzhizhanovsky's inventions enliven the text without making it sound artificial. This is less true in English. A little neologism goes a long way. So I have sometimes given a real word in English for a not-real word in Russian (e.g. 'glimmer' for *brezg*).

Other pitfalls for translators of Krzhizhanovsky are created by his plays on words. The most obvious example is: 'Yakobi i 'Yakoby'', the impossible-to-translate title of Krzhizhanovsky's first real story (1919), a 'fantasy-dialogue' between Jacobi, the German philosopher, and 'Supposedly', the sum of all human meanings. Another striking example comes from 'Autobiography': '*mezh 'ya' i 'my': yamy*'. Literally, this translates: 'between 'I' and 'we': pits' (or holes or hollows or depressions). Krzhizhanovsky's elegant play in Russian is entirely lost in translation: ''I' and 'we' are separated by gulfs.'

Gulfs certainly separated Krzhizhanovsky and the Soviet cultural establishment that came to champion socialist realism. Of the 3,000 pages he left behind, only 450 (essays, mainly) were printed in his lifetime. 'All my hard life,' he remarked in one of his notebooks, 'I have been a literary nonexistence, honestly working for existence.'

Extract
Autobiography of a Corpse

Journalist Shtamm, whose 'Letters from the Provinces' were signed Etal, among other pseudonyms, had decided to set out — on the heels of his letters — for Moscow.

Shtamm believed in his elbows and in the ability of Etal to swap drops of ink for rubles, but the matter of living space disturbed him. He knew that on the metropolitan chessboard, squares had not been set aside for all of the chessmen. People who had been to Moscow scared you: the buildings are all packed to the rafters. You have to camp: in vestibules, on backstairs, boulevard benches, in asphalt cauldrons and dustbins.

That is why Shtamm, as soon as he stepped off the train onto the Moscow station platform, began repeating into dead and living, human and telephonic ears one and the same word: a room...

But the black telephonic ear, having heard him out, hung indifferently on its steel hook. And the human ears hid from him under fur and astrakhan collars — the frost that day crackled underfoot — while the word, as though landing under more and more layers of carbon paper, grew fainter with each repetition and broke up into softly knocking letters.

Citizen Shtamm was a very nervous and impressionable person: that evening when, spun out like a top on a string, he lay down on three hard chairs determined to push him to the floor with their backs, he saw the specter of the dustbin, its wooden lid thrown hospitably open, in his mind's eye.

But there's truth in the old adage: morning is wiser than evening. Wilier, too, no doubt. Having risen with the dawn from his chairs, which went straight back to their corners to sulk, Shtamm apologized for the trouble, thanked them for the bed and trudged off along the half-deserted streets of snow- and rime-clad Moscow. But before he had gone a hundred paces, at practically the first crossroads, he met a little man mincing along in a thin and threadbare overcoat. The little man's eyes were hidden beneath a cap, his lips tightly muffled in a scarf. In spite of this, the man saw him, stopped and said:

'Oh. And you too?'

'Yes.'

'Where so early?'

'I'm looking for a room.'

Shtamm did not catch the man's reply: the words stuck fast in the scarf's double whorls. But he saw him thrust a hand inside his overcoat, feel about for something and finally pull out a narrow notebook. He quickly wrote something in it, blowing on his frozen fingers. An hour later, a three-by-four-inch slip of paper torn out of the notebook had miraculously turned into a living space measuring one hundred square feet.

The longed-for space had been found on the top floor of an enormous gray building in one of the by-streets that trace crooked zigzags between Povarskaya and Nikitskaya. The room struck Shtamm as somewhat narrow and dark, but once the electric light had been switched on, gay blue roses appeared, tripping down the wallpaper in long verticals. Shtamm liked the blue roses. He went to the window: hundreds upon hundreds of roofs pulled low over windows. Looking pleased, he turned round to the proprietress — a quiet, elderly woman with a black shawl over her shoulders:

'Very good. I'll take it. May I have the key?'

There was no key. The proprietress looked down and, pulling her shawl about her with a shiver, said the key had been lost, but that... Shtamm wasn't listening:

'Doesn't matter. For now a padlock will do. I'll go and fetch my things.'

In another hour the new lodger was tinkering with the door, screwing in the padlock's iron hasp. Elated as Shtamm was, one small detail did bother him: while securing the temporary bolt, he noticed that the old lock seemed to have been broken. Above the iron lock body he descried the marks of blows and deep scratches. A little higher up, on the wooden stock, he found the manifest marks of an axe. Feeling not a little apprehensive, Shtamm lighted a match (the corridor connecting his room to the entrance hall was dark) and made a thorough inspection of the door. But nothing else — save the legible white number 24, inscribed in the middle of the door's flat brown surface and, evidently, necessary for the house accounts — did he notice.

'Doesn't matter,' Shtamm waved the thought away and set about unpacking his suitcase.

The next two days everything went as it was supposed to go. From morning till night Shtamm went from door to door, from meeting to meeting, bowing, shaking hands, talking, listening, asking,

demanding. Come evening, the briefcase under his elbow now strangely heavy and weighing his arm down, his steps shorter, slower and less steady, Shtamm would return to his room, look blearily round at the ranks of blue wallpaper roses and sink into a black, dreamless sleep. The third evening he managed to finish somewhat earlier. The minute hand on the street-clock face jerked forward to show 10:45 as Shtamm approached the entrance to his building. He climbed the stairs and, trying not to make any noise, turned the cam of the American lock on the outer door. Then he went down the unlighted corridor to room No. 24 and stopped, fumbling in his pocket for the key. The other rooms were dark and quiet. Except for the hum — to the left, through three thin walls — of a primus-stove. He found the key, turned it inside the steel body and gave the door a shove: in that same instant a white blur by his fingers rustled, slipped down and flopped on the floor. Shtamm snapped on the light. By the threshold, having evidently fallen out of the crack in the door, lay a white paper packet. Shtamm picked it up and read the address:

Resident

Room No. 24

There was no name. Shtamm folded back a corner of the copybook inside: angular jumping letters bunched in a nervous line looked up. Puzzled, Shtamm again read the strange address, but in that instant, as he was turning the manuscript over, it slipped out of its capacious paper noose and smoothed out its folded-in-four body by itself. After that Shtamm had only to turn to the first page, which bore only these words: Autobiography of a Corpse.

No matter who you, the person in room 24, are — the manuscript began — you are the only person I shall ever make happy: you see, had I not vacated my hundred sq. feet by hanging myself from the hook in the left-hand corner by the door of your current quarters, you would hardly have found yourself a resting place with such ease. I write about this in the past tense: an exactly calculated future may be thought of as a fait accompli, that is to say, almost as the past.

We are not acquainted and now it seems too late for us ever to be so, but that in no way prevents my knowing you: you are from the provinces. Such rooms, you see, are better rented to out-of-towners with no knowledge of local affairs and press reports. Naturally, you have come to 'conquer Moscow'; you have the requisite energy and desire 'to gain a foothold', 'to make your way in the world'. In short, you have that particular ability I never had: the ability to be alive.

Well, I am certainly ready to cede my square feet to you. Or rather: I, a corpse, agree to move over a little. Go on and live: the room is dry, the neighbors quiet and peaceful, and there's a view. True, the wallpaper was tattered and stained, but for you I had it replaced: and here I think I managed to guess your taste: blue roses flattened in silly verticals: people like you like that sort of thing. Isn't that so?

In exchange for the solicitude and consideration I have shown you, the person in room No. 24, I ask only for a simple reader's consideration of this manuscript. I do not need you, my successor and confessor, to be wise and subtle: no, I need from you only one very rare quality: that you be completely alive.

For more than a month now I have been tortured by insomnias. Over the next three nights they will help me to tell you what I've never told anyone. After that, a neatly soaped noose may be applied as a radical cure for insomnia.

An old Indian folktale tells of a man made to shoulder a corpse night after night — till the corpse, its dead but moving lips pressed to his ear, has finished telling the story of its long-over life. Do not try to throw me to the ground. Like the man in the folktale, you will have to shoulder the burden of my three insomnias and listen patiently, till the corpse has finished its autobiography.

Having read up to this line, Shtamm again examined the broad paper label-band: it bore no stamps, no postmark.

'I can't understand it,' he muttered, walking to the door and standing there plunged in thought. The hum of the primus had long since quieted. Through the walls: not a sound. Shtamm glanced over at the copybook: it lay open on the table, waiting. He delayed a minute, then went obediently back, sat down and found the lost line with his eyes:

I have worn lenses over my pupils for a long time. Every year I have to increase their strength: my vision is now 8.5. That means that 55% of the sunlight does not exist for me. I have only to press

my biconcave ovals back into their case — and space, as though it too had been shut up in that dark and cramped compartment, suddenly contracts and fogs. I see only gray blurs, murk and long threads of transparent dots. Sometimes, when I wipe my slightly dusty lenses with a piece of chamois, I have an odd feeling: what if along with the specks of dust that have settled on their glassy concavities I should wipe away all of space? Now you see it — now you don't: like a sheen.

I am always acutely aware of this glassy adjunct that has stolen up to my eyes on bent wiry legs. One day I realized that it could break more than the rays of light falling inside its ovals. The absurdity I am about to describe occurred some years ago: several chance meetings with a girl I half knew had created a strange bond between us. I remember she was young, her face a delicate oval. We were reading the same books, and so we used similar words. After our first meeting I noticed that her myopically dilated pupils in fine blue rims, hidden (like mine) behind the lenses of a pince-nez, were affectionately, but relentlessly following me. One day we were left alone together; I touched her hands; they responded with a light pressure. Our lips moved closer together — and at that very moment the absurdity happened: in my clumsiness I jostled her lenses with mine: caught in a wiry embrace, they slipped off and landed on the carpet with a high, thin tinkle. I bent down to pick them up. In my hands I held two strange glass creatures, their crooked metal legs so entangled as to create one hideous four-eyed creature. Quivering specks of light, jumping from lens to lens, vibrated voluptuously inside the ovals. I pulled them apart: with a thin tinkle, the coupling lenses came unhooked.

There was a knock at the door.

I glimpsed the girl trying, with trembling fingers, to press the recalcitrant lentils back into place, against her eyes.

A minute later I was on my way down the stairs. I felt as though I had tripped over a corpse in the dark.

I left. Forever. In vain did she try to catch me up with a letter: its jumping lines begged me to forget something and promised with a naive simplicity to 'always remember'. Yes, remembering me always in my new corpselike condition could stand me in good stead, but... as I searched her note, letter by letter, I felt that the glassily transparent cold within me would not lessen.

Joanne Turnbull is co-editor of the Glas / New Russian Writing series (Moscow) and is currently working on a new selection of Krzhizhanovsky's work for the New York Review of Books' Classics.

Photos by Charlotte Bromley Davenport

Hamid Ismailov THE RAILWAY

TRANSLATED BY ROBERT CHANDLER

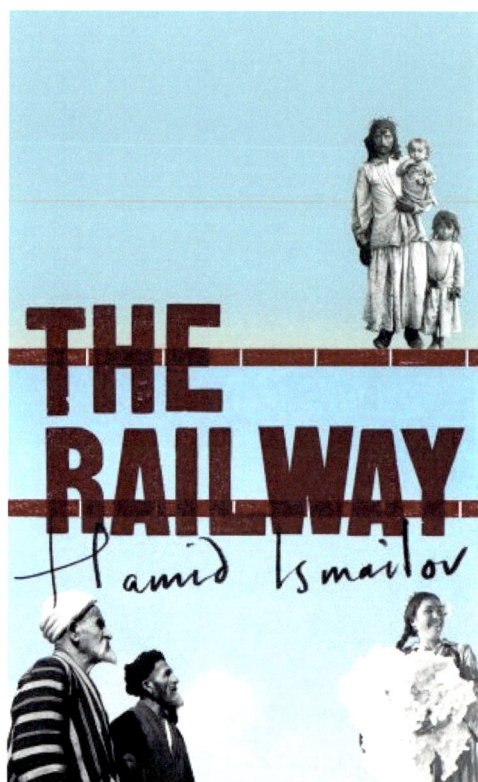

Robert Chandler for his translation of *The Railway* by Hamid Ismailov, Harvill Secker 2006, in recognition both of the merits of this particular rendition, and of the excellent work that he has done over the years in bringing Russian literature to the English reader

London:
Harvill Secker, 2006
ISBN 978-1-843-43161-0

Robert Chandler has translated the poetry of Sappho and Guillaume Apollinaire. His translations from Russian include Vasily Grossman's *Life and Fate*, Leskov's *Lady Macbeth of Mtsensk* and Alexander Pushkin's *Dubrovsky* and *The Captain's Daughter*. Together with his wife, Elizabeth, and other colleagues he has co-translated numerous works by Andrey Platonov. One of these, *Soul*, was chosen as 'best translation of the year from a Slavonic language' by the American Association of Teachers of Slavonic and East European Languages; it was also shortlisted for the Rossica Translation Prize and the Weidenfeld European Translation Prize. Robert Chandler teaches part-time at Queen Mary, University of London.

Hamid Ismailov was born in 1954. He has lived in Tashkent, Moscow, Paris, Bamberg and London, where he is now Head BBC Central Asian Service. He has written and published dozens books of poetry and novels in both Russian and Uzbek. He has also written a novel, *Hostage to Celestial Turks* in English. He was originally forced to leave Uzbekistan on political ground and his writings are still banned there. His most recent novel, *Comrade Islam* has been published in Britain but appears to be too controversial to be published in Russia, let alone in Uzbekistan. It is at present being translated into English.

The Railway

Set mainly in Central Asia between 1900 and 1980, *The Railway* introduces to us the inhabitants – which include Uzbeks, Russians, Persians, Jews, Koreans, Tartars and Gypsies – of a small town near Tashkent. Among those whose stories we hear are Mefody-Jurisprudence, the town's alcoholic intellectual; Father Ioann, a Russian priest; Kara-Musayev the Younger, the chief of police; and Umarali-Moneybags, the old moneylender. At the heart of both the town and the novel stands the railway station. Highly sophisticated yet imbued with a naive delight in storytelling, *The Railway* chronicles the dramatic changes felt throughout Central Asia in the twentieth century.

PARALLEL LINES

Part of a conversation between Hamid Ismailov, his translator Robert Chandler and Robert's collaborator, his wife Elizabeth.

R.C. **The Railway has a huge cast of characters. You once said to me that the town of Gilas is like a microcosm of the Soviet Union, or even of the world as a whole – that Gilas is a kind of Noah's ark of humanity.**

H.I. Yes, and since this Noah's ark was glued together with the help of Russian – Russian political concepts, Russian communist jargon – it made sense to write the novel in Russian rather than in Uzbek... Thinking about all this, by the way, I've realized how few truly Soviet novels there are. For the main part, Soviet literature now seems to me to have been made up of lots of little artificial reservations or theme parks: Uzbek novels, where all the characters – apart from a few Russians – are Uzbek; Russian novels, where all the characters – apart from a few token Jews or Georgians – are Russian; Georgian novels; Armenian novels, and so on... It's all a far cry from my own experience of Soviet life. But tell me: what was the aspect of the novel that you found hardest to translate?

R.C. Recreating the characters' nicknames. My wife and I knew the reader would get lost among the huge cast of characters unless we could find English equivalents to the nicknames that were memorable, informative and convincing. This was difficult but enjoyable; finding a name with the right sounds, the right rhythm, the right meaning was every bit as satisfying as coming up

with a good rhyme in a passage of verse. Often the right name emerged only after Liz and I had tried out dozens of other possibilities over the course of weeks or months. We always left someone's first (Uzbek) name the same as in the original; it was only the nickname that we translated. And we always knew when we had got it right. We were especially pleased with Abubakir-Snuffsniffer (the school caretaker), Bakay-Croc (the double amputee and leader of a disabled movement), Bolta-Lightning (the town electrician), Mukum-Hunchback (the chaikhana owner), Ortik-Picture-Reels (the cinema manager), Tolik-Nosetalk (the alcoholic manual labourer), Osman-Anon (the shadowy KGB officer who is issued every month with a new passport in a different name), Rizo-Zero (the engineer, student of shadows and supposed instigator of a terrible eclipse) or Vera-Virgo, the town prostitute... But there's something else I've always been meaning to ask. To what extent are the names your own invention, and to what extent did you take them from real life?

H.I. Nick-names like these were very common during the Soviet years. Nearly everyone in Uzbekistan had a nickname. They were based on all kinds of things: an aspect of someone's character or appearance, something to do with their profession or maybe just a particular incident in their life... Often people were stamped with these nicknames in childhood, and they carried more weight in their lives than their real names; it was as if their real names were being kept out of our everyday, vulgar life, being saved from profanation. I remember how once, when I was about twelve, a group of us were sitting in a carriage behind the locomotive and my classmate Fedka, who was by far the wittiest of us, shouted out: 'Fireman, throw in some curved logs, we're coming to a bend in the line...' Ever afterwards he was known as Fedka-Fireman. Years later I learnt that he ended up working in a fire brigade, as if trying to combat this spell that had been cast on him... I once did some study of all this. Nicknames were clearly not so common in the 19th century, before Communism, nor have they been so widely used during our last fifteen years of suddenly found independence. Nicknames seem to have been a feature of the Communist period, a time when people seemed to live two separate lives – a true one in their hearts and dreams and a false one in the real world…

L.C. (while reading the transcript of this conversation). But the nicknames aren't in the least false. Many of them embody important truths about their bearers. Are you sure they didn't arise more from a need to express individuality? Most people, I imagine, felt they were just cogs in the Communist wheel. What could be more important than a name that was all their own, or a name that individualized a colleague or neighbour they loved or hated?

H.I. Yes! Their names are both very Uzbek and very, very individual. So Uzbek and so individual that I found it hard at first to imagine they could ever be translated into English… By the way, I've often thought about a horticultural analogy for literary translation. You know the miniature tree we call *saksaul*, the only thing that grows in the very hottest and driest deserts. How can you transplant a Central Asian saksaul into an English garden? How can you get it to live in an English garden without losing its 'saksaulness' yet without looking horribly out of place? What's your recipe for that, Robert?

R.C. It is interesting that you come up with a metaphor from gardening. I am not a gardener, but Liz is a keen and sensitive gardener. She thinks a lot, she reads a lot, but she knows that there are no absolute rules. Every garden is unique. Every year and every month of every year has weather that is unique. If she were trying to find a place for your saksaul, she would think not only about such water and sunlight and soil quality but also about what other plants to put near it. What neighbours would help it to grow? What neighbours would help it to look good? Would it look best beside a plant that looks a little bit similar or a plant whose shape is completely different? Might it be best to let the saksaul stick out, to allow it a space of its own, surrounded only by sand and stones? Or might it be better to surround it by indigenous plants and hope that, if we pretend that it is natural and normal for it to be there, other people will accept its presence and not ask too many questions?

H.I. All right – but how does all this relate to what you do with words?

R.C. Sometimes I spend days looking for a synonym for a particular word or trying to improve the rhythm of a particular passage. And then, after wasting a lot of time, I realize that the problem is not in the place where I thought it was. If I change something in the previous verse or sentence, then the problem disappears just like that. I simply needed to find the right plant to put near the saksaul. But while I'm thinking about these things, I ask a lot of questions. I probably emailed you four or five hundred questions in a single year. And we spent a lot of time together, discussing everything from obscene jokes to political slogans and Sufi literature. Were there ever times when you cursed me for asking so many questions? And how does it feel to sit and watch as your own work, a work that is based on your own childhood, is slowly and laboriously taken away from the soil it sprang from, transplanted into a language that is not your own?

H.I. I spent many years of my life translating classic and modern literature from one language to another: Russian to Uzbek, Uzbek to Russian, French to Uzbek, Uzbek to French, Turkish to Russian, English to Uzbek etc. But I have never scrutinized any text so carefully as you scrutinized mine. Every single word was held up to the light. A writer is sometimes driven by some very personal association, or by the need for assonance or alliteration. As a result, he leaves some obscure places in his work. You exposed these. But you also helped to make me aware of deeper things. A professor at Tashkent conservatory used to say jokingly to me and my wife: 'I have to explain a concept to my students so many times that in the end I even begin to understand it myself…' Thanks to all Robert's questions I have sometimes begun to understand the deeper meaning of what I wrote naively. But I honestly believe that Robert now knows the novel better than I do.

R.C. Well, I don't know about that, but Liz and I have certainly found it a joy to work with an author who is always so generous. But then, as I've said in my preface, *The Railway* is a generous book. It's an open, tolerant book, a book that has room in it for everything, for history and fantasy, for anger and tenderness, for satire and reverence.

THE RAILWAY

The tone of much of the novel, as can be seen from the preceeding interview, is high-spirited. Some chapters, however, embody a remarkable depth of spirituality; even here, however, we find considerable wit and word play. The following extract is about the last months of a devout and honourable mullah who is executed in 1937, at the height of Stalin's purges. The mullah is known as Obid-Kori ('Kori' being a suffix indicating that this person has memorized the whole of the Koran.) His wife's name is Oyimcha or 'Beautiful Moon'.

[1] Many people sent to the Gulag were charged with counter-revolutionary activities, under Article 58 of the Criminal Code.

Why, why, why did life turn out this way and no other way? And what other way is there? Is there another way in the world, or is that just a dream people dream? Or a dream dreamed by Allah himself, to console people? Oyimcha appears, carrying a full basket of grapes; she appears and disappears. And nothing is left in the place of her grapes, her bright, airy grapes – only patches of sunlight among vine-leaves... vine-leaves... vine-leaves...

Calumny and the evil eye did not fall on the children – Allah be praised! Calumny and the evil eye fell on Obid-Kori. The children had gone off to the bazaar, taking with them hens' eggs for holiday egg-battles; and the youngest, Mashrab, came back in tears, saying that the son of Soat-Moneybags had smashed everyone else's eggs with an egg-like stone he had found in the Kakyr-Say river. And nobody had been able to prove that this stone was not an egg.

Nothing had been forgotten. Obid-Kori was reminded that he had studied in a hotbed of opium for the people, that he had participated in the Kokand bourgeois-nationalist congress, and that he had gone on believing in his illusory Allah during the epoch of militant materialism. He was also accused of treason towards the Motherland and betrayal of the Kirghiz people. And who, you may ask, charged him with all this under article 58?[1] Kukash-Snubnose, whom Obid-Kori had himself taught to read and write. This green-eyed young Sart – now a Kirghiz NKVD officer – was interrogating Obid-Kori every other day in the main jail.

*

Oyimcha had been carrying a full basket of grapes, bright bunches of bright grapes, grapes, grapes, when Shir-Gazi had come with four policemen to arrest Obid-Kori.

And the children were at the bazaar, and the yard was empty, and only patches of light, patches of light lay on the ground, which was covered by the shade of vine-leaves... vine-leaves... vine-leaves... Oyimcha wept. Obliged as she was to hide from these profane ones, she cried from deep in the house; her tears fell like grapes, grapes, grapes and her wordless howl carried far beyond the gate...

Grapes lay scattered over the yard. Shir-Gazi and the four policemen trampled over them in their

boots, pressing, squashing, stamping them down like patches of light, patches of light in a deserted court... court... courtyard...

Yes, life turned out this way and how else could it have turned? Words can turn out other ways, words can be replayed and re-plied, relayed and re-lied, rehearsed and re-versed; words can be the tools of a green-eyed Judgment-Day-Devil like Kukash-Snubnose – but life is one, and life is from Allah. And what do we know of it? It cannot be sensed or weighed between words any more than the rays of the sun can be sensed between leaves... leaves... leaves... And only the leaves' shadow catches the little patches of light, surrounds, frames, defines, confines, arrests.

Life happens in words. One person says or thinks of another: 'they did right' or 'they did wrong'. But what is this 'right' or 'wrong' outside of words? Or if words are turned upside down, turned head over heels? If, instead of leaves casting a shadow imposed by the light, the shadow gives birth to the leaves and light is the leaves' product?

The iron grating in the small prison window Obid-Kori looked through after saying his prayers had precisely this relationship to the sky and its blue, to its sun and its occasional white clouds. The grating was formed by two verticals and six rusty crossbars.

*

And after each interrogation by the Judgment-Day-Devil, when everything he said was turned back against him, old Obid-Kori, refusing to understand anything at all, sat on the stone ledge beneath the grating and, between his repeated prayers, which gave words back their meaning, remembered a family legend told him by Oyimcha... Oyimcha...

Oyimcha's maternal grandfather, Mullah Tusmuhammad-Okhun, had studied as a young man in the Miri-Arab madrasah in Bukhara – the madrasah where Obid-Kori had studied fifty years after him. One winter, after reading the Koran in his cell, Tusmuhammad realized that it had been snowing. It had been snowing so thickly that he could no longer open the door. Snow fell for three days and three nights. Or maybe longer – Tusmuhammad, barely pausing in his studies, ate his entire store of food, all his thin porridge. And it went on snowing. There was no food left in the cell, and time did not stop. And

Tusmuhammad prayed and read the Koran... prayed and read the Koran... He lost count of the days and nights. And it went on snowing. And during one of these countless days or countless nights he was sitting and listening to the falling snow and thinking about the might of Allah, who had sent people down on this earth just as he sends down snow, snowflake after snowflake, snowflake after snowflake, when he heard a strange noise in a corner of his cell. And he saw a shining hen. Together with seven golden chicks, she walked across the cell and out of the door, the snow dissolving before her as the door silently opened. The sun was shining and the muezzin was calling the faithful to their prayers. And the sky's blue, blue, blue pierced Mullah Tusmuhammad-Okhun's eyes so deeply that Obid-Kori was able to see traces of that celestial blue in them even after Tusmuhammad had gone blind in his old age.

Mullah Tusmuhammad-Okhun's teacher had told him that seven generations of his family would live under the protection of Allah, and Oyimcha, poor Oyimcha had believed this as if it were holy writ.

*

Oyimcha came every week, staying with relatives who lived opposite the prison and bringing sometimes prayer beads, sometimes flatbreads, once a jug for Obid-Kori's ablutions, once a secret note from their children. Her male relatives bribed the prison guards and passed her gifts on to Obid-Kori; there was even one occasion when Oyimcha threw a veil over her face and got as far as the prison gates herself – but a Russian standing there with a rifle drove her away, making the air thick with his swearing and cursing.

What, in any case, did it matter if calumny and the evil eye had fallen on Obid-Kori? Even little Mashrab was already fully-grown, already a fine young man – Allah be praised! Mashrab at least had been like a golden chicken, protected from calumny and the evil eye. But Obid-Kori himself had evidently been unworthy to marry a descendant of the Prophet – may he be praised!

Repeated interrogations, repeated prayers, repeated thoughts were beginning to confuse Obid-Kori. Why had life turned out...

One night, when a sudden light fell on the metal grating (those two verticals and six crossbars)

and the harsh clanking of cell doors made him rise from his iron bed (the same iron grating, the same two verticals and six horizontals, covered by a mattress Oyimcha had stuffed) Obid-Kori's torments came to an end. The wing of a night bird flashed outside the window and he was led into the prison yard. Seven Black Marias were waiting there, and the guards were leading men out, leading men out.

Obid-Kori took in deep lungfuls of the night mountain air – as relieved to be leaving his cell as Mullah Tusmuhammad-Okhun had been when the snow finally melted.

'Val Zukha, val laili iza sadja,
Ma vadda'aka rabbuka va ma kala...

'I swear by the bright shining of the day
And by the night, when her darkness is spread wide,
Your Lord never left you, nor is he displeased...'

Obid-Kori whispered to himself, and tears rolled down the thin beard on his cheeks.

Oyimcha, Oyimcha was sitting in the middle of the summer courtyard, beating cotton wool, spinning it with long switches... switches... switches... In their broad white linen sleeves her arms were like fluttering wings and the cotton wool clinging to the slow, slow, slow switches flew high into the air, into the air, like celestial clouds... clouds... clouds...

The prisoners were loaded into Black Marias and taken off to the station in Gorchakov. There they were transferred to a goods wagon, with the same small grating as in the prison (two verticals and six crossbars) and taken silently-slowly down the iron road. Through chinks and holes in the floor of the wagon they could see two never-ending metal rails and those same short crossbars, repeated again and again and again, to infinity, and it seemed as if the earth herself had been put behind bars, framed, bound, confined, arrested, or as if they, in their goods wagon with the metal grating, had been separated from the earth for ever.

*

Why had life... The soul of Obid-Kori was flying over the earth, leaving Oyimcha behind, and the children were running after Oyimcha, Oyimcha, Oyimcha, whose long hair streamed behind her like bunches of grapes... grapes... grapes...

LEO TOLSTOY

WAR AND PEACE

TRANSLATED BY ANTHONY BRIGGS

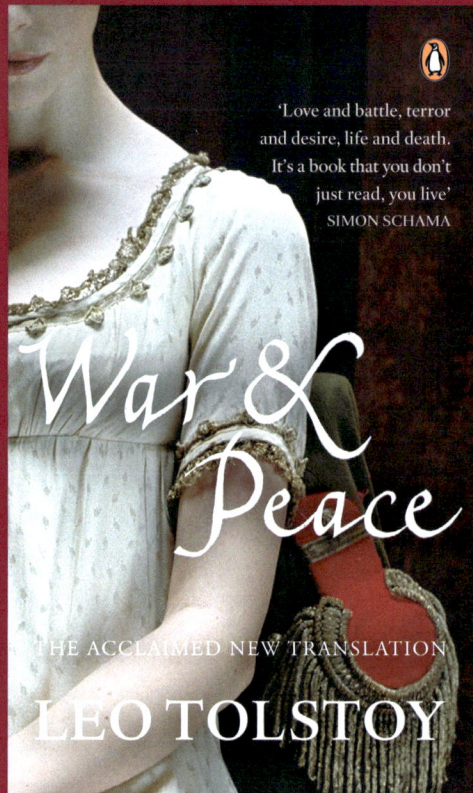

'Love and battle, terror
and desire, life and death.
It's a book that you don't
just read, you live'
SIMON SCHAMA

War &
Peace

THE ACCLAIMED NEW TRANSLATION
LEO TOLSTOY

Lev Nikolaevich Tolstoy (1828-1910) is Russia's most famous novelist and moral philosopher best known for *War and Peace*, *Anna Karenin* and *Resurrection*, which are celebrated for their compelling narrative interest and strong characterisation, especially of women. He also wrote many stories, plays, essays, commentaries and translations.

Underlying all of his work is a search for religious truth, and in his later years he challenged the church, government and general public in a series of uncompromising moral positions involving non-resistance to evil, the renunciation of property, the abolition of government and ecclesiastical authority, but an ultimate belief in God and love.

War and Peace, often described as the world's greatest novel, stands alone in its vast scope and intimate detail, its immense diversity and final unity. Against a background of alternating peace and war, Tolstoy unfolds many stories involving three aristocratic families and more than 500 hundred individually rendered characters. The novel's epic qualities are seen in the depiction of Napoleon's invasion of Russia in 1812, but most readers are even more captivated by the personal destinies of young people growing through their youthful uncertainties and struggling towards a mature understanding of life. Natasha Rostov has been described as 'the most wonderfully made character in any novel'.

Professor Tony Briggs was educated at King Edward VII School, Sheffield, and the Universities of Cambridge (MA) and London (PhD). He has been Head of Russian at the Universities of Bristol and Birmingham. As well as many articles, he has written, edited or translated more than twenty books, including five on Alexander Pushkin, on whom he is the country's leading authority, and six edited volumes of English poetry. Penguin Books will soon publish his edition of *The Death of Ivan Ilyich and Other Stories*, and he is now translating Tolstoy's *Resurrection*. He is also preparing for a double celebration of Edward FitzGerald's *Rubaiyat of Omar Khayyam* in 2009, including a new edition of that work.

London:
Penguin Books, 2005
ISBN 978-0-141-02511-7

Ilya Repin
Portrait of Leo Tolstoy
1887
State Tretyakov Gallery

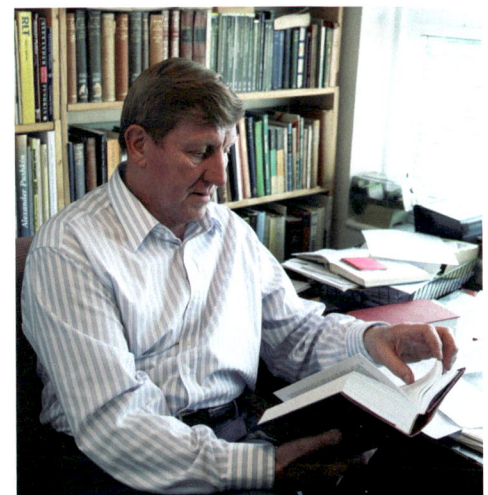

CORRECTING TOLSTOY

THE RIGHTS AND WRONGS OF TRANSLATING TOLSTOY Tony Briggs

Leo Tolstoy was no stickler for accuracy and exactitude. R.F.Christian reminds us that 'Rules irked him, and the student will not find his prose a model of grammatical conformity ... he neither knew nor cared much about formal grammar.' He gives examples of Tolstoy's grammatical mistakes and stylistic lapses, particularly repetition. There are also plenty of factual errors in *War and Peace*, such as when Pierre sees the comet of 1812 in 1811, or when Tolstoy sometimes remembers and sometimes forgets that Kutuzov had only one eye.

The question of what to do with these aberrations puts the translator in an impossible situation. If you were to correct every lapse and tidy up the style pedantically you would certainly give a false impression of Tolstoy's mode of writing. On the other hand, the concept of 'silent adjustment' can be invoked justifiably from time to time. To take a single example, all seven translators of *War and Peace* have broken down Tolstoy's longest sentence (of 230 words) into smaller units. So, some quiet improvement does go on, as it should.

It is, however, equally possible that a translator does the opposite and makes poor phrases even worse. Witness, for example, a description of Berg as 'assistant to the head of the staff of the assistant of the chief officer of the staff of the commander of the left flank of the infantry of the first army...' (III, 1, 16, emphasis supplied). This version by

the admirable Constance Garnett manages to exaggerate Tolstoy's only slightly clumsy original sentence, which has more variation and fewer genitives. It is not difficult to smooth this out: Berg was 'assisting the Head of Staff commanding the First Army Infantry, left flank ...'

But there is one important section in the novel where Tolstoy both writes rather badly and also makes a mistake that matters; the whole section really does need tidying up, and the earlier translators have not done that. In III, 1, 19 he describes Pierre's procrustean attempts to link his own destiny with Napoleon's through a strange mixture of biblical prophecy and numerology. Tolstoy's account of what Pierre did is confusing and inaccurate. This is what the author says, literally translated: 'The French letters, in the manner of the Hebrew numerical system, by which units are determined by the first ten letters, and tens by the others, have the following significance: ...' We shall set aside the impossibility of using the phrase 'French letters' (though an early translator did so). This sentence has a solid meaning but it is not clearly expressed, and it contains an error. Units can be represented only by the first nine letters of the alphabet because the tenth letter denotes the first of the tens.

Of the previous translators only Weiner stays with the incorrect 'ten'; Bell, Dole, Garnett, the Maudes, Edmonds and Dunnigan (some copying from a predecessor) make the necessary silent correction. So we are agreed on the need for that. But they fail in their further duty to expand and clarify. For instance, it is not helpful to read, 'The French alphabet written out with same numerical values as the Hebrew …' The Hebrew what? The Hebrew alphabet? There is no Hebrew alphabet. Most of the existing versions seem to suggest this, which adds to the confusion. Garnett comes close to an explanation, but her style is awkward: 'If the French alphabet is treated like the Hebrew system of enumeration …' She is right to mention numbers, but 'treated like' tells us nothing useful.

This passage does need remedial treatment. Letters are being ranged against numbers, and we need to suggest that. The numbers are Hebrew ones, but that won't mean much to a western reader. We speak of Arabic numerals, which are the same. So in our translation we should either drop 'Hebrew' or at least mention 'Arabic'. Hence our preferred version:

'The French alphabet, laid out alongside the Hebrew (or Arabic) numerical system, with the first nine letters representing units, the next tens, and so on, gives the following values: …'

There is an amusing irony in this. It is doubtful whether anyone has ever noticed how obscure the previous English versions have been (and the Russian before them), for one good reason. Stretched out across the page are the 25 letters of the French alphabet ('i' and 'j' counting as the same letter) with the Arabic numerals neatly ranged below them. They grab your attention as soon as you turn the page, and you can see instantly what it is all about: a = 1, b = 2 … etc.

The system is clear in the mind before you get down to its verbal explanation, which does not need to be assimilated. So the busy eye skates over the inadequate English without stopping to ask questions. Still, it is time somebody put it right. Would anyone claim that this small piece of text (Russian or English) would be better left in its primeval state?

Not all the possible corrections and adjustments are as easy to decide on. Most of them are a matter of opinion and quick decision. (You can't phone a friend very often when you have 600,000 words to get through). Occasionally there comes a mistake which must on no account be corrected. When Pierre says, ungrammatically, 'All I said was – we could make better sacrifices when we know what the needs are' (III, I, 23) he is harassed and confused, and it would be wrong to tidy him up.

Professor Christian's close study of Tolstoy's language has been helpful in setting a translation strategy for the whole work. One comment is particularly useful: 'Tolstoy thought aloud, transferred his thoughts to paper and sometimes forgot that he was writing, not talking.' This judicious observation not only warns us away from excessive meddling and correction, it also justifies a gentle tendency towards the colloquial not only in the dialogue but even in the narrative passages. This is not to risk modernisms or slang; all it means is the use of easy, normal, natural speech, which is the common currency of *War and Peace*.

Volume 3

Part One

Chapter 19

War & Peace

Following her suicide attempt and subsequent depression Natasha has been comforted by Pierre Bezukhov. This is the beginning of their love for each other, though many months will pass before it matures into an intimate relationship. Meanwhile disaster threatens Russia, and Pierre wonders how to involve himself in the destiny of his country.

Ever since the day Pierre had driven home from the Rostovs with Natasha's look of gratitude still fresh in his mind, stared up at the comet in the sky and felt the range of new possibilities opening up before him, he had stopped worrying about the agonizing problem of the vanity and senselessness of all earthly things. The terrible questions, 'Why?' 'What's it all about?', which had always assailed him whatever he was doing, had now been replaced, not by different questions or answers to the old ones, but by an image of her. If he heard people prattling on about nothing, or did so himself, if he read or heard about something that reminded him of human wickedness or folly, he no longer despaired; he had stopped wondering why people bothered with anything at all when life was so short and uncertain. He had only to think of her as he had last seen her, and all his doubts melted away, not because she had any answers to the questions that had been haunting him, but because her image transported him instantly into another realm of sweetness, light and active spirituality, where there was no question of being in the right or in the wrong, a region of beauty and love well worth living for. If he came across some worldly abomination he would say to himself, 'So-and-so's robbing the state and the Tsar while the state and the Tsar weigh him down with honours, is he? Well, let him get on with it – she smiled at me yesterday, she asked me round, and I love her, and nobody will ever know.'

Pierre still went out a good deal, he hadn't stopped drinking and he led the same kind of idle, dissipated life, because apart from a few hours spent with the Rostovs he had to get through the rest of his time somehow, and the habits and friendships formed in Moscow kept drawing him back inexorably to the same old life. But in recent days, with rumours from the theatre of war sounding more ominous by the day, and with Natasha's health much improved, which meant that she no longer required the same degree of sympathy and pity, he had found himself increasingly overwhelmed by an inexplicable feeling of restlessness. His present position was

untenable, he thought, and, sensing the approach of some disaster that was going to change the whole course of his life, he cast around impatiently on all sides watching for signs of it. One of his brother masons had revealed to Pierre a certain prophecy concerning Napoleon, taken from the Revelation of St John the Divine, where, in chapter xiii, verse 18, we read:

Here is wisdom. Let him that hath understanding count the number of the beast: for it is the number of a man; and his number is Six hundred threescore and six.

And in the fifth verse of the same chapter:

And there was given unto him a mouth speaking great things and blasphemies; and power was given unto him to continue forty and two months.

The French alphabet, laid out against the Hebrew (or Arabic) numerical system, with the first nine letters representing units, the next tens, and so on, gives the following values:

a b c d e f g h i k l m n o p q r s t u v w x y z
1 2 3 4 5 6 7 8 9 10 20 30 40 50 60 70 80 90 100 110 120 130 140 150 160

If you use this system to write out the words *l'empereur Napoléon* numerically, the sum of the letter-numbers comes to 666 (allowing 5 for the e omitted from le), which makes Napoleon the beast prophesied in the Apocalypse. More than that, if you apply the same system to the French number forty-two, *quarante-deux*, (the span of months allotted to the beast that spoke 'great things and blasphemies'), you get 666 once again, from which it emerges that Napoleon came to a peak in 1812, a French Emperor forty-two years old. This prophecy made a great impression on Pierre, and he began wondering what could possibly put an end to the power of the beast that was Napoleon. Using the same system of taking the numerical values of letters and adding them up, he set out to solve this problem. He wrote down possible answers: *l'empereur Alexandre? La nation russe?* He added up the letters, but they came to much more or much less than 666. Once he applied the system to his own name in its French version,

'Comte Pierre Besouhoff,' but the total was miles out. He changed the spelling, substituting z for s, added de and the article le, but he still couldn't get what he wanted. Then it occurred to him that if the answer he was looking for was to be found in his name, surely his nationality ought to be mentioned as well. He tried *Le russe Besuhof* and this came to 671, only five too much and 5 was the value of e, the letter dropped from the definite article in *l'empereur Napoléon*. Dropping the e again (quite unjustifiably) Pierre got the answer he was after in the phrase *l'russe Besuhof* – exactly 666! This discovery shook him. How, and by what means he was connected with the great event predicted in the Apocalypse, he couldn't tell, but the connection was there beyond doubt. It was all there: his love for Natasha, Antichrist, Napoleon's invasion, the comet, the number 666, *l'empereur Napoléon* and *l'russe Besuhof* – all these things were going to gestate together and something would suddenly emerge from them to help him break out of that vicious circle created by the petty concerns of Moscow that had so enthralled him, and lead him forth to some mighty achievement and true happiness.

The day before the Sunday when the new prayer was read out, Pierre was due to carry out his promise to the Rostovs by calling on Count Rostopchin to collect a copy of the Tsar's appeal to the country and also pick up any late news from the army. On his arrival at Count Rostopchin's that morning Pierre ran straight into a special courier just back from the army. The courier was a familiar figure on the Moscow ballroom scene and Pierre knew him well.

'For heaven's sake, can you take something off me?' said the courier. 'I've got a sackful of letters to parents.'

These included a letter from Nikolay Rostov to his father. Pierre took that, and Count Rostopchin gave him a copy of the Tsar's appeal to Moscow, fresh off the press, the last army orders, and his own most recent bulletin. A quick glance through the army announcements, including lists of the dead and wounded, and also recent honours, told Pierre that Nikolay Rostov had been awarded the Order of St. George, Fourth Class, for outstanding bravery at Ostrovna, and that Prince Andrey Bolkonsky had been placed in command of a regiment of chasseurs. Although reluctant to reawaken the Rostovs' memories of Bolkonsky, Pierre couldn't resist the temptation to raise their spirits by handing on the news of their son's decoration, so he sent the printed announcement and Nikolay's letter straight round to the Rostovs, holding back the Tsar's appeal, Rostopchin's bulletin and the other announcements so he could take them along at dinner-time.

The conversation with Rostopchin, who looked so worried and hard-pressed, Pierre's encounter with the courier, who had let it drop so casually that the army was in a terrible state, rumours of spies being caught in Moscow and a pamphlet in circulation stating that Napoleon had sworn to be in both capitals by autumn, together with the Tsar's impending arrival the next day – all things conspired to rekindle with new intensity in Pierre that feeling of excitement and anticipation that had never really left him since the appearance of the comet, and had flared up again at the beginning of the war.

The idea of doing some military service had occurred to Pierre long before this, and he would have done something about it but for two things: in the first place, he was a sworn member of the Masonic brotherhood committed to peace on earth and the abolition of war, and secondly, one look at the great mass of Muscovites who had gone into uniform as self-proclaimed patriots, and for some reason he squirmed with embarrassment at the idea of doing the same thing. But the main reason for not carrying out his intention to join up was the rather vague idea that he, *l'russe Besuhof*, was associated with the number of the beast, 666, and his role in putting an end to the power of the beast 'speaking great things and blasphemies' had been predetermined from time immemorial, which meant that his was not to go about doing things, his was to sit there and wait for the inevitable to happen.

LEO TOLSTOY
THE DEATH OF IVAN ILYICH

TRANSLATED BY HUGH APLIN

Hugh Aplin studied Russian at Emanuel School, London, and the University of East Anglia, and lived for three years as a student in the Soviet Union in Voronezh, Leningrad and Moscow. He has been Head of Russian at Westminster School for almost two decades, encouraging dozens of pupils over that period to continue with their study of Russian at university. His translation of Mikhail Bulgakov's *The Fatal Eggs* was shortlisted for the inaugural Rossica Translation Prize, won by a former pupil. Among his other translations are Tolstoy's *Hadji Murat*, upon which a BBC radio adaptation was based, and *The Forged Coupon*.

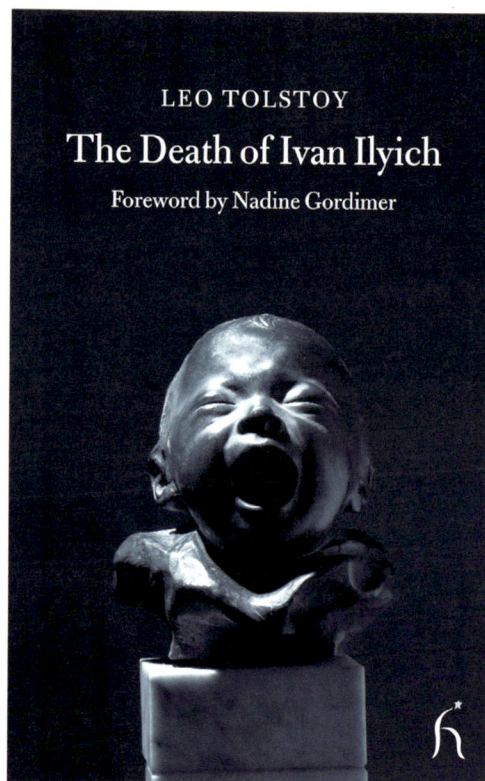

Lev Nikolayevich Tolstoy scarcely needs any introduction: he is challenged perhaps only by Dostoevsky and Chekhov for the position of most famous Russian writer in the English-speaking world. Best known for his weighty novels, he was nonetheless also a master of the short story and novella, and after 1880, as a result of increasing dissatisfaction with the longer genre that has ensured his literary immortality, he devoted much of his creative energy to shorter fiction. In these works of his last three decades many facets of Tolstoy's personal spiritual struggles were exposed to his readership to striking artistic effect.

The Death of Ivan Ilyich is presented in the shortlisted volume together with The Devil, and between them these stories from the late 1880s deal with two of the major recurrent themes in the fiction of Tolstoy's latter years – sexual love and death. But *The Death of Ivan Ilyich* is also concerned with arguably his most important question of all: how a man should live his life. Thus thematically it has much in common with his non-fictional religious writings from *A Confession* onwards. The grand historical sweep of *War and Peace* is renounced in favour of the bleak spiritual landscape of a single soul facing extinction.

TOLSTOY'S FABRIC OF LIFE   by Hugh Aplin

**The Death of Ivan Ilyich begins with the
immediate aftermath of a man's death at 45.
We are privy to the reactions of colleagues,
and learn of the situation in his household. In
the second chapter, however, Tolstoy begins
to dissect the life that preceded the death,
a life characterised as 'the most simple and
ordinary and most dreadful'. I have chosen
this passage as exemplary of the work as a
whole – deeply committed, didactic maybe,
but artistically effective and powerful.**

The point of view employed by Tolstoy is third-person omniscient throughout the story, so the translator does not have to contend with a variety of narrative voices or a dominant non-literary register. Even dialogue is kept to a minimum, so although a servant of peasant origin, Gerasim, is a very significant figure in the ideological structure of the piece, his language, which is distinct from that of the educated middle-class characters who otherwise predominate, features but little, and there is minimal demand for a differentiated voice even for him.

Thus the central aim for the translator here (along, of course, with accuracy) is arguably to seek to replicate the characteristic texture of Tolstoy's prose, which in this particular story seems to me ideally suited to the subject-matter, doing much to account for the work's undoubted power. Much of the narrative is comprised, as is apparent in the chosen extract, of quite dense Russian, where the long and syntactically complicated sentences involving numerous subordinate clauses serve to reflect the language of the world of the legal bureaucracy that is the setting. Equally, this complex prose is used to impressive effect in Tolstoy's exploration of the psychological fabric of both the individual and his personal and social environment, revealing painful and tortuous realities through appropriately

convoluted sentences. If at times the English text seems heavy, cumbersome, then in the circumstances that is perfectly justified: reading the Russian text is by no means an experience that is 'easy and pleasant' – the phrase Tolstoy uses to describe the morally bankrupt way of life he exposes.

Certain difficulties are thrown up before anyone translating prose of this nature by the fact that English is not a highly inflected language like Russian. For example, Tolstoy uses a large number of participial clauses in his writing, and where in the original it is the ending that indicates which word a participle is referring to, in English the word-order becomes much more significant. The temptation can sometimes be to simplify matters by breaking sentences up. Ideally that ought to be resisted in order to remain as close to Tolstoy's own sentence structure as possible.

Another feature of Tolstoy's writing that can tempt the translator to stray from the original is his propensity for repetition. There are times when this can seem simply careless, when a word of no great 'significance' recurs several times in a single sentence, but even then the translator should, I believe, remain faithful, and not look to edit. In *The Death of Ivan Ilyich*, numerous instances can be found of such 'non-significant' repetitions. Take, for example, conjunctive phrases repeated more than once in a short paragraph. These are very much a part of the texture of Tolstoy's writing. More 'significant' repetitions can actually be more troublesome, and there are quite a number of words and phrases that Tolstoy quite deliberately deploys over and over again, within a sentence, a paragraph, or throughout the work as a whole – such as the 'easy and pleasant' mentioned above.

Particularly important within this story are the notions of decency, decorum, seemliness, respectability, propriety, that Ivan Ilyich adheres

London:
Hesperus Press, 2005
ISBN 1-84391-127-2

to in ordering his life up until his illness. This is nicely illustrated with the excerpt I have selected. Here we meet more than a dozen occurrences of words in various grammatical forms relating to decency, decorum, etc. They are usually, but not exclusively based on the Russian noun prilichie. It could be argued that one equivalent English word should be chosen and used throughout, say, 'decorum', and thus 'decorous', 'decorously', 'indecorous', 'indecorously', and 'indecorum' or 'indecorousness'. These last two words, however, seem unnecessarily obscure in comparison with the perfectly standard Russian neprilichie and, unsurprisingly, are not listed in the Russian-English dictionary. Similar problems with alternative renderings of prilichie and its derivatives finally made me decide to use more than just one word, employing synonyms where appropriate. Wherever the repetition of this leitmotif was immediate, I did seek to use a single English word and its derivatives. Tolstoy's insistent deployment of these words encouraged my adoption of this approach. In many other works, where the repetition of significant words and phrases is less constant, being subtly used, for instance, to link characters or events which are not obviously associated, it would certainly be far more difficult to defend.

Features of specifically Russian life can often present the translator with problems – is a rough equivalent better than a more precise but unwieldy description or a footnoted transliteration when, for example, dealing with items of clothing? In this story, however, the terms relating to the judiciary actually work rather well if they remain obscure for the reader. Since Tolstoy wanted Ivan Ilyich's career to be seen as divorced from what life ought to be, any feeling of uncertainty about the exact difference between an examining magistrate and a deputy public prosecutor and their functions, or about any other such details, can even be regarded as positively helpful in accentuating their estrangement from the universal realities which Ivan Ilyich is ultimately forced to confront beyond his comfort zone of work. And it is, of course, the universality of Tolstoy's great themes of life and death that makes this story essential reading in any language.

THE DEATH OF IVAN ILYICH

In the provinces Ivan Ilyich immediately organised for himself just as easy and pleasant a situation as his situation in the law school had been. He worked, forged a career, and at the same time had fun in a pleasant and respectable way; he would occasionally travel out to rural districts on the orders of his superiors, where he conducted himself with dignity with both high and low, and with a precision and incorruptible honesty of which he could not help but be proud, and carried out the commissions entrusted to him, predominantly on matters concerning schismatics[1].

In official matters he was, despite his youth and his penchant for mild fun, extremely restrained, formal and even severe; but in social matters he was often playful and witty and always good-natured, decorous and *bon enfant*[2], as the governor and his wife, with whom he was like one of the family, said of him.

In the provinces there was also a liaison with one of the ladies who threw herself at the rather stylish lawyer; there was also a milliner; there were also drinking bouts with visiting aides-de-camp and trips after dinner to a distant street; there was also obsequiousness to the governor and even to the governor's wife, but it all bore such an elevated tone of respectability that bad words could not have been used to describe it all; it all fitted only the rubric of the French saying: *il faut que jeunesse se passe*[3]. Everything took place with clean hands, in clean shirts, with French words and, most importantly, in the very highest society, and therefore with the approval of people in high places.

Ivan Ilyich served thus for five years, and a change of work arrived. New judicial institutions appeared; new men were needed.

And Ivan Ilyich became this new man.

Ivan Ilyich was offered a post of examining magistrate and Ivan Ilyich accepted it, despite the

[1] The Schism in the Russian Orthodox church occurred in the 17th century, but numerous sects of Old Believers continued to flourish 200 years later

[2] A good chap (Fr.)

[3] Youth must have its day. (Fr.)

fact that the post was in a different province and he had to give up established relationships and establish new ones. Ivan Ilyich was given a send-off by his friends, they had a group photograph taken, presented him with a silver cigarette-case, and he left for his new post.

Ivan Ilyich was just as *comme il faut*[4] and decent an examining magistrate, adept at dividing his official duties from his private life and inspiring universal respect, as he had been an officer for special commissions. And in itself the work of a magistrate was of much greater interest and attractiveness for Ivan Ilyich than his former work. In his former work it had been pleasant to stroll in a free and easy way in his uniform jacket from Scharmer's past trembling petitioners awaiting an audience and functionaries who envied him, straight into the governor's office, and to sit down with him for tea and a cigarette; but the people directly dependent on his authority were few. Such people were only rural police chiefs and schismatics when he was sent with a commission; and he liked to treat such people who were dependent on him courteously, almost in a comradely way, he liked to let them feel that here he was, capable of crushing them, but treating them amicably and simply. Such people then had been few. But now, as an examining magistrate, Ivan Ilyich felt that all, all without exception, the most pompous, self-satisfied people – all were in his hands, and that he only had to write certain words on a piece of headed paper, and this pompous, self-satisfied man would be brought to him in the capacity of the accused or a witness, who would, if he did not want to let him sit down, stand before him and answer his questions. Ivan Ilyich never abused this power of his, on the contrary, he tried to emolliate its manifestations; but the consciousness of this power and the possibility of emolliating it comprised for him the main interest and attraction of his new work.

In the work itself, specifically in investigations, Ivan Ilyich very quickly assimilated the technique of dismissing from his mind all circumstances unrelated to work and of dressing any case, even the most complex, in a way such that only the externals of the case would be reflected on paper, and such that his personal view would be completely excluded and, most importantly, all the required formality would be observed. This was something new. And he was one of the first men to work out in practice the application of the Code of 1864.

On moving to the new town to the post of examining magistrate, Ivan Ilyich made new acquaintances, liaisons, set himself up in a new way and adopted a rather different tone. He set himself up at a certain dignified distance from the provincial authorities and chose the best circle of magistrates and wealthy gentlefolk living in the town, and adopted a tone of mild discontent with the government, of moderate liberalism and urbane civic-mindedness. At the same time, without in the least altering the elegance of his dress, Ivan Ilyich in his new position stopped shaving his chin and allowed his beard the freedom to grow where it liked.

Ivan Ilyich's life turned out very pleasantly in the new town too: society opposed to the governor was friendly and good; his salary was higher, and no small pleasure in life was then added by whist, which Ivan Ilyich began to play, having a capacity to play cards cheerfully, weighing things up quickly and very subtly, so that on the whole he always won.

After two years working in the new town Ivan Ilyich met his future wife. Praskovya Fyodorovna Mikhel was the most attractive, intelligent and brilliant girl of the circle in which Ivan Ilyich moved. Among the other amusements and ways of relaxing from the labours of a magistrate Ivan Ilyich established a playful,

4 Correct (Fr.)

easy relationship with Praskovya Fyodorovna.

While he was an officer for special commissions, Ivan Ilyich had generally danced; but as an examining magistrate he now danced as an exception. He now danced in the sense that 'I may indeed be in the new institutions and in the fifth grade, but if it's a matter of dancing, I can prove that in that respect I can do better than others.' Thus at the end of an evening he would occasionally dance with Praskovya Fyodorovna and it was primarily in the course of these dances that he made his conquest of Praskovya Fyodorovna. She fell in love with him. Ivan Ilyich had no clear, definite intention to marry, but when the girl fell in love with him he asked himself this question. 'Indeed, why on earth shouldn't I get married?' he said to himself.

The unmarried Praskovya Fyodorovna was of good gentle birth and not bad-looking; there was a little property. Ivan Ilyich could have counted on a more brilliant match, but this was a good match too. Ivan Ilyich had his salary, she, he hoped, would have just as much. A good family connection; she was nice, pretty and a perfectly respectable woman. To say that Ivan Ilyich married because he came to love his fiancée and found in her sympathy to his outlook on life would be just as incorrect as to say that he married because people of his social group gave this match their approval. Ivan Ilyich married for both reasons: he was doing something pleasant for himself in acquiring such a wife, and at the same time was doing what people in the highest places considered right.

And Ivan Ilyich got married.

The process of getting married itself and the first period of married life, with conjugal caresses, new furniture, new crockery, new linen, passed very well up until his wife's pregnancy, so that Ivan Ilyich was already starting to think that not only would marriage not disrupt the nature of a life that was easy, pleasant, cheerful and always seemly and approved by society, the nature Ivan Ilyich considered characteristic of life as a whole, but would further intensify it. Yet at this point, from the first months of his wife's pregnancy, there appeared a certain something that was new, unexpected, unpleasant, trying and unseemly, which could not have been expected and of which it was quite impossible to be free.

His wife, without any grounds, as it seemed to Ivan Ilyich, *de gaîté de coeur*[5], as he said to himself, began to disrupt the pleasantness and decorum of life: without any reason she was jealous of him, she demanded that he be attentive towards her, she found fault with everything and made unpleasant and vulgar scenes.

At first Ivan Ilyich hoped to rid himself of the unpleasantness of this situation with that same easy and decent attitude to life which had helped him out previously – he tried ignoring his wife's frame of mind, continued to live easily and pleasantly just as before: he invited friends round to make up a hand of cards, tried going out himself to the club or to see acquaintances. But on one occasion his wife began abusing him in vulgar terms with such energy and then continued so persistently to abuse him every time he failed to carry out her demands, evidently firmly resolved not to stop until he submitted, that is, until he stayed at home and until he was just as miserable as she was, that Ivan Ilyich was horrified. He realised that married life – at least with his wife – did not always promote the pleasantness and seemliness of life, but, on the contrary, often disrupted them, and that it was therefore essential to protect himself from these disruptions. And Ivan Ilyich began seeking out ways of doing this. His work was the one thing that impressed Praskovya Fyodorovna, and Ivan Ilyich, by means of work and the obligations that stemmed from it, began to battle with his wife, fencing off his own independent world.

With the birth of the child, attempts at feeding and various failures at it, with illnesses real and imaginary of the child and the mother, in which sympathy was demanded of Ivan Ilyich, but of which he could understand nothing, Ivan Ilyich's

[5] Out of sheer wantonness (Fr.)

need to fence off for himself a world outside the family became still more pressing.

As his wife became more irritable and demanding, so Ivan Ilyich shifted his life's centre of gravity more and more towards work. He began to like his work more and became more ambitious than he had been previously.

Very soon, no further than a year after the wedding, Ivan Ilyich realised that married life, while presenting certain comforts in life, was, in essence, a very complicated and difficult business, in relation to which, in order to fulfil one's duty, that is, to lead a decent life, approved by society, one had to work out a definite attitude, just as one did to work.

And Ivan Ilyich did work out such an attitude to married life for himself. He demanded of family life only those comforts of home cooking, a hostess, a bed, that it could give him, and, most importantly, the seemliness of external forms which were defined by social opinion. And for the remainder he sought cheerful pleasantness, and if he found it, he was very grateful; but if he met with a rebuff and grumpiness, he would immediately go off to his separate world of work that he had fenced off, and in that he would find pleasantness.

Ivan Ilyich was valued as a good, experienced worker, and after three years he was made deputy public prosecutor. New duties, their importance, the possibility of bringing anyone to trial and putting them in gaol, the public nature of his speeches, the success that Ivan Ilyich had in this – it all attracted him to work even more.

Children arrived. His wife became ever grumpier and crosser, but the attitude to domestic life that Ivan Ilyich had worked out made him almost impervious to her grumpiness.

After seven years working in the same town Ivan Ilyich was transferred to the post of public prosecutor in another province. They moved, there was little money, and his wife did not like the place to which they had moved. Although the salary was, indeed, higher than the previous

one, life was more expensive; and besides, two of the children died, and so family life became even more unpleasant for Ivan Ilyich.

For all the misfortunes that occurred in this new place of residence Praskovya Fyodorovna reproached her husband. The majority of topics of conversation between husband and wife, especially the upbringing of the children, led to questions about which there were memories of quarrels, and quarrels were ready to flare up at any moment. There remained only those rare periods of amorousness which came over the spouses, but which did not last long. These were islets to which they would put in for a time, but then they would launch themselves again into the sea of suppressed enmity, expressed in their alienation from one another. This alienation might have distressed Ivan Ilyich, if he had considered that things ought not to be this way, but now he already acknowledged this situation not only as satisfactory, but even as the objective of his activity within the family. His objective consisted in freeing himself more and more from this unpleasantness and lending it a harmless and seemly character; and he went about achieving this by spending less and less time with his family, but when he was forced to do so, he would try to safeguard his position with the presence of third parties. But the most important thing was that Ivan Ilyich had his work. For him the whole interest of life was concentrated in the world of work. And this interest engrossed him. The consciousness of his power, of the possibility of destroying anyone he might wish to destroy, his importance, even externally, on his arrival in court and at meetings with subordinates, his success before superiors and subordinates and, most importantly, his skill in conducting cases, which he could sense – it all gratified him and, along with talks with colleagues, dinners and whist, it filled his life. And so all in all Ivan Ilyich's life continued to go along in the way he considered it ought to have gone along: pleasantly and decently.

Ilya Ilf & Evgeny Petrov

Ilf and Petrov's American Road Trip
the 1935 Travelogue of Two Soviet Writers

Translated by Anne O. Fisher

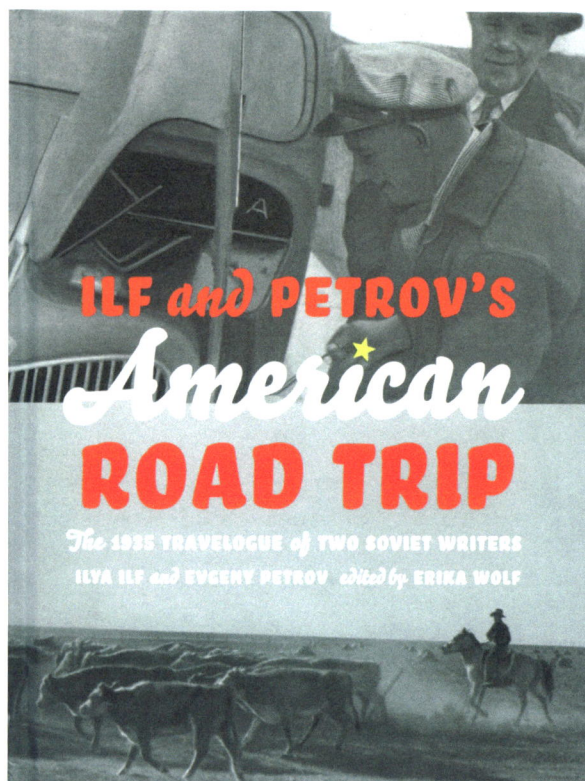

In the winter of 1935-1936, the popular Soviet writing duo Ilya Ilf and Evgeny Petrov came to America on assignment from *Pravda* to add their two cents' worth to a continuing Soviet discussion on America. Unlike other Soviet writers who had toured America, however, they spent four months in the country, two of them on a transcontinental road trip, Ilf snapping over 1000 amateur photographs along the way. Back home the writers published a photographic essay about their trip which is remarkable for its text-image interplay, its perceptive critique of American life, and its trenchant observations on race, religion, and popular entertainment in Depression-era America.

New York: Princeton Architectural Press & Cabinet Books, 2006
ISBN 978-1-56898-600-5

Ilya Ilf (1897-1937) and **Evgeny Petrov** (1903-1942) were born and raised in Odessa, a cultural melting pot known to this day as a vibrant centre of Russian and Jewish humour. Although most Russian-speakers now consider Ilf and Petrov an inseparable unit (Ilf's daughter, Aleksandra Ilf, humorously refers to herself as 'the daughter of Ilf and Petrov'), the two did not meet until 1925, when they were both working as journalists in Moscow. Petrov's older brother, an established writer, introduced the two and suggested that they work together, even giving them the plot of their first co-written novel, *The Twelve Chairs* (1928). This picaresque satire on the late NEP period jump-started Ilf and Petrov's career largely due to the appeal of the main character, a con man named Ostap Bender whose wit strongly suggested his creators' Odessan verbal flair. Quips by Bender such as 'How much does opium of the people cost?' and 'What, do you want the key to a room full of money, too?' quickly became part of everyday speech. Ilf and Petrov continued to write a sequel, *The Golden Calf* (1931), but were discouraged in 1932 from writing a third novel about the now-problematic Bender. By then, however, they had branched out from journalism to reviews, screenplays, and stories, and were fully established writers working for *Pravda* and *Literaturnaia gazeta*. Both promising careers were soon cut short; Ilf died from tuberculosis in 1937, while Petrov died in an accident while covering WWII in 1942.

Anne O. Fisher took Russian in her Oklahoma high school as a way of introducing some exoticism into her life. She studied for a year abroad in Russia while pursuing her B.A. at the University of Oklahoma; there she was introduced to *The Twelve Chairs*, a popular 1920s novel written jointly by two authors called Ilf and Petrov. Since then she has written a PhD dissertation at the University of Michigan on this book and its sequel, arguing that these popular books and their authors embody a particularly Soviet process of reading, writing, and publishing. In the fall of 2007 Fisher will be teaching at Williams College.

A Serious Look at America by Soviet Russia's Funniest Writers

Anne O. Fisher

Ilya Ilf and Evgeny Petrov published 'American Photographs,' a series of eleven photographic essays devoted to their four-month journey to America, in 1936 in the popular weekly magazine *Ogonek*. 'American Photographs' was never republished. A year later the writers released a book-length revision of their travelogue with no photographs, called *One-Storied America*. Although one edition of *One-Storied America* which included some of Ilf's photographs appeared in 1947, it has since become a bibliographic rarity. Thus the two writers' doubled vision of America, marked by the interplay of photographs and text, was effectively forgotten, replaced by a text-only narrative.

Much was lost as a result. Art historian Erika Wolf came across 'American Photographs' while working on the early Soviet photographer and theorist Aleksander Rodchenko; she recognized the value of Ilf and Petrov's photo-essay and began rescuing it from oblivion, inviting me in 2006 to translate the text for an English-language recreation. With the help of Ilf's daughter Aleksandra Ilf, Wolf devoted much time and effort to tracking down prints and negatives in Moscow, only to find that all the archived negatives were lost, perhaps destroyed, and many of the surviving prints suffer from neglect and deterioration. In her words, Ilf and Petrov's American Road Trip 'resurrects a significant body of work in the history of Soviet visual culture and even in the history of documentary images of the United States.'

Hear, hear. As translator, I can add that the text of 'American Photographs' is no less worthy of rescue, in part because of the inclusive, engaging narrative which the text-image interplay encourages Ilf and Petrov to create. This narrative is also notable for its characteristic humour, as well as for its fascination with American English, particularly advertising, which Ilf and Petrov treat as the American counterpart of the omnipresent Soviet political rhetoric they mocked

All photographs from Ilf and Petrov's photo-journal, which provides illustrations for the book so memorably in their novels about Ostap Bender. This translation was also interesting for me as an American since it required me not just to reverse-translate into 1930s American English, but to convey the evident amusement with which these foreign travellers heard and recorded that English.

The presence of Ilf's photographs changes the nature of the narrative, allowing readers to stand next to Ilf and Petrov and observe a vista or person along with them. Ilf once half-jokingly described himself as a *zevaka* or rubbernecker, but it is the process of observing and evaluating on which his and Petrov's art is based, and it is this process which these photographs allow us to share. Thus the writers' exhortations, observations, and asides are directed to us, as when they groan at the advertising for *The Crusades*, an epic by Cecil B. DeMille: 'Comrades and brothers, let's walk on by! God will be their judge, these Cecils!' This conversational immediacy, the shared gaze at the American other, and the implicit assumption that readers agree with Ilf and Petrov's value judgments all create a sense of community between narrator and narratee and reinforce the importance of accurately reproducing the narrative's informal, oral texture.

It is impossible to discuss Ilf and Petrov's writing without mentioning their rich palette of humour. Much of it depends on structure and contrast, as with one of their favourite structures, a list in which the final element doesn't fit with the others. This specimen, a description of the co-writers' first encounter with a burrito in Santa Fe, is paired with exaggeration: 'Judging by the taste, the pancakes were apparently filled with onion, red pepper, and thinly sliced gunpowder. A bonfire caught fire in our mouths and burned for at least three days.' Another structural figure they use to create humorous contrast is the parallel construction. They use it to convey their first impressions upon entering the harbour at New York, where 'two things caught our attention. One was small and green; we were later told that it was the Statue of Liberty. The other one was huge and insolent; it was a billboard advertising Wrigley's Chewing Gum.' Ilf and Petrov also vary their tone to humorous effect. Sometimes they employ a sort of faux-naïve sarcasm, as when they claim that if there were no advertising in America, 'life would become unbelievably complicated.

People would have to think for themselves about every single thing they did. No sir, it's definitely better with advertising.' Sometimes they stick to deadpan asides, as when they describe the 'vulgar' Hollywood habit of capturing movie stars' handprints in concrete: 'This is, so to speak, the triumph of civilization.' In terms of their most characteristic mode of humour, ironic quotation or appropriation of official discourse, they were at a slight disadvantage, since only Petrov spoke English. Still, they paid careful attention to the two kinds of discourse they encountered most frequently on their trip: road signs, which they generally appreciate, and advertising, which they mock relentlessly in the chapter of the same name.

Ilf and Petrov's portrayal of American speech was also, I suspect, not quite straightforward. Here's an example, in which Ilf and Petrov's entourage asks a passer-by for directions:

- Боже ты мой! Дорогу на Кливлэнд! – говорил он горячо. – Да ведь я родился в Кливлэнде. Уж я-то знаю дорогу на Кливлэнд. Еще бы! На меня вы можете смело положиться. Ай-яй-яй! Дорогу на Кливлэнд! Нет, вам положительно повезло, что вы напали на меня.

'Oh my goodness! The way to Cleveland!' he was saying excitedly. 'After all, I was born in Cleveland. If anybody knows the way to Cleveland, it's me. I'd say so! You can count on me for sure. Oh, my, yes. The way to Cleveland! Yep, you really got lucky when you ran into me.'

One senses that they were as tickled by the word 'Cleveland' as they were by the local yokel's eagerness to please. And I confess that I was surprised to find that 'Ai-yai-yai' is, or was, an interjection to be heard from a native of the Midwest.

Some parts of Ilf and Petrov's narrative are hopelessly dated or overtly politically correct, while others, for better or worse, still ring true. Ilf and Petrov's *American Road Trip* has preserved their candid portrait of America so that we may not only contemplate what we looked like to them seventy years ago, but consider what we'll look like to other curious foreign guests in another seventy years.

Ilya Ilf and Evgeny Petrov, *Ilf and Petrov's American road trip*
The 1935 travelogue of two Soviet writers

Extract

On the fifth day of travel across the Atlantic Ocean we saw the gigantic buildings of New York. America was before us.

But when we had been in New York for a week and had begun, as we thought, to understand America, we were suddenly and unexpectedly told that New York isn't America at all. We were told that New York is a bridge between Europe and America and that we were still just on the bridge.

Then we went to Washington, being firmly convinced that the capital of the United States would, undoubtedly, be America. We spent a day there and by evening we had fallen in love with that purely American city. However, that very evening we were told that on no account could Washington be considered America. We were told that it is the city of government clerks, while America is something completely different.

Bewildered, we went to Hartford, a city in the state of Connecticut, where the great American writer Mark Twain spent his mature years. Much to our horror, the locals announced in unison that Hartford isn't exactly the real America either. They couldn't say for certain where the actual America is located. Some said that the real America is the southern states, while others maintained that it is the western ones. A few didn't say anything at all – they just pointed their fingers vaguely into space.

Then we decided to act in an organized fashion: to travel the entire country by car, to cross it from the Atlantic Ocean to the Pacific and to return by another road along the Gulf of Mexico, reasoning that indeed somewhere we'd be sure to find America.

We returned to New York, bought a Ford (travelling in your own car is the cheapest way to travel in the United States), insured it and ourselves, and one chilly November morning we set out from New York for America.

ix. Advertising

Advertising has so permeated American life that if one fine day Americans woke up and found that all advertising had disappeared, the majority of them would be in a desperate position. It would be impossible to figure out things like:

Which cigarettes to smoke?

Which store to buy clothes at?

Which refreshing drink to quench your thirst with – Coca-Cola or Ginger Ale?

Which whiskey to drink – White Horse or Johnny Walker?

Which company's gasoline to buy – Shell or Standard Oil?

Which God to believe in – the Baptist one or the Methodist one?

In general, everything would go to hell without advertising. Life would become unbelievably complicated. People would have to think for themselves about every single thing they did.

No sir, it's definitely better with advertising. An American doesn't have to think about anything. Big business thinks for him.

He doesn't have to sprain his brain choosing a refreshing drink.

'Drink Coca-Cola!'

'Coca-Cola refreshes a dry throat!'

'Coca-Cola stimulates the nervous system!'

'Coca-Cola is good for you!'

In general, everything will come up roses for the person who drinks Coca-Cola!

The average American, notwithstanding his apparent energetic activity, is actually very passive by nature. You have to give everything to him pre-cooked. Tell him which drink is better, and he'll drink it. Tell him which political party is more in his interest, and he'll vote for it. Tell him which God is the 'real' one, and he'll believe in him. But whatever else you do, don't force him to think. He doesn't like to and is not very good at it. And so that he'll believe your words, you have to repeat them as often as possible. All American advertising is built that way, both commercial and political, all of it.

And advertising lurks in wait for you everywhere: at home and at your friends' homes, on the street and on the highway, in taxis, in the subway, in trains, in planes, in ambulances, everywhere.

We were still on board the ocean liner Normandie and tugboats were just pulling the steamship into New York Harbor when two things caught our attention. One was small and green;

later we were told that it was the Statue of Liberty. The other one was huge and insolent; it was a billboard advertising Wrigley's Chewing Gum.

From that time on the little green mug with the enormous megaphone followed us all over America, convincing, begging, urging, cajoling, and demanding that we chew Wrigley's, the flavourful, incomparable, first-class gum.

We withstood it for a month. We didn't drink Coca-Cola. We even held out for another month. But then advertising finally got to us. We experienced the drink. We can speak with clear consciences. Yes, Coca-Cola does refresh the throat, stimulate the nerves, and has a salutary effect on a weakened constitution. How could we not say that, when for three months it's been drilled into our skulls every day, every hour and every minute?

Cigarette advertising is even more terrible, insistent, and shrill than advertising for chewing gum and refreshing drinks. Chesterfield, Camel, Lucky Strike, and other tobacco products are advertised with a frenzy otherwise found only in the dances of whirling dervishes or in the now no longer observed celebration of Shakhsei-Vakhsei, the celebrants of which wildly stabbed themselves with knives and covered themselves with blood in honor of their deity.[1] The fiery writing burns all night long above America, and all day long the garish billboards hurt your eyes: 'The Best in the World! Toasted Cigarettes! They Bring You Success! The Best in the Solar System!'

Perhaps this is a monument to a horse that

[1] This is a reference to the Shi'a observance of the Muslim holiday Aashurah; some Shi'a celebrate this holiday with a traditional flagellation ritual.

perished heroically in the war between the North and the South to free the Negroes? Alas, no! This horse with the inspired eyes is advertising the whiskey White Horse. The consumer can find out more information about this drink if he goes to the White Tavern, which is located adjacent. There he will discover that you can get dead drunk on this whiskey in five minutes, that the wife of whoever drinks it will never cheat on him, that his children will grow up safe and sound, and that they'll even get good jobs. The distinguishing characteristic of American advertising is its grotesque exaggeration, designed to provoke a smile from potential customers. The most important thing is that they read the announcement. Then everything's all set. It'll do its job in time, like a slow-acting oriental poison.

Drinks aren't the only things that get advertised. Whole towns advertise themselves. Next to the road stands a colossal sign on which the town of Carlsbad, New Mexico state, conveys information about itself: '23 miles to Carlsbad. Paved road. Famous mineral springs. Good churches. Theatres. Free bathing beach. Lots of shade. Splendid hotel. Drive into Carlsbad.' The town is invested in getting you to go there. Even if you're not interested in the mineral springs, you'll definitely buy some German

gasoline for the road or have dinner while you're in town. So you'll have left a few dollars, anyway. Every little bit helps. And maybe you'll drop by one of Carlsbad's good churches. Then God will get to feel good too.

Churchgoers don't lag behind the laity one bit. Neon signs burn all night, announcing entertainment of both a spiritual and a non-spiritual nature to the visitors for whom it has been arranged. The Baptist church tempts you with a school choir, while the Congregational church beckons with a social hour. 'Come by! You'll be satisfied with our service.'

The American word publicity, denoting advertising, actually has a wider meaning. It means not only actual advertising, but also every single mention of the advertised object or person at all. If, for example, they are doing publicity for some actor, then even an article in the paper about how he just had a successful operation and is well on his way to recovery is also considered advertising. One American told us with a certain amount of envy that the Lord gets great publicity in the United States. Fifty thousand clergymen talk about him every day.

Advertising billboards are always popping up along the road. Sometimes there's a whole series of them spread out along the road for

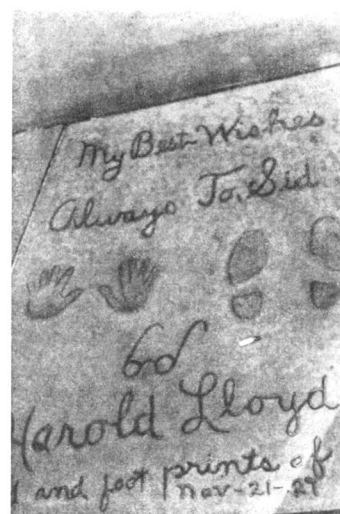

several miles, something like a riddle game. Absolutely identical yellow placards with black letters ask travellers questions and then in a hundred feet give the answers. There are Bible verses, jokes, and various informative facts of a geographic or historical nature. As a result, the traveller finds the name of a warmly recommended shaving soap on the exact same kind of little yellow placard from which, bored, he was hoping to extract a few more useful facts. With disgust he realizes that that name will be stuck in his head for the rest of his life.[2]

Once we saw a sign that was inspired not by commercial considerations alone. Some benefactor of humanity, with the help of the Viking Press company, had placed the following dictum on the road: 'Revolution is a form of government that is only possible abroad.'[3] The best thing about this daring assertion is that revolution is supposedly a 'form of government.' Incidentally, the very fact of such a sign's presence shows that there are people who need to be convinced that there can never be a revolution in America.

Whether he looks straight ahead, to the right, or to the left, the American sees advertising everywhere. But he even sees advertising when he raises his eyes to the heavens. An airplane

dashingly writes out words upon the blue sky, making publicity for somebody or something.

Even on roads running through the desert, advertising acts with full force. Come mountains, cliffs, or chasms, the traveller must know that oil from Shell is an excellent oil, as these three jolly mice can testify. This oil is so good that the cute little mice just can't help but dance from joy.

Sometimes the private initiative of some small gas-station owner takes its place alongside national advertising campaigns. Here, he has hung above his establishment a comical little man made from empty oil cans. The man sways in the wind, clanks, and moans. In this manner sound is added to visual advertising.

And of course, as with everything in America, the film industry sets the standard for vulgarity.

The footprints and handprints of movie stars are preserved in concrete slabs outside the entrance to one of Hollywood's film studios. The little hands and little feet of Mary Pickford, Harold Lloyd's paw prints and hoof prints. There are prints of other movie stars' extremities, too. This is, so to speak, the triumph of civilization.

[2] This is a description of the immensely successful and highly visible Burma Shave signs, a staple of American highway culture from the 1920s to the 1960s.

[3] The qualifier 'that is only possible' has been inserted into the Russian description of this sign – an addition that was necessary for this interpretation. Again the joke was on Ilf and Petrov. This is an ad for Boners, a highly popular humor anthology illustrated by Dr. Seuss that was first published in 1931.

LUDMILA ULITSKAYA

SONECHKA: A NOVELLA AND STORIES

TRANSLATED BY ARCH TAIT

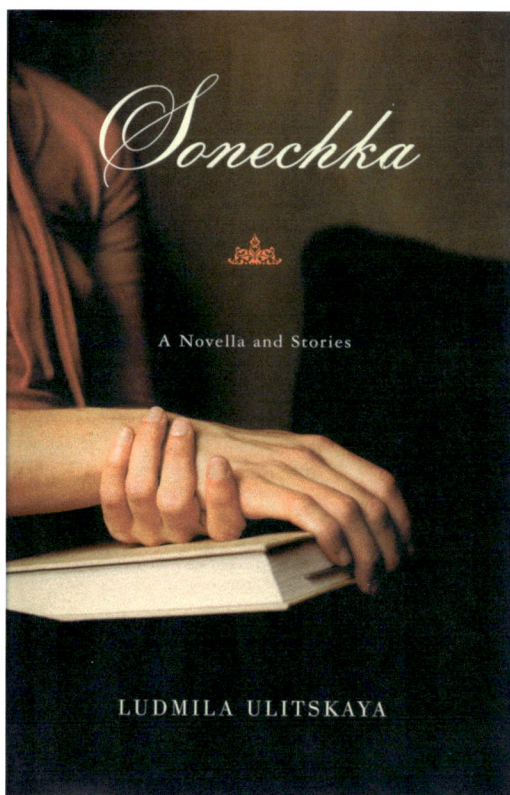

Sonechka: A Novella and Stories

This collection of short fiction was published by
Schocken Books (Random House), New York in
2005 and brings together Ludmila Ulitskaya's
masterpiece, the novella 'Sonechka', and the
stories 'The Queen of Spades', 'Zurich', 'The Beast',
'Angel', and 'The Orlov-Sokolovs' (reprinted in the
New Yorker). 'If living well is the best revenge [on
a totalitarian regime] then Ludmila Ulitskaya's
characters, in choosing to embrace the unique
gifts that their lives bring them, are small heroes
of the quotidian, their stories as funny and tender
as they are brilliantly told'.

New York: Schocken
Books, 2005
ISBN 0-8052-4195-7

Ludmila Ulitskaya was born in 1943 in the Urals. She graduated from Moscow University with a Master's Degree in Biology and worked at the Institute of Genetics as a research scientist. Shortly before perestroika, in 1979-82, she became Repertory Director of the Hebrew Theatre of Moscow and took up script writing. She is the author of twelve books of fiction, which have sold over 1.2 million copies, of three volumes of tales for children and of six plays. Ludmila won the Russian Booker Prize in 2002 for her novel *The Kukotsky Case*, and has won other major literary prizes in Italy, France, Russia and China.

Arch Tait learned Russian at Latymer Upper School, London; Trinity Hall, Cambridge; and Moscow State University. He has a PhD in Russian literature from Cambridge and began translating in earnest in 1986 after a meeting with Valentina Jacques, then editor of the magazine *Soviet Literature*. From 1993-2003 he was the UK editor of the *Glas New Russian Writing* translation series, whose editor-in-chief was Valentina's successor, Natasha Perova. To date he has translated 14 books, 30 short stories and 25 articles by most of the leading Russian writers of today. His translation of Anna Politkovskaya's *A Russian Diary* was published in April 2007 by Harvill Secker.

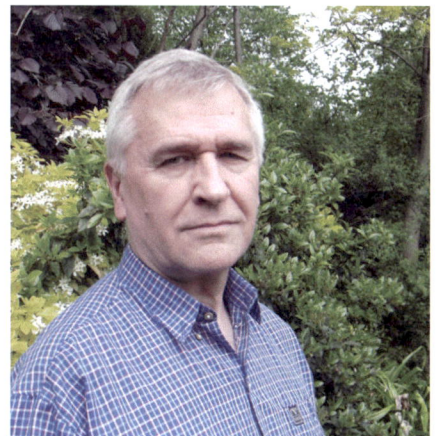

Arch Tait ON ELUDING FALSE CERTAINTIES

Since 1993 I have translated a novel, a novella, and eleven short stories by Ludmila Ulitskaya, and have always found them a delight. She won the Russian Booker Prize in 2002, and has also won the Penne Prize (Italy) in 1997 and 2006; the Medici Prize (France) in 1998; Novel of the Year Prize and Best Writer of the Year Ivanushka Prize (both Russia) in 2004; the National Literature Prize (China) in 2005; and the National Olympia Prize of the Russian Academy of Business in 2007.

Ludmila chooses as her heroines, and occasionally heroes, people who were completely marginal in the USSR, hence unsovietised, and who managed to wring a victory out of their highly unpromising circumstances: a teenager in a communal apartment who falls in love with a man in his sixties and bears him a succession of fine sons while the neighbours puzzle over how she can be getting pregnant; an unremarkable provincial lady librarian who marries an exiled artist and turns adversity into success when, in old age, he becomes infatuated with a much younger woman; an Uzbek nurse whose Russian husband abandons his family when their mentally retarded daughter is born, and who, when terminally ill, finds a way of ensuring her daughter's future; or one of the last Pontic Greeks left in the Crimea, overlooked during Stalin's deportation because her married name is Mendez, who contrives to welcome a vast and ramified family to her home each year. It has been said that, in her stories, love and life are lived 'under the radar of oppression. If living well is the best revenge, then Ludmila Ulitskaya's characters, in choosing to embrace the unique gifts their lives bring them, are small heroes of the quotidian'. Lesley Chamberlain wrote, 'Ulitskaya's fresh, delicately sensual writing, full of the joys and pitfalls of everyday, is a world away from gloomy, fear-driven reflections on the plight of human beings under the Soviet heel… With Ulitskaya, Russian fiction rediscovered a consoling and universal normality'. Zinovy Zinik observed that, 'In her intelligent narratives human dignity triumphs against all odds over misery and oppression'.

Ulitskaya's prose is also peopled by villains, most of whom have been corrupted by the blandishments of fake success offered by the Soviet system: a vampire-like femme fatale who sucks the life out of her family as she pursues gratification; an ageing paedophile professor who marries a cleaning lady with a handsome young son; an intellectually arrogant young couple whose ambitions enable the Soviet system to take them away from producing the family they were predestined to have; a schoolteacher who loiters around an international conference and snares a Swiss businessman, herself becoming successful but empty.

Ludmila's style is very literary. Her references, often to medicine and physics, can be arcane, and her sentences long and serpentine. An appreciative reviewer really did write that 'Arch Tait's translation faithfully captures Ulitskaya's carefully constructed colloquial style'. There is usually a strong narrative presence in her writing, and the stories have an implied moral to the effect that disregarding ancient wisdom leads to an abyss of meaninglessness: a Judaic illustration of the law of karma. As efforts are strenuously being made to return all the most corrupting features of the Soviet system, her writing reminds us of the unwisdom of building palaces on sand.

I have chosen an excerpt from the short story 'The Queen of Spades', which has four principal female characters, belonging to four generations. Great-grandmother was a society belle before the revolution and had no trouble changing landmarks. Her daughter is a conformist but good-hearted eye surgeon, her granddaughter a wilful woman with a secret lovelife, and her great-granddaughter an equally self-willed young girl. The eye surgeon married her student, who was obliged to emigrate, but many decades later he returns to the Soviet Union as perestroika is getting underway to meet the grandchildren he has never seen. This passage has a lot of dialogue, which is always fun to translate, and gives a great sense of the unease which the loosening of tyranny brought to many who had relied for so long on false certainties.

THE QUEEN OF SPADES

EXTRACT

The children wanted to see him back to the hotel. He was staying nearby, in what had been the Hotel Balchug. It had been transformed over the last few years into something quite magnificent, like the crystal bridge in the fairy tale which in a single night spans from shore to shore.

'No, let's decide that we have said goodbye,' he announced with unexpected firmness and Grisha, who would whine about anything, usually until he got his way, immediately accepted the situation.

Marek wound his unendurably red scarf round his neck and kissed the children for the last time as naturally as if it were not a mere five days before that he had first met them. Then from the hallstand he took Anna's fur coat, which was balding on the breast, and said in that inexorable voice,

'Let's go for one last walk.'

For some reason Anna submitted, although a minute before she had had no intention of going down to the street with him. Without a word she squeezed into the coat, and put round her neck a shawl which was a present from Orenburg. She accepted presents if she was offered them: boxes of chocolates, books, envelopes with money. She took them and thanked the givers in a reserved way. She never named the price for her own operations and in that respect, although she was quite unaware of it, she was following exactly in her late father's footsteps.

In the street he took her arm. From Lavrushinsky Lane they came out on to Ordynka. The street was clean, snowy white, and virtually deserted. The few passers-by looked round at the lean foreigner wearing only a light-coloured jacket and walking unhurriedly along with an elderly citizen packaged in a thick fur coat. They couldn't relate her to him in any way: she looked too educated to be his cleaner, and she was too old and badly dressed to be his wife.

'What a lovely city. For some reason I was remembering it as gloomy and dirty.'

'There are different sides to it,' Anna responded politely.

'Why did you come back?' she was wondering.

'Turning everything upside down, unsettling everyone ...' But she did not say it out loud.

'Let's go and sit down somewhere,' he suggested.

'Where? At night?' she asked in surprise.

'There are any number of places open at night. There's a marvellous restaurant quite near here. We had lunch there yesterday with the children.'

'You have to be up at the crack of dawn tomorrow,' Anna said evasively.

Marek was going back on an early flight, and she herself had to get up at half past six. The reference to tomorrow calmed her. He would leave, everything would get back to normal, all this turmoil in the family would come to an end.

'I would like to invite the children to come to Greece for the summer. Would you mind?'

'Not at all.'

'You are an angel, Anelia. And my greatest loss.'

Anna said nothing. Why on earth had she come out with him? It could only be because she had been used to doing as she was told at home for so many years. She really should have refused.

He detected her wordless irritation and caught hold of her puffy mittens with his thin glove.

'Anna, do you think I don't see or understand anything? Emigration is a hard school, very hard, and I have experienced it three times. From Polish to Russian, from Russian to Hebrew, and for the last fifteen years I have been speaking English. Each time you have to learn your way into a new life again from scratch. I have been through all sorts of things. I have fought in wars, starved ... I have even been in prison.'

What a sweet boy he used to be, a student in the third year, so different from the hearty males performing the robust ritual of the dog's wedding beside her mother. As part of her duties as a postgraduate she had been conducting an undergraduate seminar at the time, and their romance began among the retorts and the bacilli. For a long time she meticulously concealed their relationship from everyone. It was embarrassing that he was so young, but it was precisely his youthfulness, the absence of aggressive meat, that subconsciously attracted her to him. He had a white, hairless chest and a constellation of birthmarks, the dipper of Ursa Major to the left, near the nipple. To this day he was the only man there had been in her life, but she never regretted either that, or the fact that it had been him. She always knew, though, that marriage was not central to her life. She was around sixteen when she decided never to get married. She knew nothing more repugnant than the purring voice, the sexually aroused laughter and the drawn-out moaning proceeding from her mother's bedroom. The eternal sex hunt, animals on heat. For a moment she relapsed into an immensely powerful childish sense of the irredeemable filthiness of sex, when it was an embarrassment to look at any married couple because you immediately imagined them, sweating and grunting, getting on with that dirt. How fine to be a nun, dressed all in white, pure, without any of this. But what a joy it was, all the same, that Katya existed.

Marek was talking, saying something, but it flew past her like the snow. She was suddenly jolted back to herself by his faltering words.

'... a real miracle how a curse can turn into a blessing. This monster, this daemon of egoism, the Queen of Spades, has destroyed everything, has put everyone in their graves. And how do you bear it? You are simply a saint.'

'Me? A saint?' Anna stopped in her tracks as if she had walked into a lamppost. 'I am afraid of her ... and there is my duty ... and I feel sorry for her.'

He brought his face close to hers, and she could see that he was not by any means so young. His skin was that of an old man, with little incised wrinkles and senile dark freckles beneath the year-round suntan.

'How can I help you? What can I do for you?' She waved a grey mitten at him:
'See me back home.'

Marek called from his Johannesburg more frequently than her friends called from Sviblovo. Grisha waited frantically for his calls, pouncing on the telephone and shouting to absolutely anyone who rang, 'Marek! Is that you?' Lenochka devoted herself exclusively to the study of English and to readying herself for the journey abroad. She became remarkably businesslike, not an

attribute which had been much in evidence up till then. She set about selecting the location for her future studies with intelligence and discernment. Even Katya, always calm and a little indolent, was expecting indefinable changes which would relate in some way to the reappearance of her father. She seemed to have cooled a little towards her secret lover who, for his part, began making non-committal remarks about possibly leaving his family.

Marek enthusiastically set about fulfilling his Christmas promises. The first to materialise was shoes of an uncompromisingly orthopaedic appearance for Mour. They were exceptionally ugly and, probably, no less exceptionally comfortable, and they were brought directly to their home by an old friend of Marek's who was practically a first secretary at the Israeli Embassy. Mour did not even try them on, merely muttered something. They had schoolgirl heels and were elasticated, as befitted footwear for the elderly. For the past seventy years Mour had worn only court shoes with heels as elegant as the latest fashion allowed.

The pair of shoes was followed by a pair of small computers, their size in inverse proportion to their cost. He also took time to find computer games for Grisha. Lenochka had yet to get over the amateur ciné camera he had left her before departing. She was still in thrall to that special perspective on the world revealed by a viewfinder when her new present arrived, demanding that she should promptly learn to do all the things which were now possible with its magical assistance.

Finally, six weeks after Marek's departure, there came an invitation from Thessaloniki, signed by a certain Evangelia Daoul who was a close friend of Marek's wife. Of Marek's wife all that was known was that she had a Greek friend who would send them an invitation.

The wording of the invitation left it open to them to come at any time between June and September.

Grisha, delighted to seventh heaven by the mere sight of the envelope with its rectangular window, rushed round the apartment with it until he collided with Mour who was steering towards the kitchen in her metal contraption. He waved the envelope in her face.

English translations include Sonechka and Other Stories, 1998; The Funeral Party, 1999; Medea and Her Children, 2002; Sonechka: A Novel and Stories, Schocken, 2005.

Ludmila Ulitskaya's work has been translated into twenty-five other languages.

'Look, Mour, we're going to Greece, to the Island of Seriphos. Marek has invited us.'

'What nonsense!' Mour snorted. She never made concessions of any kind to age. 'You're going nowhere.'

'We are, we are!' Grisha shouted, jumping up and down in excitement.

Mour wrenched her hand from the rail of her walker and stuck it with great aplomb under the nose of her eight-year-old grandson in an obscene gesture, the bright red nail of her thumb jutting out between the fingers of her clenched fist. With her other hand she deftly snatched the invitation from the grasp of the startled boy, who had not been expecting such an audacious attack. Leaning her elbows on the rails, she screwed up the envelope and threw it in a ball as solid as a good snowball straight at the front door.

'You foul old witch!' Grisha howled and rushed to the door.

Katya jumped out of her room, seized her son, not knowing what had transpired between him and her grandmother. Grisha was straightening out some kind of paper and continuing to shout wholly unexpected words:

'You god-forsaken old crow! You fucked-up old bitch!'

Lowering her eyelids, Mour reproached her granddaughter more in sorrow than in anger:

'Remove your little bastard, my dear. My dear, one really does have to teach children a modicum of good manners.' Her wheels squeaking, she proceeded to the kitchen.

Katya, still unaware of what the scrap of paper was that the sobbing Grisha was trying to straighten out, dragged him off to her room from whence his sobs were to be heard for a long time afterwards.

That day Anna returned from work more tired than usual. Some things are more draining than work itself. A seriously injured girl had been brought in. They had no suitably qualified doctor in the paediatric department for her. She was about Grisha's age and had a shrapnel wound. The operation had been very distressing.

Putting the blood-pressure cuff back in its case, Anna wondered where Mour got her energy from. With those readings she should have been feeling weak and sleepy, but instead she was aggressive and acute in her reactions. Other mechanisms were evidently coming into play. Ah, well, gerontology …

'You're not listening to me! What are you thinking about? I'm against it, do you hear? I was never in Greece. They are going nowhere!' Mour was tugging at Anna's sleeve.

'Yes, yes, of course. Of course, Mama.'

'What do you mean, of course? Don't you mama me!' Mour shrieked.

'Everything will be just as you wish,' Anna said in a soothing tone.

'No, my dear mother. Not this time!' Anna decided emphatically, for the first time in her life. The word 'no' had not yet been uttered, but it already existed. It had already broken through like a puny shoot. She decided simply to face her mother with the fact of her family's disobedience without any preliminary discussion. One could only imagine what kind of hullabaloo this bloodless insect would raise when it became apparent that the children had left.

By early June they had obtained external passports for travel abroad and the necessary visas. Air tickets to Athens had been booked for the twelfth of June. That same day, in accordance with Anna's ingenious plan, had been chosen for the move to the dacha. Everything had been thought through down to the last detail. In the morning Katya and the children would go to Sheremetievo Airport, which should rouse no suspicion because Katya always went on ahead to the dacha in order to prepare it for Mour's arrival. A taxi had been ordered for twelve to take Mour and Anna there. Anna hoped the turmoil of the move would soften the blow, the more so since preparations to go to the dacha would disguise the great escape. Grisha and Lenochka were simply bursting with excitement, especially Grisha. His semi-Greek grandfather had turned up at just the right moment. All Grisha's classmates had been abroad. He was almost the only one who had never been taken further then Krasnaya Pakhra. A photograph of his grandfather with his curly white hair standing on board a white yacht had been shown to the entire class and successfully made up for the absence of a father of his own.

GLAS BOOKS =
NEW RUSSIAN WRITING

The Moscow publisher GLAS, run by Natasha Perova, is a collaboration between UK and US translators with Russian editors and critics, who believe that the great Russian literary tradition lives on.

Editors: Natasha Perova and Joanne Turnbull

'GLAS gives us a sense of Russian literature in motion. If it cannot perhaps mercifully convey fully what it is like to live in Russia at present, GLAS at least gives us a taste of what it is to be a reader there' – Times Literary Supplement

www.russianpress.com/glas

War & Peace
Contemporary Russian Prose
ISBN 5-7172-0074-9

Young authors' stories about the modern-day Russian army (War) and stories by and about women (Peace). Together they provide a thought-provoking exposé of post-post-perestroika Russia.

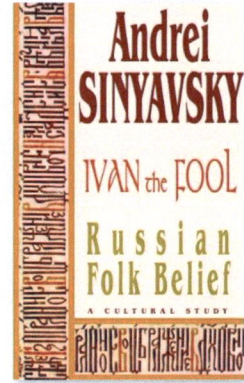

Ivan the Fool: Russian Folk Belief
By Andrei Sinyavsky
Translated by Joanne Turnbull
ISBN 978-5-7172-0077-6

A masterly and extremely readable survey covering folk superstitions and customs, house and nature spirits, pagan gods, Christianization, saints, the Schism, Old Believers, religious sects, and the symbolism in Russian fairy tales.

The Grassy Street
By Asar Eppel
Translated by Joanne Turnbull
ISBN 5-7172-0039-0

The portrait of a moldering Moscow outskirt in the 1940s, The Grassy Street is fascinating for the picture Eppel paints – with his remarkable tenderness, humor and challenge

Master of the Grass
By Nina Gabrielyan
Translated by Kate Cook
ISBN 5-7172-0066-8

A short novel about the drama of a narcissistic man who is irresistibly drawn to his own reflection in the mirror, his best companion since childhood and throughout life.

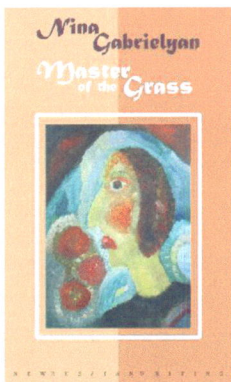

Skunk: A Life
By Peter Aleshkovsky
Translated by Arch Tait
ISBN 5-7172-0033-1

'Aleshkovsky is a highly talented Russian writer with a powerful sense of the disorders and conflicts of his society. Here is a strong and exciting voice in the lively world of Russian fiction.' – Malcolm Bradbury

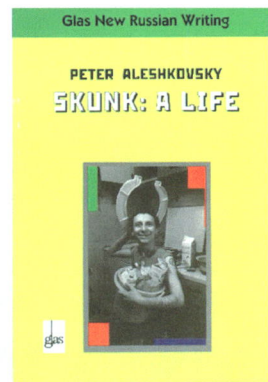

The Road to Rome
By Nikolai Klimontovich
Translated by Frank Williams
ISBN 5-7172-0069-2

Naughty autobiographical narratives about semi-underground life in Moscow in the 1970s and '80s: 'a veritable Moscow Decameron,' 'the Soviet Casanova.'

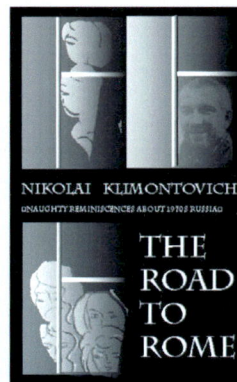

The Scared Generation:
The Old Arbat by Boris Yampolsky
The Manhunt by Vasil Bykov
ISBN 5-7172-0071-4

These two novels, in their different ways, explore the inner powerlessness of the victims of Stalinism. Written in an intense, suffocating style they make powerful reading.

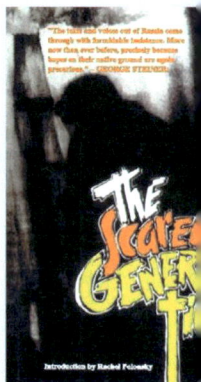

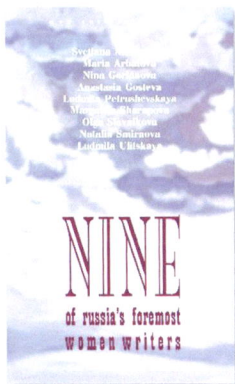

The Portable Platonov
Translated by Robert Chandler

ISBN 5-7172-0046-3

This collection presents various facets of Platonov's genius: three chpters from the novel Chevengur; his best play Fourteen Little Red Huts; two folktales; and the story 'Among Animals and Plants'. 'In the 20th century the best Russian prose has been written by our poets and Platonov.'
– Joseph Brodsky.

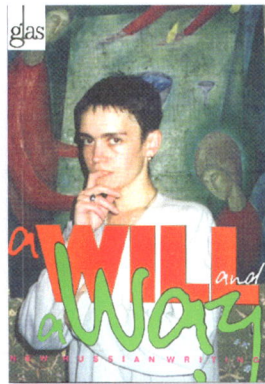

Stamp Album: A Collection of People, Things, Relationships and Words
By Andrei Sergeev
Translated by Joanne Turnbull

ISBN 5-7172-0059-5

Winner of the Russian Booker Prize, Stamp Album is a pastiche of memories about growing up in Stalin's Russia, 'illustrated' with family documents, newspaper clippings, slogans, letters, children's rhymes and irreverences.

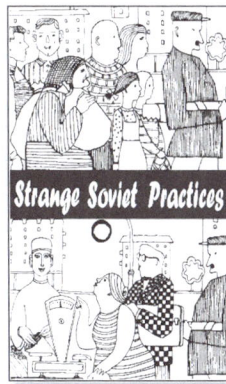

Here I Am, Essays and Performance Poems
By Lev Rubinstein
Translated by Joanne Turnbull

ISBN 5-7172-0058-7

A leader of Moscow Conceptualism, Rubinstein parodies the idiocy of daily life in the USSR by treating it as something incredibly serious and important.

A Novel Without Lies
By Anatoly Mariengof
Translated by Jose Alaniz

ISBN 5-7172-0049-8

The story of Mariengof's extraordinary friendship with the extraordinary poet Sergei Esenin in the upside down world of post-revolutionary. 'You should read Mariengof's marvelous novel about the half-glamorous, half-wretched 1920s.' TLS

Nine of Russia's Foremost Women Writers

ISBN 5-7172-0063-3

Included in this collection are Svetlana Alexiyevich, a Byelorussian dissident; Maria Arbatova, 'Russia's Erica Jong'; Ludmila Petrushevkaya, an internationally known author, Olga Slavnikova, a Russian Booker winner; Ludmila Ulitskaya and others.

A Will & A Way, Women's Stories

ISBN 5-7172-0029-3

The heroines range from a wide-eyed child to a 95-year-old sculptress in love with a man sixty years her junior, a noblewoman adrift in Moscow to an old woman forgotten in an abandoned village, from a gynecologist to a fairytale princess. Maria Arbatova, Ludmila Petrushevskaya, Dina Rubina, Larissa Miller and others.

Strange Soviet Practices

ISBN 5-7172-0068-4

A collection of short stories and documents illustrating some typically Soviet phenomena. This collection answers to some extent the questions most often asked by people in the West about the incomprehensible ways of the artificial and inhuman Soviet system.

Captives

ISBN 5-7172-0072-2

Collected in this anthology are stories, which have long become classics in Russian literature and are representative of the exciting and turbulent 1990s. Authors include Victor Pelevin, Vasily Aksyonov, Yevgeny Popov, Vladimir Makanin, Vasily Grossman, and Georgy Vladimov.

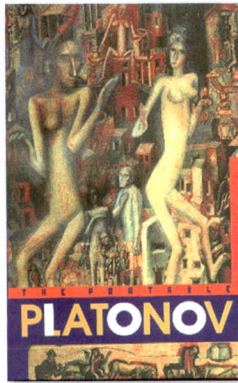

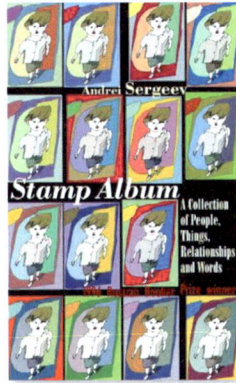

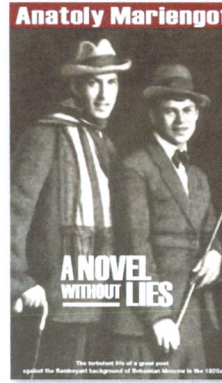

THE VALUE AND VALUES

OF LITERARY TRANSLATION

Amanda Hopkinson

I received what passed for a normal literary education. My mother told me the tales of Hans Christian Andersen, Lafontaine and Perrault; my father, who had had a classical formation, recited Aesop and Homer. I spent holidays in France in company with Asterix and Tintin; in Austria with the Brothers Grimm; in Italy with Pinocchio. I fell in love with Young Werther and the poems of Seferis, Akhmatova, Villon and Ovid; tackled insomnia with the *1001 Nights* or, more pessimistically, with the *Inferno*; and giggled at the sexual antics as described by Rabelais and Eskimo Nell. I studied Chaucer, who became a writer through translating the *Roman de la Rose* and Shakespeare, who stole not only the sonnet, but most of the plots for his comedies from Petrarch. I learnt that, while Don Quixote might have been the first novel, it took another couple of centuries for the Great Novel to arrive, composed by authors with names such as Schiller and Goethe; Manzoni and Eça de Quieroz; Knut Hamsun and de Maupassant; Zola and Balzac; Tolstoy, Dostoevsky, and Pasternak.

So far so average, with little that suggested that what I was reading was 'foreign' (with the possible exception of Brer Rabbit, whose southern states inflections were hard to follow). The surprise was the reverse: that on entering secondary school and in an obligatory Scripture lesson, I discovered that the rest of the class thought the Bible was originated in English. Today we might just react by thinking: 'How like the member of the Republican Party who thought that if 'English was good enough for Jesus, it'll do for me''. Then I realized that I actually had no idea how many languages had to be translated to provide us with one of the greatest works of the English canon, the King James edition of the Old and New Testaments; nor where the Arabic of the Qu'oran came from; still less the languages of origin for those latterly fashionable philosophical texts, the *Bhagavad Gita* or the *Epic of Gilgamesh*. At least Aurelian epithets were shorter.

That was when I began to wonder at the monumentality of the translator's task in conveying not only a text but a context – at times an entire belief system – across space and time, into that classroom in Camden Town.

Писатель и переводчик

Drawing by
Alexander Florensky:
Writer & Translator

What never occurred to me was that there was anything inherently more difficult about following the words of the Psalms than those, similarly sonorous, in the *Book of Common Prayer*. Nor that the pranks of Lazarillo de Tormes or Till Eulenspiegel were more incomprehensible than those of the similarly picaresque characters in *The Canterbury Tales* or the *Knights of the Round Table*. Indeed, the recent fashion for contemporary poets to retranslate classics of Middle English literature – Seamus Heaney in the case of *Beowulf* or W.S. Merwin and Simon Armitage in that of *Sir Gawain and the Green Knight* – re-connects an entire new generation with works of the canon otherwise lost to them. But for them to be read as 'naturally familiar' simply by belonging to that national literature would have been as sensible as to assume that Julian Barnes' *Metroland*, Ian McEwan's *Amsterdam*, even Colm Toibin's *South* or Chico Buarque's *Budapest*, were about geographical places.

For the world of the imagination is far wider and stranger than that described by national borders. Despite all this, and until at least the 1980s, there was rampant prejudice against books by authors with 'funny names' – particularly on the part of chain booksellers who, bewilderingly, claimed they were hard to rack. Then, with the rise of the post-colonial novel, Britain was suddenly rich in best-sellers by Salman Rushdie, Ben Okri, Jung Chan, Arundhati Roy, VS Naipaul, Chinua Achebe, Wole Soyinka, Benjamin Zephaniah – all originated in English and most by British authors. Close behind came the revival of regional literatures: the Scottish romance of the Waverley novels supplanted by violent estates of another kind in Irvine Walsh; the Welsh pastorals of RS Thomas by the urban wastelands described by Niall Griffiths. 'The particular in the universal' had been the cry of the seventeenth century Metaphysical poets: now, all of a sudden, it had taken on a new meaning, better expressed by saying the opposite. What was universal was now most clearly expressed by a process of honing down in a locally specific place of origin.

This literary diversity went hand-in-hand with apparently contradictory social change. As post-War Britain became increasingly culturally diverse, so Britons themselves were denied a breadth of linguistic heritage by continual restructures of the

**Drawings by
Alexander Florensky:
Andrei Bitov
Daniil Yuvachev
Sergei Dovlatov**

educational system. Within a generation Classics were no longer part of the core State curriculum; another generation and Modern Languages have gone the same way. At the same time London grew into the world capital of linguistic diversity with over 350 distinct languages[1] spoken in its primary schools. After English, the most commonly spoken are Portuguese and Yoruba. The children who now grow up multilingual are now those with the benefit of immigrant or second generation parents who conserve and transmit their cultural heritage.

The outsider status of incoming families serves to shake up an atrophied relationship with what used to be called 'foreign' languages. In 2001, poets and translators Daniel Weissbort and Stephen Watts together edited a special issue of the seminal quarterly, *Modern Poetry in Translation*. Called "Mother Tongues", it included verse by poets whose first language ranged from Somali to Czech, Punjabi to Russian, Arabic to Bulgarian. As part of a collaborative exercise, many were translated by fellow poets including Anthony Rudolf, Clive Wilmer, George Szirtes, Jonathan Griffin and Keith Bosley. Equally impressive was the writers' tour, sponsored by the Arts Council and co-ordinated by Sian Williams,

[1] Aka the linguist Prof. David Crystal, Radio 4 interview on 30th April 2007.

which brought the two groups together. In each region poets whose languages predominated (Urdu in Leeds, Punjabi in Birmingham, Turkish in North London) would read with their translators. At the session I attended in the British Library, members of the audience rose to their feet (some stood on their seats) to respond to the words of 'their' poets while more respectable (and passive and British) members sat rapt to listen to both the original and its translation.

Britain seems to be a land where only between 2-3% of the 160,000 books published annually are works of literary translation. As against some 14% in Hungary and France and nearer 40% in Spain and Holland. If one focuses on certain genres – contemporary or historical novels, say – then over half of those sold in Italy and Germany are translated, the great majority from English. Conversely the translated books that sell well here tend to be of even more specific kinds: Eurocrime, of which several independents have lists; or female porn, for which a sudden recent vogue seems gradually to be fading.

The standard response to the lack of contemporary translations available to British readers is along the lines of 'we can read the world in English, so why bother with reading

Флоренский

СЕРГЕЙ ДОНАТОВИЧ ДОВЛАТОВ 1941-1990

something second-hand' The clear implication is that it will be second-rate: James Fenton said as much, when interviewed by Christine Patterson for the *Independent* newspaper in December 2006. Explaining his process of selection of works for *The Faber Book of Love Poems*, he says he decided not to include translations 'because they're so rarely to the same standard as the other things'[2]. With prejudices like these amongst those who should know much, much better, literary translators have a great deal more to do to teach even the supposedly converted.

In so doing, we have to be content with taking small steps to raise the profile of literary translation and literary translators. Seven years ago, the Independent Foreign Fiction Prize was revived with the support of the Arts Council. It is the only award shared equally between writer and translator, but has encouraged an expansion of the Translation Prizes given annually by the Translators' Association, working with the British Centre for Literary Translation [BCLT]. Recent additions have included the Porjes Prize (Hebrew); the Banipal (Arabic); and, since 2005, the Rossica Translation Prize – shortly to be joined by one mooted by the Polish Book Institute. The readings which accompany the award ceremonies draw growing audiences and media interest.

Translators within the Society of Authors have full authorial status, as they do within the School of Creative Writing at the University of East Anglia, home of the BCLT. Arch Tait, previously short-listed for the Rossica Translation Prize reminds us that as long ago as 1976, UNESCO's general conference declared 'the status of translators should equal that of authors'; also that the 1988 Copyright, Designs and Patents Act recognized the translator as the creator of a literary work. He adds: 'And yet... Translating feels qualitatively different from writing, and substantially less original. Is a translation really an original, autonomous literary work, or is it just a variant of painting by numbers?'[3]

I confess myself puzzled by this. Having no imagination to compose either poetry or fiction, I have nonetheless written extensively across the medium: from mainstream radio and print journalism to academic reviews; historical biography to contemporary interviews; and provided texts for numerous catalogues, monographs and specialist literary and photographic publications. I've also curated at least a dozen exhibitions. In every case felt I was engaged in an activity comparable to translating.

[2] From 'James Fenton: Songs of experience', an article published in *The Independent* on 8 December 2006.

[3] Translating Hurramabad, in *Rossica*, Issue 15, p. 19

ИОСИФ
БРОДСКИЙ
(1940 – 1996)

похоронен в
Венеции на
кладбище
Сан – Микеле.

А.Э.

In short, all my 'original' work is predicated on being the conduit for the work of another, and I take it absolutely as seriously if the end 'product' is a translation or an exhibition, the story of a life or of an epoch.

That translators work with an existing text does not render their undertaking a purely mechanical one. We have all seen the ludicrous results of feeding a piece of even the plainest prose through the translation software of a computer programme. English words published as the outcome of my endeavours are my words, not the original author's. We each have our own task: different but equal. Just as I don't need to lead the life to write the biography, I don't need to write the Spanish or Portuguese version to provide an English one. But, since every translation is an act of recreation, one writer deserves another. Hence the number of poets currently busy at work on their own and others' poems. To name but a few: Ciaran Carson, David Constantine, George Szirtes, Gwyneth Lewis, Jo Balmer. And sometimes one writer deserves himself: what could be wittier than either Beckett or Nabokov recreating their own work through translation?

Susan Sontag, who wrote: 'Translations are

like buildings. If they're any good, the patina of time makes them look better: Florio's Montaigne, North's Plutarch, Motteux's Rabelais... (Who was it who said, 'The greatest Russian writer of the century, Constance Garnett'?) The most admired, and long-lived, are not the most accurate.'[4] Actually, Constance Garnett was accused of being the most Victorian Russian writer: another misnomer for her style was nothing if not High Edwardian. Nonetheless, Constance not only won her crown as the only literary translator to have a biography written of her and, in modern terms of critical evaluation, has more websites than any fellow translator too. All this for a long life dedicated to bringing the works of Pushkin, Turgenev, Dostoyevsky, Tolstoy, Chekhov, Gorky, and Pasternak to an entirely new readership. No subsequent translator can afford to ignore her and Anthony Briggs, whose fresh translation of *War and Peace* appeared in 2005, followed by *Resurrection* a year later, acknowledges her due. Oscar Wilde famously greeted her early translations by announcing that what endowed Russian literature with greatness was that it was commensurate with 'the pity they put in them'[5]. Orlando Figes concludes Tony Briggs' edition with

[4] Susan Sontag,
Where the Stress Falls,
(Jonathan Cape, 2002)
'On Being Translated', p. 344

[5] *The Epigrams of Oscar Wilde*,
ed. by Alvin Redman
(Bracken Books, 1995), p. 86.

М. З. Ломоносов (с портрета худ. Л. С. Миропольского, 1787 года)

Флоренский

**Drawings by
Alexander Florensky:
Joseph Brodsky
Mikhail Lomonosov**

[6] Leo Tolstoy, *War and Peace*, 'Afterword' (Penguin, 2005), p.1392

[7] As a Modern History major at Warwick University, *War and Peace* was the first book on the reading list. The concept was that Tolstoy, whose literary career began in 1851 when he first joined a regiment in the Caucasus, and who fought in the Crimean War, commanding a battery at Sebastopol, was the best possible guide to nineteenth century Russian history. Initially preferable, in any case, to any contemporary historian.

an Afterword stating: 'English readers will learn more about the Russians by reading *War and Peace* than they will be reading perhaps any other book. But they will also find in it the inspiration to make them think about the world and their own place in it. For *War and Peace* is a universal work and ... [typically] of the Russian tradition, it functions as a huge poetic structure for the contemplation of the fundamental questions of our existence.'[6]

So, or as much in so many words, say the overwhelming number of castaways on the popular British radio programme *Desert Island Discs*, who make *'W&P'* their book of choice. This is, presumably, because Tolstoy brings not only what he believed to be most important – his philosophy, the fruit of a lifetime's profound thought and action – but what the reader most desires – epic history[7] in which the violent intensity of the battlefield and the bedroom are parallel determinants – home to all of us. If the universal significance of a work of literature can in any sense be estimated by the number of its translations then, like Flaubert's *Madame Bovary*, *War and Peace* is a repeated challenge, and all the more so because of its length.

We all have our personal libraries, partly shelved inside our homes, partly internalized inside our heads, and while mine may have more translations than some, I've yet to meet one that had none at all. For the reader is truly a book's first translator, taking the text off the page and rephrasing it in her own mind, according to her own imagination. For millennia, before we had books and across centuries when they were rare and expensive artifacts, we depended on others to transmit our stories and histories. It so happened that these intermediaries were oral storytellers. Through them, fables have girdled the world, each with local variants, all with themes common to the human condition.

Like the storytellers, literary translators relay words, assessing the precise degree of their required impact, their importance for an audience. For, barring the obvious disqualifications – a failure either to comprehend the source text or write competently in the target language – who is to say the translator isn't at least as adequate an interpreter as a fellow reader?

Vladimir Nabokov on the balcony of the Palace Hotel in Montreux, 1960s. Photo by Horst Tappe

Traditore tradutore

Nabokov's inimitable 1941 note on translation is, as one would expect, merciless towards what he considers the lazy, ignorant and mediocre. It was Nabokov, after all, who dismissed the equally grand and self-regarding Edmund Wilson in an increasingly acrimonious discussion of 'Yevgeny [or, as Nabokov insists, Eugene] Onegin' with the greatest put-down of all such dismissive remarks: Why should I continue discussion with someone who, it turns out, cannot even scan Russian verse?

That magisterial, occasionally contemptuous, tone is also present here. His comments would not be so intriguing or stimulating if that remained the dominant tone. Nabokov was not only a writer but also the translator of his own works. The attempt to render Lolita*, originally composed in English, into a genuinely live form of literary Russian, for instance, proved such a demanding and baffling experience that in addition to his Russian version it gave rise to a unique dictionary,*

illustrating a stage beyond dictionaries where style, idiom and larger aspects of culture come into play.

A third element is biographical. Nabokov Sr, famously killed in Berlin by a bullet intended for fellow liberal Milyukov, was a thorough-going Anglophile and in Speak, Memory *the younger Vladimir describes the succession of English and Scottish governesses who taught the children. In the early 1920s Nabokov found himself at Cambridge and, for the first time, in constant contact with that much-admired culture. From that period, when the young 'Sirin' produced his Russian translation of* Alice in Wonderland *began the humbling experiences of linguistic recalcitrance described here. Through battling with lines by Pushkin or a single resonant phrase from A.E. Housman Nabokov arrived at his own set of principles and conclusions regarding literary translation.*

On the Art of Translation

Vladimir Nabokov

Three grades of evil can be discerned in the queer world of verbal transmigration. The first, and lesser one, comprises obvious errors due to ignorance or misguided knowledge. This is mere human frailty and thus excusable. The next step to Hell is taken by the translator who intentionally skips words or passages that he does not bother to understand or that might seem obscure or obscene to vaguely imagined readers; he accepts the blank look that his dictionary gives him without any qualms; or subjects scholarship to primness: he is as ready to know less than the author as he is to think he knows better. The third, and worst, degree of turpitude is reached when a masterpiece is planished and patted into such a shape, vilely beautified in such a fashion as to conform to the notions and prejudices of a given public. This is a crime, to be punished by the stocks as plagiarists were in the shoe buckle days.

The howlers included in the first category may be in their turn divided into two classes. Insufficient acquaintance with the foreign language involved may transform a commonplace expression into some remarkable statement that the real author never intended to make. 'Bien être general' becomes the manly assertion that' it is good to be a general'; to which gallant general a French translator of *Hamlet* has been known to pass the caviar. Likewise, in a German edition of Chekhov, a certain teacher, as soon as he enters the classroom, is made to become engrossed in 'his newspaper', which prompted a pompous reviewer to comment on the sad condition of public instruction in pre-Soviet Russia. But the real Chekhov was simply referring to the classroom 'journal' which a teacher would open to check lessons, marks and absentees. And inversely, innocent words in an English novel such as 'first night' and 'public house' have become in a Russian translation 'nuptial night' and 'a brothel'. These simple examples suffice. They are ridiculous and jarring, but they contain no pernicious purpose; and more often than not the garbled sentence still makes some sense in the original context.

The other class of blunders in the first category includes a more sophisticated kind of mistake, one which is caused by an attack of linguistic Daltonism suddenly blinding the translator. Whether attracted by the far-fetched when the obvious was at hand (What does an Eskimo prefer to eat-ice cream or tallow? Ice cream), or whether unconsciously basing his

Чудище обло, озорно, огромно, стозевно и лаяй.   Флоренский

СПб   Радищев   Москва

**Collages by
Alexander Florensky:
Alexander Radishchev
Gavrila Derzhavin**

rendering on some false meaning which repeated readings have imprinted on his mind, he manages to distort in an unexpected and sometimes quite brilliant way the most honest word or the tamest metaphor. I knew a very conscientious poet who in wrestling with the translation of a much tortured text rendered 'is sicklied o'er with the pale cast of thought' in such a manner as to convey an impression of pale moonlight. He did this by taking for granted that 'sickle' referred to the form of the new moon. And a national sense of humour, set into motion by the likeness between the Russian words meaning 'arc' and 'onion,' led a German professor to translate 'a bend of the shore' (in a Pushkin fairy tale) by 'the Onion Sea'.

The second, and much more serious, sin of leaving out tricky passages is still excusable when the translator is baffled by them himself; but how contemptible is the smug person who, although quite understanding the sense, fears it might stump a dunce or debauch a dauphin! Instead of blissfully nestling in the arms of the great writer, he keeps worrying about the little reader playing in a corner with something dangerous or unclean. Perhaps the most charming example of Victorian modesty that has ever come my way was in an early English translation of *Anna Karenin*. Vronsky had asked Anna what was the matter with her. 'I am *beremenna*' (the translator's italics), replied

Anna, making the foreign reader wonder what strange and awful Oriental disease that was; all because the translator thought that 'I am pregnant' might shock some pure soul, and that a good idea would be to leave the Russian just as it stood.

But masking and toning down seem petty sins in comparison with those of the third category; for here he comes strutting and shooting out his bejewelled cuffs, the slick translator who arranges Scheherazade's boudoir according to his own taste and with professional elegance tries to improve the looks of his victims. Thus it was the rule with Russian versions of Shakespeare to give Ophelia richer flowers than the poor weeds she found. The Russian rendering of

There with fantastic garlands did she come
Of crowflowers, nestles, daisies and long purples

if translated back into English would run like this:

There with most lovely garlands did she come
Of violets, carnations, roses, lilies.

The splendour of this floral display speaks for itself; incidentally it bowdlerized the Queen's digressions, granting her the gentility she so sadly lacked and dismissing the liberal shepherds; how anyone could make such a botanical collection beside the Helje or the Avon is another question.

ГАВРИЛА
РОМАНОВИЧ
ДЕРЖАВИН
(1743 – 1816)
писал торжествен-
ные оды, пронизанные
сильной
идеей государственности

где тут у вас, братец, нужник?

But no such questions were asked by the solemn Russian reader, first, because he did not know the original text, second, because he did not care a fig for botany, and third, because the only thing that interested him in Shakespeare was what German commentators and native radicals had discovered in the way of 'eternal problems.' So nobody minded what happened to Goneril's lapdogs when the line

Tray, Blanche and Sweetheart, see, they bark at me

was grimly metamorphosed into

A pack of hounds is barking at my heels.

All local colour, all tangible and irreplaceable details were swallowed by those hounds.

But, revenge is sweet – even unconscious revenge. The greatest Russian short story ever written is Gogol's *Overcoat* (or *Mantle*, or *Cloak*, or 'She-nel'). Its essential feature, that irrational part which forms the tragic undercurrent of an otherwise meaningless anecdote, is organically connected with the special style in which this story is written: there are weird repetitions of the same absurd adverb, and these repetitions become a kind of uncanny incantation; there are descriptions which look innocent enough until you discover that chaos lies right round the corner, and that Gogol has inserted into this or that harmless

sentence a word or a simile that makes a passage burst into a wild display of nightmare fireworks. There is also that groping clumsiness which, on the author's part, is a conscious rendering of the uncouth gestures of our dreams.

Nothing of these remains in the prim, and perky, and very matter-of-fact English version (see – and never see again – *The Mantle*, translated by Claude Field). The following example leaves me with the impression that I am witnessing a murder and can do nothing to prevent it:

Gogol: ... his [a petty official's] third or fourth-story flat ... displaying a few fashionable trifles, such as a lamp for instance – trifles purchased by many sacrifices ...

Field: ... fitted with some pretentious articles of furniture purchased, etc ...

Tampering with foreign major or minor masterpieces may involve an innoÐcent third party in the farce. Quite recently a famous Russian composer asked me to translate into English a Russian poem which forty years ago he had set to music. The English translation, he pointed out, had to follow closely the very sounds of the text – which text was unfortunately K. Balmont's version of Edgar Allan Poe's *Bells*. What Balmont's numerous translations look like may be readily understood when I say that his own

Оставив по не совсем ясным причинам университет, Лермонтов в 1832 году переезжает из Москвы в Петербург и поступает в школу гвардейских подпрапорщиков и кавалерийских юнкеров. Выпущен корнетом

Лейб-гвардии гусарского полка в 1834 году Место высокой поэзии занимает непечатное стихотворство («ЮНКЕРСКИЕ ПОЭМЫ»), а место трагического избранника — циничный бретер.

Михаилъ Юрьевичъ Лермонтовъ.
(1814—1841).

А. Ф.

**Collages by
Alexander Florensky:
Mikhail Lermontov
Alexander Griboedov**

work invariably disclosed an almost pathological inability to write one single melodious line.

Having at his disposal a sufficient number of hackneyed rhymes and taking up as he rode any hitch-hiking metaphor that he happened to meet, he turned something that Poe had taken considerable pains to compose into something that any Russian rhymester could dash off at a moment's notice. In reversing it into English I was solely concerned with finding English words that would sound like the Russian ones. Now, if somebody one day comes across my English version of that Russian version, he may foolishly retranslate it into Russian so that the Poe-less poem will go on being balmontised until, perhaps, the *Bells* become *Silence*. Something still more grotesque happened to Baudelaire's exquisitely dreamy *Invitation au Voyage* (Mon enfant, ma soeur, / Songe à la douceur …) The Russian version was due to the pen of Merezhkovski, who had even less poetical talent than Balmont. It began like this:

> My sweet little bride,
> Let's go for a ride;

Promptly it begot a rollicking tune and was adopted by all the organ-grinders of Russia. I like to imagine a future French translator of Russian folksongs re-Frenchifying it into:

> *Viens, mon p'tit, / A Nijni*

and so on, ad malinfinitum.

Barring downright deceivers, mild imbeciles and impotent poets, there exist, roughly speaking, three types of translators – and this has nothing to do with my three categories of evil; or, rather, any of the three types may err in a similar way. These three are: the scholar who is eager to make the world appreciate the works of an obscure genius as much as he does himself; the well meaning hack; and the professional writer relaxing in the company of a foreign confrere. The scholar will be, I hope, exact and pedantic: footnotes – on the same page as the text and not tucked away at the end of the volume – can never be too copious and detailed. The laborious lady translating at the eleventh hour the eleventh volume of somebody's collected works will be, I am afraid, less exact and less pedantic; but the point is not that the scholar commits fewer blunders than a drudge; the point is that as a rule both he and she are hopelessly devoid of any semblance of creative genius. Neither learning nor diligence can replace imagination and style.

Now comes the authentic poet who has the two last assets and who finds relaxation in

А. С. Грибоедов
автор пьесы
«ГОРЕ ОТ УМА»
(1790 (по другим
сведениям – 1795)
† 1829).
русский писа-
тель и ди-
пломат.

В 1828 году на-
значен послом в
Персию, где вскоре
и был убит пер-
-сидскими фана-
тиками.

Флоренский

translating a bit of Lermontov or Verlaine between writing poems of his own. Either he does not know the original language and calmly relies upon the so-called 'literal' translation made for him by a far less brilliant but a little more learned person, or else, knowing the language, he lacks the scholar's precision and the professional translator's experience. The main drawback, however, in this case is the fact that the greater his individual talent, the more apt he will be to drown the foreign masterpiece under the sparkling ripples of his own personal style. Instead of dressing up like the real author, he dresses up the author as himself.

We can deduce now the requirements that a translator must possess in order to be able to give an ideal version of a foreign masterpiece. First of all he must have as much talent, or at least the same kind of talent, as the author he chooses. In this, though only in this, respect Baudelaire and Poe or Jhukovski [Zhukovsky] and Schiller made ideal playmates. Second, he must know thoroughly the two nations and the two languages involved and be perfectly acquainted with all details relating to his author's manner and methods; also, with the social background of words, their fashions, history and period associations. This leads to the third point: while

having genius and knowledge he must possess the gift of mimicry and be able to act, as it were, the real author's part by impersonating his tricks of demeanour and speech, his ways and his mind, with the utmost degree of verisimilitude.

I have lately tried to translate several Russian poets who had either been badly disfigured by former attempts or who had never been translated at all.

The English at my disposal is certainly thinner than my Russian; the difference being, in fact, that which exists between a semi-detached villa and a hereditary estate, between self-conscious comfort and habitual luxury. I am not satisfied therefore with the results attained, but my studies disclosed several rules that other writers might follow with profit.

I was confronted for instance with the following opening line of one of Pushkin's most prodigious poems[1] :

Yah pom-new chewed-no-yay mg-no-vain-yay

I have rendered the syllables by the nearest English sounds I could find; their mimetic disguise makes them look rather ugly; but never mind; the 'chew' and the 'vain' are associated phonetically with other Russian words meaning beautiful and important things, and the melody of the line with

[1] In literal prose equivalent: 'I remember the wondrous moment / You appeared before me / As a passing vision / as the spirit of pure beauty.' 1825 poem dedicated to Annie Kern whom Pushkin met at a ball in Petersburg before his exile to the south.

улица Гоголя

В 1828 году Гоголь отправился в СПб, где безуспешно искал место. Только в 1829 году ему удалось стать чиновником департамента с ничтожным жалованьем. По ходатайству Пушкина и Жуковского

Гоголь получил место адъюнкт-профессора в СПб университете, но вскоре разочаровался в научной и педагогической деятельности. По подаренному Пушкиным сюжету Г. написал пьесу «Ревизор».

Я. Френский

**Collages by
Alexander Florensky:
Nikolai Gogol
Ivan Krylov**

the plump, golden-ripe 'chewed-no-yay' right in the middle and the 'm's and 'n's balancing each other on both sides, is to the Russian ear most exciting and soothing – a paradoxical combination that any artist will understand.

Now, if you take a dictionary and look up those four words you will obtain the following foolish, flat and familiar statement: 'I remember a wonderful moment.' What is to be done with this bird you have shot down only to find that it is not a bird of paradise, but an escaped parrot, still screeching its idiotic message as it flaps on the ground? For no stretch of the imagination can persuade an English reader that 'I remember a wonderful moment' is the perfect beginning of a perfect poem. The first thing I discovered was that the expression 'a literal translation' is more or less nonsense. 'Yah pom-new' is a deeper and smoother plunge into the past than 'I remember', which falls flat on its belly like an inexperienced diver; 'chewed-no-yay' has a lovely Russian 'monster' in it, and a whispered 'listen', and the dative ending of a 'sunbeam', and many other fair relations among Russian words. It belongs phonetically and mentally to a certain series of words, and this Russian series does not correspond to the English series in which 'I remember' is found. And inversely, 'remember',

though it clashes with the corresponding 'pom-new' series, is connected with an English series of its own whenever real poets do use it. And the central word in Housman's 'What are those blue remembered hills?' becomes in Russian 'vspom-neev-she-yes-yah', a horrible straggly thing, all humps and horns, which cannot fuse into any inner connection with 'blue', as it does so smoothly in English, because the Russian sense of blueness belongs to a different series than the Russian 'remember' does.

This interrelation of words and non-correspondence of verbal series in different tongues suggests yet another rule, namely, that the three main words of the line draw one another out, and add something which none of them would have had separately or in any other combination. What makes this exchange of secret values possible is not only the mere contact between the words, but their exact position in regard both to the rhythm of the line and to one another. This must be taken into account by the translator.

Finally, there is the problem of the rhyme. 'Mg-no-vain-yay' has over two thousand Jack-in-the-box rhymes popping out at the slightest pressure, whereas I cannot think of one to 'moment'. The position of 'mg-no-vain-yay' at the

end of the line is not negligible either, due as it is to Pushkin's more or less consciously knowing that he would not have to hunt for its mate. But the position of 'moment' in the English line implies no such security; on the contrary he would be a singularly reckless fellow who placed it there.

Thus I was confronted by that opening line, so full of Pushkin, so individual and harmonious; and after examining it gingerly from the various angles here suggested, I tackled it. The tackling process lasted the worst part of the night. I did translate it at last; but to give my version at this point might lead the reader to doubt that perfection be attainable by merely following a few perfect rules.

ADDENDUM: POET AND SCHOLAR

Professor of Latin at University College, London, and then at Cambridge, A.E. Housman was author of several volumes of lyric verse, including translation from the Latin. The phrase cited by Nabokov comes from the following poem in *A Shropshire Lad* (first published 1896)

Into my heart an air that kills
From yon far country blows

What are those blue remembered hills,
What spires, what farms are those?

That is the land of lost content,
I see it shining plain,
The happy highways where I went
And cannot come again.

Housman had his own definite and well-informed ideas about translation.

'There is a predicable rivalry', notes the *Oxford Book of Classical Verse in Translation* 'between the scholar and the poet. A.E. Housman spoke as both ... when he caught a hapless translator of Propertius prematurely asserting that,

"Scholars will pardon an attempt, however bald, to render into English these exquisite love poems. "

To which Housman, baldly and unanswerably: "Why?" ('Tremenheere's Cynthia of Propertius', *The Classical Review*, May 1900)'

Translating Russian Literature

Peter France

[1] For details see M. B. Line, A. Ettlinger and J. M. Gladstone, *Bibliography of Russian Literature in English Translation to 1945* (Totowa, NJ,1972)

[2] Donald Davie, *Russian Literature and Modern English Fiction* (London/Chicago, 1965)

The translation of Russian literature is in good heart today. For this year's Rossica Translation Prize there were some thirty entries, ranging from a new version of War and Peace to slim bilingual editions of little-known poets. But it was not always so. Go back 200 years – by 1807 no more than half a dozen pieces of Russian imaginative literature had found their way into English.[1]

The nineteenth century was to see a great opening up to Russian culture – so much so that Donald Davie once wrote that the 'awakening of the Anglo-Saxon people to Russian literature' was 'a turning point no less momentous than the discovery of Italian literature by the generations of the English Renaissance'.[2] The great period of this awakening came at the end of the nineteenth century, but the way was prepared by pioneers from many walks of life.[3] Their translations ranged from traditional folk tales and ballads to the new literature of Pushkin or Tolstoy.

The first of the pioneers was John (eventually Sir John) Bowring (1792-1872), who in 1820 issued the first of his two volumes of Specimens of the Russian Poets. As a translator from Russian he had been preceded by the anonymous translator of Catherine the Great's 'Ivan Czarowicz, or, The Rose

without Prickles that Stings not', published in the Edinburgh magazine *The Bee* in the 1790s, and by the Dane A. A. Feldborg, who translated some of Nikolay Karamzin's stories and travels from the German. But it was Bowring who brought Russian writing to the attention of the British literati, as is shown by the numerous reviews of his anthology, which amounts to about 400 pages in all.

Born in Exeter, he started travelling and learning languages early in life, as a merchant trading in wine and herrings. Though translation helped to launch his career, it was only a small part of the very busy life of this high-principled but prickly and vain man. Politically he was a disciple of the philosopher Jeremy Bentham, who in 1824 made him political editor of the new radical quarterly, the *Westminster Review*, for which he wrote copious articles. Later he travelled abroad on public service, made forays into the world of industry, was twice a Member of Parliament, and in 1848 became British consul in Canton and later governor of Hong Kong.

Bowring was in St Petersburg for some months in 1819-20, during which he claimed to have met Karamzin and the fabulist Ivan Krylov and to have heard folk songs sung 'in the wooden huts of the cottagers'. He composed the second volume of his Russian anthology when

[3] For further details, see Peter France, 'Literatures of Central and Eastern Europe', in Peter France and Kenneth Haynes, eds., *The Oxford History of Literary Translation in English*, vol. 4: 1790-1900 (Oxford, 2006), pp. 308-319

THE PIONEERS

he was in prison in France in 1822, suspected of spying and subversive activities. It was the first of a series of anthologies, which later included the poetry of Serbia, Bohemia, Hungary, Holland and Spain. *The Dictionary of National Biography* notes that Bowring had schemes for 'writing the history and giving translated specimens of the popular poetry, not only of the Western, but of the Oriental world'. He himself saw his mission as 'one of benevolence', saying that he had never left his native land 'but with the wish to return to it, bearing fresh olive branches of peace and fresh garlands of poetry'.[4] Translation was a much-needed exercise in mutual understanding, since it was all too easy to 'despise what we do not comprehend'.

Given the number of languages he translated, Bowring's claims to comprehension were wide indeed, and have sometimes been mocked. George Borrow, in some ways a similar figure, with whom Bowring collaborated on a Scandinavian project before falling out with him, declared in an acid pen-portrait of 'The Old Radical' in *The Romany Rye* that he was 'slightly acquainted with four or five of the easier dialects in Europe'.[5]

As far as Russian is concerned, he acknowledged help received from Friedrich Adelung, who provided him with German and English prose cribs. However, he knew enough Russian to cite Russian originals in his discussion of poetic form, and he insists on the genuineness of his enterprise by citing five lines of the poet Batyushkov in Cyrillic script on his title page. His anthology is well-informed, containing poems by 23 poets, some of them very recent, as well as some 50 pages of folk songs. His conscientious rhymed versions have not worn particularly well, but they lasted well enough to be included in the American Leo Wiener's *Anthology of Russian Literature* at the beginning of the twentieth century. Here are a few lines of his translation of Batyushkov's 'Shade of a Friend':

The dancing surge, the evening breezes falling,
And through the sails and shrouds those breezes whistling shrill,
And to the watch the active helmsman calling,
The watch, who, midst the roar, sleeps tranquilly and still.
All seemed to rock itself to gentle thought.

More interesting for us now, perhaps, is what Bowring says in his Introduction. He sees modern Russia emerging 'as it were instantaneously, from a night of ignorance'. Being the good radical he is, he deplores the continuing despotism in Russia, the yawning chasm between the privileged classes and the serfs, but affirms that 'the foundation is now laid, on which the proud

Photograph of Constance Garnett, a pioneer of Russian literary translation

[4] John Bowring, *Poetry of the Magyars* (London, 1830), p. viii.

[5] George Borrow, *Works*, ed. by Clement Shorter, (London, 1923-4), VI, 315

ИВАН ТУРГЕНЕВ

«Муму» и др.)

Николай Алексеевич Некрасов, поэт начало 1860-х годов. В 1847–66 гг. Некрасов редактировал и издавал журнал «Современник», а с 1868 г. – «Отечественные записки»

А.Ф.

[6] *Ivan Turgenev in Britain*, ed. by Patrick Waddington, (Oxford, 1995), p. 2

[7] Borrow's Russian translations, including most notably an unrhymed version of Pushkin's *The Gypsies*, are discussed by John Crowfoot.

edifice of civilization will be raised'. Even if most of the nation is still sunk in its old barbarity, 'the immense political influence which Russia has acquired [as a result of the Napoleonic wars], and seems likely to maintain, will be less appalling, at all events to the moralist if not to the statesman, than if wholly unaccompanied by a spirit of literature'. And since poetry expresses something of the national character, statesmen will do well 'to study the tendency and the character of that fountainhead whose waters will spread over generations of men, and over the widest empire in the world.' The need to know more about the giant in the East is a theme that will recur in the history of translation up to our own day; some thirty years after Bowring's anthology 'the Crimean War did miracles for Turgenev's fortunes in Britain, as indeed for those of Russian culture in general.'[6]

Pushkin emerged on the scene just too late to be included in Bowring's volumes. One of his first translators was in fact Bowring's rival, the larger-than-life George Borrow, who spent some two years working for the English Bible Society in Russia and published two volumes of translations from many languages, *Targum* and *The Talisman*, in St Petersburg in 1835.[7] Generally speaking,

the difficulty of translation meant that Pushkin's poetry did not occupy a very important place in the nineteenth-century British vision of Russian literature (the stories in prose are another matter – there were many versions of such texts as 'The Queen of Spades' and 'The Captain's Daughter'). There was just one translation of *Eugene Onegin*, which is rather better than Vladimir Nabokov's acid comments might lead one to suspect. It was the work of the tantalizingly shadowy figure of Lieutenant Colonel H. Spalding, who must have lived in a Russian-speaking environment and who translated direct from the Russian. (As we have seen in the case of Bowring, it was – and remained – common practice to translate from Russian via French or German.)

There is, however, one other pioneer of Pushkin translation who deserves a mention: Thomas Budd Shaw (1813-62). Unlike Bowring and Borrow, Shaw actually made his career in Russia, and is described by Patrick Waddington in the *Oxford Dictionary of National Biography* as unique in his ability to interpret British culture to the Russians and Russian culture to the British. The son of a famous architect, he took himself off to Russia as an escape from insolvency, and

А.И. ГЕРЦЕН
и его газета «колокол»

THE BELL
КОЛОКОЛЪ

[8] *The Autobiography of Arthur Ransome*, ed. by Rupert Hart-Davis (London, 1976), p. 157

Drawings by Alexander Florensky:
Ivan Turgenev
Nikolay Nekrasov
Alexander Herzen

made his way as a private tutor to grand dukes, as teacher of English at Pushkin's old lycée in Tsarskoe Selo, and eventually as Professor of English in St Petersburg. He wrote textbooks on English literature, but also an entry on St Petersburg for the *Encyclopedia Britannica*. His translations included Russian popular novels, Gogol, and Lermontov. And in 1845 he published three articles entitled 'Pushkin, the Russian Poet' in Blackwood's *Edinburgh Magazine* (one of the periodicals which did most to bring foreign literature to the English-speaking public). They draw on private knowledge of the poet derived from his surviving friends and are accompanied by a substantial selection of poems, diligently rendered in something like the original metres and in the same kind of padded translationese that we see in Bowring and Borrow.

The real star of Russian literature in the English-speaking world, at least until Tolstoy's dramatic arrival on the scene in the 1880s, was Ivan Turgenev, who was greatly admired by Henry James and the Americans and seen by some British critics as the greatest novelist then writing. And through Turgenev we can meet three other pioneers of Russian translation, W.R.S. Ralston

(1828-1889), Isabel Hapgood (1850-1928), and Constance Garnett (1861-1946). Unlike the translators mentioned so far, Ralston learnt his Russian in London, becoming an expert on Russian culture during his many years working at the British Museum. He also travelled frequently to Russia and was made a corresponding member of the Imperial Academy of Sciences in St Petersburg in 1886. He was on friendly terms with Turgenev, keeping his name in the public eye, attacking bad translations of his works (including those done by way of French), making abortive plans for a jointly written political novel, and producing one of the best contemporary translations of his work, Liza, a version of *Dvorianskoe Gnezdo* (A Nest of Gentlefolk).

Ralston wrote for literary periodicals and was by all accounts a witty talker and gifted story-teller. He was also – like many of his contemporaries – deeply interested in folk art, publishing collections of Tibetan tales, of 'the songs of the Russian people' and of Russian folk tales. The last of these, a scholarly work based on the recent researches carried out in Russia by the great Afanasyev and others, had an interesting afterlife. When the young Arthur

МИХАИЛ ЕВГРАФОВИЧ
САЛТЫКОВ – ЩЕДРИН
(с оригинала работы
худ. И.Н. Крамского
исполнил худ:
Флоренский А.О.)

9 See the introduction by J. W. Mackail to the London reissue of this book in 1915

Ransome was seeking inspiration for his own story telling, he chanced upon Ralston: 'In the London Library I had come across Ralston's *Russian Folk Tales*, and, while disliking what seemed to me the unsuitable "literary" prose in which they were written, saw what rich material there was there.'[8] So Ransome went off to Russia, learned Russian, worked as a journalist (and possibly a spy), married Trotsky's secretary, and (among other things) wrote the marvellous *Old Peter's Russian Tales*, a reworking for children of the kind of story he had found in Ralston.

While Ralston only translated one Turgenev novel, the two outstanding female translators of the late nineteenth century, Isabel Hapgood in America and Constance Garnett in England, both published complete editions of his novels and stories – and lots more besides. Hapgood's name is less familiar now, but her output was almost as impressive as Garnett's, and in her day hers was a name to conjure with. She translated from French and German as well as Russian, and according to *The Nation*, her work set 'a new standard for fidelity in translation'. In addition to the complete Turgenev, she did early versions of works by Gogol and Tolstoy. Her translations of Dead Souls and Taras Bulba were immediately pirated on

this side of the Atlantic by the publisher Henry Vizetelly; they appeared in lightly revised and unacknowledged form in his pioneering 'Russian novels' series, which also included the first British versions of Dostoevsky, each subtitled (as a warning to the timid) 'a Russian realistic novel'.

Hapgood was born in Boston, learnt French and Latin at school, then taught herself several other languages including Polish, Russian and Old Church Slavonic before embarking on a career as a literary translator. One of her first translations was her pioneering *Epic Songs of Russia* (1885), prose versions of byliny (folk epics) such as the wonderful Sadko, the subject of Rimsky-Korsakov's opera. Although these had little success at first, they were intended for popular reading, in the hope of dispelling the 'dense ignorance' of Russia that prevailed in the West.[9] She herself visited Russia with her mother in 1887. Her *Russian Rambles* of 1895 explains how the reality of Russia differed from the ideas derived from her 'preliminary knowledge of the Russian language'. As she describes her meetings with poets and writers including Tolstoy, whose fame was at its peak, she emerges as a curious, humorous, intelligent person. Later on she produced a *Survey of Russian Literature* (1902) and a service book for

ФЕДОР
ДОСТОЕВСКИЙ

(«Бесы»,
«Братья Ка-
рамазовы»,
«Идиот»,
«Крокодил,
или Пассаж
в пассаже»)

род. в 1821
✝ в 1881г.

**Drawings by Alexander
Florensky:**

**Mikhail Saltykov-Shchedrin
Fedor Dostoevsky**

[10] See G. Jean-Aubry, Joseph
Conrad: Life and Letters
(London, 1927), vol. II, p. 192

[11] See Patrick Waddington's
entry on Garnett in the Oxford
Dictionary of National Biography

the Orthodox Church and made a further visit to Russia in order to collect church music.

Isabel Hapgood was a considerable figure then, but for British readers at least it was the great Constance Garnett who dominated early translation from Russian – and her story takes us into the twentieth century. Because of the general neglect of translation, you will barely find her mentioned in most histories of English literature. Yet her innumerable translations had a far greater impact on the development of British and American literary culture than that of all but a few 'original' writers. Her achievement was celebrated by some of the greatest English writers – thus Joseph Conrad wrote in May 1917: 'Turgenev for me is Constance Garnett, and Constance Garnett is Turgenev. She has done the marvellous thing of placing the man's work inside English literature and it is there that I see it – or rather that I feel it.'[10]

Constance Black was born in Brighton, the daughter of a solicitor and the granddaughter of a man who designed a steamship for the Russian government but died on delivering it to Kronstadt. After a childhood plagued by illness and family unhappiness, she studied classics at Cambridge and worked as a tutor and librarian

before marrying the man of letters, Edward Garnett . She learnt Russian from a political exile and met a number of exiled revolutionaries, one of whom, Sergey Stepniak, became her literary collaborator, making an arrangement in 1893 to correct her translations in return for 20 per cent of her earnings – but alas, he died two years later. She continued to consult Russians for many years, although of course her knowledge of Russian improved greatly, particularly after a visit to Russia in 1893 (including again the usual visit to Tolstoy).

It could be said that she learnt on the job, her first assignment, Goncharov's A Common Story, being undertaken as a translation exercise. But this exercise led on to great things: 15 volumes of Turgenev, 6 of Gogol, 6 of Tolstoy, 6 of Herzen, 15 of Chekhov (the stories and the plays) and above all (in terms of impact) 12 of Dostoevsky, all in a period of 40 years, making nearly two volumes a year. As can be imagined, she worked fast and intensely, damaging her eyesight and eventually having to recourse to amanuenses to whom she could dictate. While she was still in her prime, D. H. Lawrence watched in fascination as she wrote page after page, throwing them on to the floor as she finished them.[11]

With the exception of Leskov, she thus gave

АНТОН
ЧЕХОВ

(« Чайка »,
« Дама с собачкой »,
« Пала-
та № 6 »,
« Крыжов-
ник »,
« Хаме-
леон »,
« Злоумыш-
ленник »
и др.)

English literature almost the full cohort of major nineteenth-century prose writers, and, for the first half of the twentieth century at least, the classic Russian novels read by English speakers were almost invariably filtered through the mind and the language of Constance Garnett. Of course her near-monopoly, beneficent as it was, could not last for ever. Sometimes her translations were revised (a process that has continued to this day), more often new translations were produced, in increasing numbers, as every popular series (Penguin, Signet, World's Classics, etc) wanted to have different versions of familiar texts.

At the same time, Garnett's translations began to be criticized as inaccurate (which they rarely are) and as outdated (which may be the case, though the question of the right idiom for translating Turgenev remains an open one). In particular, and with some justification, she was reproached with 'smoothing out' the often idiosyncratic language of her originals, above all Dostoevsky.[12] But even if modern translators may now be able make translations which do greater justice to the texture of these constantly challenging novels, their work does not take away from the huge achievement of the frail

woman who with her eloquence made them an enduring part of our heritage. When her *Brothers Karamazov* hit London in 1912, the critic Middleton Murry wrote that it was 'the most successful translation in the history of English literature'. He was perhaps thinking of the shock effect of scenes like the one at the end of the novel where Grushenka confronts Katya:

Katya moved swiftly to the door, but when she reached Grushenka she stopped suddenly, turned as white as chalk and moaned softly, almost in a whisper:
'Forgive me!'
Grushenka stared at her and, pausing for an instant, in a vindictive, venomous voice, answered:
'We are full of hatred, my girl, you and I! We are both full of hatred! As though we could forgive one another! Save him, and I'll worship you all my life.'

There were other pioneers, but there is only space to mention one more, again a woman. Unlike the other Russian translators we have encountered, Louise Shanks was actually born in Russia – in Moscow in 1855, into a Quaker family engaged in the jewellery trade. In 1884, she married Aylmer Maude, three years her junior,

12 See for instance A. N. Nikoliukin, 'Dostoevskii in Constance Garnett's Translation', pp. 207-227 in *Dostoevskii and Britain*, ed. by W. J. Leatherbarrow, (Oxford/Providence, USA, 1995)

ГРАФ
ЛЕВ ТОЛСТОЙ

написал
«Анну Каренину»,
«Войну и мир»,
«Воскресение»,
«Акулу» и
мн. др.

р. 1828
† 1910

**Drawings by Alexander
Florensky:
Anton Chekhov
Count Leo Tolstoy**

who had been living in Moscow since he was sixteen. Together they were to form a long-lived husband-and-wife team known above all for their translations of Tolstoy, culminating in the Oxford University Press centenary edition (1928-37, 21 volumes), which dominated the English-language Tolstoy market in the twentieth century. The Maudes got to know Tolstoy in 1888, becoming friends and disciples whom the great man trusted to produce reliable translations of his work. On their return to England in 1897, they lived for a time in a Tolstoyan commune, and Aylmer visited Canada accompanying a group of Dukhobors, the radical Christian sect supported by Tolstoy (though he confessed to taking a first-class cabin). Later they were active in the Fabian Society and the co-operative movement, and supported Marie Stopes's campaign for contraception.

In translating, Aylmer concentrated on the philosophy, Louise on the fiction (both of which were equally important for the early impact of Tolstoy in Britain). Louise's first venture was *Resurrection*, which with the author's approval and cooperation was published simultaneously in Russian and English in 1899-1900. The English version came out in the labour journal *Clarion*

and in thirteen 'pocket parts' costing a penny each and published by the Tolstoyan Brotherhood Publishing Company (a far cry from the straightforward commercial world that Constance Garnett worked for). It was very successful and was often reprinted. Louise donated £150 from her royalties to helping the Dukhobors in North America, but when they discovered what wicked deeds were described in the novel, the Dukhobors returned the cash.

In the century since the heyday of Isabel Hapgood, Constance Garnett and Louise Maude there have been many remarkable translators of Russian literature, and the post-Perestroika years have seen no decline in numbers or in quality. The translations of the pioneers have been largely superseded; only scholars now look into Bowring, and even Garnett's classic renderings are no longer the automatic first port of call for those wanting to read Turgenev or Dostoevsky. But all modern translators owe an immense debt of gratitude to these men and women who in their different ways strove to come to terms with a new and often alien culture, and whose labour of love started the snowball rolling.

A Writer in the Making:
George Borrow's Months in Russia

John Crowfoot

On 31 August 1833 the paddle steamer *Nikolai* docked in St Petersburg, after three days at sea from Travemünde. Those waiting at the wharf, or passing by, could hardly fail to notice one of its passengers. Almost as tall as Tsar Nicholas himself, the new arrival was a young man but already quite grey haired. George Borrow had arrived in Russia.

He stayed for less than two years. Yet this was the journey, of all Borrow's many travels, that would enable him, eventually, to fulfil his single aim of the past ten years, to become successful and admired as an author. 'During the whole of Borrow's manhood there was probably only one period when he was unquestionably happy in his work and content with his surroundings,' says a 1912 biographer. The years in Russia, Portugal and Spain helped transform him, writes Herbert Jenkins, from 'an unknown hack writer, who hawked about unsaleable translations of Welsh and Danish bards, a travelling tinker and a vagabond Ulysses' into a person 'of considerable importance'. Borrow's time in Russia produced nothing to compare with the *Bible in Spain*, his

first literary triumph, or with *Lavengro* (1851) and the *Romany Rye* (1857), where his youthful wanderings were so intriguingly transmuted. Yet the Petersburg months did have literary consequences, both then and at a tantalisingly undefined later moment.

While Borrow was in Russia a new collection of Pushkin's verse appeared. Drawn to Borrow's attention by J.P. Hasfeldt, the interpreter at the Danish legation who was his constant companion in the Imperial capital, George set about translating a handful of the poems in that volume. These were published in Petersburg in a tiny print run as *The Talisman* and before Borrow's return to England a copy was given to the author.

The incongruous but, one suspects, mutually sympathetic couple are easily pictured together. The one tall, eccentrically-dressed and grey-headed (a 'mullo' or ghost, as a Gypsy opponent described him), the other short and dapper, with his curly dark mop of hair ... One can just imagine them sharing a glass of the wine that helped Borrow to keep periodic attacks of 'the horrors' at bay. Sadly, they did not meet. Nor did the Pushkin translations reach a wider public's attention

George Borrow in 1843
Born at Pudding Green,
East Dereham 1803,
of mixed Cornish and East
Anglian parentage;
died at Oulton, nr.
Yarmouth 1881

until 1924 when the Norwich edition of Borrow's collected works appeared. The poet passed a message of thanks to Borrow for his translation (personally handed to him by Hasfeldt) and expressed the regret that they had not become acquainted.

Talisman includes the poem of that name and three others. The 1835 Russian volume of Pushkin's works also included longer pieces of verse, among them 'The Gypsies', composed ten years before. We must presume the book returned with the translator to Borrow's native East Anglia. For, at some moment during the next 10-15 years, he also set about rendering that work into English.

The unrhymed 'Tzigany' (Borrow's preferred title) is still well worth reading. It is mentioned with approval in the recent new translation by Antony Wood, though he wrongly states that Borrow completed his version during Pushkin's lifetime. Together with the small Petersburg volume *Talisman* it is the earliest tribute in English to Russia's great poet. That in itself is an illustration of the mysterious, chance confluence of circumstance and sympathy that seem to lie

behind many translations. Borrow's translation the Gypsies and its subsequent fate may not justify Pushkin's aphorism that 'translation is the post-horse of civilisation'. As Anthony Briggs has pointed out, it was a version in French by Prosper Merimée that cantered off into a different existence, ultimately disguised and universally promoted, in print and on the stage, as *Carmen*. After publishing *The Talisman* Borrow turned to Russian literature only once again as a source of inspiration and none of his efforts reached a wide audience.

The tale of Borrow's journey to Petersburg and back is, nevertheless, deserves recounting. For it says a great deal in passing about the two countries, then and now and reveals lesser known aspects of two inimitable authors. In the telling, it confirms much about the often marginal role of the translator: *auteur manqué*; someone who must earn their living in different (often, very different) ways; someone fuelled by a passion and determination that over-ride the hurdles of low pay (or none), the indifference of publishers and all but a small circle of fully appreciative readers; an

Видели его на ярмарке в красной рубашке с косым воротом и в таковых же портах. Перед ним и за ним были друзья его нищие. В правой и левой руке держал он по апельсину.

ПОЭТ А. ПУШКИН 1799 - 1837 Творчество пушкина весьма разнообразно. Поэт, драматург, прозаик, мемуарист, критик, публицист, он с одинаковой силой владел всеми литературными жанрами, и ещё неплохо рисовал.

А.Ф.

individual who feels at home in several cultures – or in none ...

Borrow's case also conjures up the nightmare of collaboration between different breeds of translator, as categorised memorably by Nabokov in his 'Art of Translation'. For the organisation that sent him, with his first ever regular salary to St Petersburg (and, subsequently, to the Iberian peninsula) was the British and Foreign Bible Society; and the task entrusted to him in the Russian capital was one that no fiction could invent. Apart, that is, from the phantasmagoric and semi-fictional status Russia often seems to be awarded in the Western imagination (and, one may add, in its own).

On the morning of 4 January 1833 the caretaker at Earl Street found George waiting for the Bible Society to open its doors and for the society's secretary, Reverend Joseph Jowett, to arrive and interview him. Had he slept well? Borrow replied that he was not aware of having slept overnight. In fact he had walked for just over 27 hours, from

Norwich to London, a distance of 112 miles.

Once offered the job in St Petersburg, Borrow set about learning the language necessary for the work. He was given six months to do so and at the end of that period he gave convincing proofs of his achievement. Among those who helped him prepare for the journey was Mr Joseph Venning, a retired Russia merchant who now lived in Norwich. The language essential to the task ahead was not Russian, however. The energetic if unconventional young man who had 'read the Bible in 13 languages' was just the person, Jowett decided – how translators, editors and publishers, must wince to read this – to complete a task begun by another translator many years before: the rendition of the Bible into the language of the Chinese Imperial Court, 'Mandchou' as it was then termed.

A certain Mr Lipovtsov in Russia had begun the task, after five years of painstaking study to acquire that demanding tongue. Type had even been cast in St Petersburg in order to print there – only for the Neva to flood its banks, in 1824,

ЕВАНГЕЛИ... ЧЕСКО – ЛЮТЕРАНСКАЯ ЦЕРКОВЬ, ЧТО НА НЕВСК... ОМ ПРОСПЕКТЕ

Drawings by Alexander Florensky: The Evangelical Lutheran Church, Nevsky Prospect, St Petersburg

and penetrate the vaults where the type were stored. There they had lain, in the mud and filth, rusting away ever since.

The transformation wrought in the 27-year-old Borrow over the next seven years from 1833 to 1840 is movingly conveyed by Herbert Jenkins, his most sympathetic biographer: 'He developed an astonishing aptitude for affairs, a tireless energy, and a diplomatic resourcefulness that aroused silent wonder in those who had hitherto regarded him as a failure.' His later missionary work in Spain and Portugal was referred to in the House of Commons by Sir Robert Peel as 'an instance of what could be achieved by courage and determination in the face of great difficulties'.

This had its roots and beginnings in those brief months in Petersburg. There Borrow experienced a welcome and acceptance from the 'expatriate' British community that cheered and sustained him. Unlike other short-term visitors, then and now, he rapidly made contacts with the people of the country itself. In one of his numerous

letters to his doting and ever-patient mother in Norwich, Borrow wrote 'the Russians are the best-natured, kindest people in the world and though they do not know as much as the English [he was not referring to the Petersburg Colony] they have not their fiendish, spiteful dispositions'. Later, when in Portugal he wished himself 'back in Russia … where I had left cherished friends and warm affections'. Among these friends were, of course, Hasfeldt, with whom he continued to correspond for several years afterwards; Nikolai Grech, the grammarian; and Friedrich von Adelung who helped him with books and manuscripts in Oriental languages. Mr Lipovtsov – or Lipovzoff, as Borrow wrote – was a rather different matter.

To Borrow he seemed curiously indifferent to the fate of his translation but, as Jenkins rightly notes, Lipovtsov was also, and primarily, an official in the Russian Ministry of Foreign Affairs who reacted with bewilderment to the 'impetuosity and determination foreign to Russian official life' with which the striking young Englishman pursued his appointed task. The distribution of bibles

Drawing by Alexander Florensky: The Universal Cosmorama was brought to St Petersburg by enterprising foreigners but at first it did not stir much of a reaction among spectators in Russia. Which was odd, since all of Paris had flocked to admire its views of Moscow and Petersburg.

translated into Russian had been allowed under Emperor Alexander I. His brother and successor Nicholas forbade such activities. Borrow was taken aback to find that this ban did not inhibit German Lutherans or non-conformist societies from handing out Bibles in Russian with a regularity that put the Church of England, parent body of the Bible and Foreign Society, to shame. The problems facing the Manchu translation of the Bible, as Borrow later discovered, were less apparent but eventually proved insuperable. There was a Russian reluctance to give offence to the Chinese authorities. However, it was 'not in Borrow's nature to exist outside his occupations' (Jenkins) and so he progressed, against all obstacles, from translation to printing, and from printing to the question of distribution. In February 1834 he wrote to the Reverend Jowett, suggesting that it would be far better to introduce the Manchu Bibles

into China from the West, and not merely to the European-influenced or controlled seaports: 'About five thousand miles from St Petersburg, on the frontiers of Chinese Tartary ... stands the town of Kyakhta ... the emporium of Chinese and Russian trade. Chinese caravans are continually arriving and returning, bringing and carrying away articles of merchandise.' Borrow considered this an ideal base for his operations and strove for several months for permission to travel there.

In this proposal we can see both the old Borrow and the new: the young man who walked and rode about England for two years in the company of Gypsies, tinkers and other travellers, and on further undocumented travels (as far as India? Perhaps), and the older and accomplished literary man who would turn such travels into much imitated by never equalled tales of Spain, England and Wild Wales.

The Manchu Bible would eventually be printed, and at a reasonable cost; the same small Petersburg printing works ran off a hundred copies each of *Talisman* and its companion volume *Targum* ('Metrical translations from Thirty Languages and Dialects'). Borrow acquired a reputation that served him well not only with the Bible Society but with its supporters throughout England. Neither the bibles nor Borrow travelled east to Kyakhta. Both instead returned to England. Five more years and Borrow was an established author and could marry and settle at Oulton Broad, near Yarmouth.

Borrow today enjoys a justifiably high reputation. The George Borrow Society plays its part in increasing appreciation for that extraordinary man's life and numerous achievements and I am grateful to the Society for responding patiently to basic queries concerning books I first read, like many others, as a teenager. How could I forget (though I did) the wonderful exchange between Borrow and the now blind Jasper Petulengro? It was Petulengro, in reality the Gypsy Ambrose Smith, who first named Borrow 'The Philologist' (Lavengro) and 'Romany Rye' or Gypsy Gentleman.

'What is your opinion of death, Mr Petulengro?' Said I, as I sat down beside him.

P: Life is sweet, brother.

B: Do you think so?

P: Think so! There's night and day, brother, both sweet things; sun, moon and stars, brother, all sweet things; there's likewise the wind on the heath. Life is very sweet, brother; who would wish to die?

B: I would wish to die –

P: You talk like a Giorgio – were you a Romany Chal you would talk wiser. Wish to die, indeed! A Rommany Chal would wish to live for ever!

B: In sickness, Jasper?

P: There's the sun and stars, brother.

B: In blindness, Jasper?

P: There's the wind on the heath, brother; if I could only feel that, I would gladly live for ever.

Dosta, we'll now go to the tents and put on the gloves; and I'll try to make you feel what a sweet thing it is to be alive, brother!

From his teens Borrow was an ardent pugilist and well able to defend himself.

Rather literal-minded critics have raised doubts about the 'veracity' of Borrow's account of events that, by his own admission, took place twenty years earlier. A necessary caution, perhaps, but hardly a weakness. Of more interest to the present theme is the coincidence in time between Pushkin's dalliance with the Gypsies of Bessarabia and that of Borrow.

Near contemporaries, they both took up with the Romany in their twenties. It seems probable that each knew of Meg Merrilies who, thanks to Keats, is far more famous than *Guy Mannering*, the anonymously published 1817 novel by Walter Scott in which she appears. It was real contact with the travelling community, however, that drew both Pushkin and Borrow to vanish for a while from respectable society and return with a vivid tale of their experiences. In Pushkin's case, the disappearance was brief -- as noted by his brother Lev, a matter of days. Borrow took to the road for months and became thoroughly immersed in Romany language and culture.

Years later, when he was slowly composing *Lavengro*, he recalled Pushkin's poem of 1825 and wrote out in manuscript form his own version. Not only that. As Dr Ann Soutter has discovered, one famous passage in Lavengro bears an uncanny resemblance to part of Pushkin's work – a case of sympathy and, even, unconscious re-working rather than any less laudable borrowing. It is a tribute to Pushkin in general and, in particular, to the conviction of the acute vision he conjured from short acquaintance of passion and disillusion among 'The Gypsies'.

How does Borrow's version compare with the latest translation of the work? The friend of his later years, Edward FitzGerald, translator of the *Rubaiyat of Omar Khayyam*, 'the most famous verse translation ever made into English'

ЦЕРКОВЬ ЗАЛОЖЕНА В 1753 ГОДУ И СТРОИЛАСЬ НА ДЕНЬГИ БОГАТОГО ОТКУПЩИКА ЯКОВЛЕВА. ЕЁ АВТОРОМ, ВОЗМОЖНО, БЫЛ ЗНАМЕНИТЫЙ Б. РАСТРЕЛЛИ(ОН ЖЕ ПОСТРОИЛ НЕПОДАЛЕКУ ОСОБНЯК ЯКОВЛЕВА)

церковь успения

торговый павильон

городская улица

Успенский

Drawing by Alexander Florensky:
Church of the Assumption, St Petersburg
The Alexander Nevsky Lavra, St Petersburg

expressed a pithy requirement of any version in another language: 'at all cost' he wrote, 'a Thing must live: ... better a live Sparrow than a stuffed Eagle'. Which of the two translations is more successful? Which flies or only limps along? Does one barely take to the air? It is, of course, a matter of personal choice. Perhaps, if one reads Russian the English rhyme must seem weaker, almost invariably. If, on the other hand, the English version is the only access one has to this rhythmic vision, a prose equivalent may well appear flat and unconvincing.

> 'Father,' declares the girl, 'I found
> A guest out there, beside a mound;
> I've asked him home to stay with us.

Says Zemfira in Antony Wood's version (2002). The old man invites Aleko

> Be one of us and live our life –
> The threadbare freedom of the road.
> We're off tomorrow with our load;
> Choose a trade to suit your flair,
> Blacksmith, singer, or the bear.

A literal prose translation by John Fennell (1964): Father, says the girl, I am bringing a guest: I

found him in the waste land beyond the mound and I have called him to the camp to spend the night.

Old Man: ... Be one of us, accustom yourself to our lot, to wandering poverty and freedom ... forge iron, sing songs or go around the villages with the bear.

In Borrow's hands these words became

> My father, says the girl,
> I bring you a guest. I found him in the wilderness
> Behind the hill
> And invited him to the camp for the night.

Old Man: Be ours. Accustom yourself to our lot
> Our wandering poverty and freedom.
> Adopt the trade you like the best:
> Forge iron or sing songs
> Or go about the villages with the bear.

The various and unresolved arguments over the right way to translate were summarised in contrasting demands by Theodore Savery (1957): Should a translation read like a translation – or like an original work? Should it give the words of the original or the ideas of the original? Should it translate verse into verse, or verse into prose? And

Александро-Невская лавра ✝

речка Монастырка

Флоренский

so on ... Plausible arguments have been made, in theory and in practice, on either side of the coin.

For his part Borrow has one most definite comment about translation and its shortcomings. In *Lavengro*, the 18-year-old hero is recalled as doubting his claim to immortality or, as he more precisely expresses that vague desire, 'a reputation of a thousand years'. He has translated from Welsh and Danish, he had learnt many more tongues and acquired some knowledge of Hebrew and Arabic. Were he to continue in this way until he was forty he would then be very learned but the prospect distressed him: '...all this is mere learning and translation, ... Translation is at best an echo, and it must be a wonderful echo to be heard after the lapse of a thousand years.' He chose, instead, the surer path to lasting fame by becoming an author in his own right.

And the Manchu bibles? At first sight their fate is an ironic footnote to this tale of travel, translation and failure transformed into success. They became the very emblems of the futile and unremarked activity that all translators secretly dread. The bibles liberated Borrow from obscurity and frustration and accompanied him back to England. Yet the formidable task of their production proved, ultimately, misplaced and misguided.

In contemporary China, it turned out, the court had long ceased to speak Manchu. It preferred to converse in Mandarin Chinese, enjoy literature and other entertainments in that language. The ancestral tongue of the dynasty was confined to the writing of official documents.

It is unlikely that Borrow was greatly upset and certainly not for long. His passion for languages was sufficient in itself. Each opened a new doorway between different worlds and cultures that beckoned and intrigued him. Compared to his lifelong passion for Wales and its bards, his acquaintance with Russia and its great poet was brief. Yet it was characteristically wholehearted and left behind a monument that has weathered remarkably well.

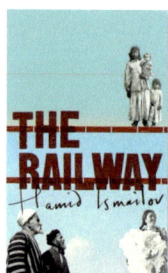

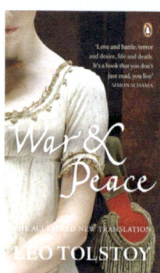

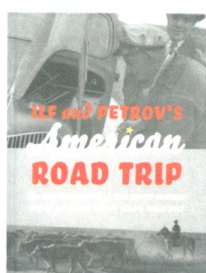

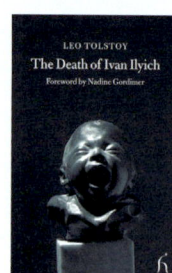

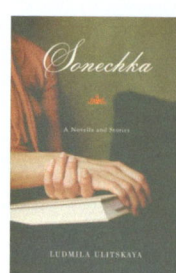

Премия Rossica 2007

Международная Премия за литературный перевод с русского языка на английский

Премия Rossica была учреждена фондом Academia Rossica в 2004. Премия вручается раз в два года; она присуждается как переводчику, так и издателю перевода, который члены Жюри признают лучшим среди изданных за последние два года. Премия Rossica уникальна — она является единственной в мире премией за литературный перевод с русского языка на английский.

Переводы русских писателей в конце XIX и начале XX века на английский язык стали важным событием для британской культуры, сравнимым по масштабу с влиянием Италии эпохи Возрождения на Англию времен Шекспира и Марлоу. Поэтому неудивителен постоянный и глубокий интерес английских читателей, издателей и переводчиков к русской литературе.

Мы надеемся, что Премия Rossica станет стимулом для издания большего числа литературных переводов широкого круга авторов, жанров и периодов, способствуя таким образом распространению лучших образцов русской словесности в англоязычном мире. Учреждение Премии Rossica также признание важности работы переводчиков, своим трудом выстраивающих мосты между различными языковыми культурами.

Премия Rossica была впервые присуждена в 2005 году. С тех пор многие страны последовали этому примеру: Франция учредила премию 'Русофония' за лучшие переводы с русского на французский, вскоре подобная премия возникла и в Испании, а Британский Совет учредил в Москве премию 'Лев и Единорог' за лучший перевод прозы и поэзии с английского языка на русский.

Поскольку премия дается за перевод, а не за оригинальный текст, разнообразие книг, участвующих в конкурсе, необычайно широко: от великих и всемирно знаменитых классиков XIX века до романов века XXI, от путевых дневников до поэзии. Как отмечали судьи премии, рядом со знакомым и предсказуемым нередко случаются открытия: новые авторы, забытые работы, новые литературные стили — так и должно быть, ведь Премия Rossica отражает богатые традиции и живое развитие русской литературы.

Победитель Премии Rossica 2007

Джоанн Тернбулл и GLAS/New Russian Writing
(Москва, 2006)
за перевод 'Семи рассказов' Сигизмунда Кржижановского Сборник удивительных, причудливых басен советского писателя 20-х годов, лишь недавно ставшего известным. Этот смелый и тонкий перевод настолько точно передает мир и атмосферу рассказов Кржижановского, что кажется, что они были написаны по-английски.

Специальная награда Жюри

Роберт Чандлер и Harvill Secker (Лондон, 2006)
за перевод романа Хамида Исмаилова 'Железная дорога' В знак признания достоинств этого перевода, а также в знак признания блестящих заслуг Роберта Чандлера, в течение многих лет знакомящего англоязычного читателя с лучшими произведениями русской литературы.

Шорт-лист Премии Rossica 2007

Энтони Бриггс и Penguin Books (Лондон, 2005)
перевод романа Льва Толстого 'Война и мир'

Хью Аплин и Hesperus Press (Лондон, 2005)
перевод книги рассказов Льва Толстого 'Смерть Ивана Ильича'

Арч Тейт и Schocken Books (Нью-Йорк, 2006)
перевод книги Людмилы Улицкой 'Сонечка: новелла и рассказы'

Анн О. Фишер и Princeton Architectural Press & Cabinet Books (Нью-Йорк, 2006)
перевод путевых заметок Ильи Ильфа и Евгения Петрова, 'Путешествие Ильфа и Петрова по дорогам Америки: путевые заметки двух советских писателей, 1935 год'

Памяти Бориса Николаевича Ельцина, Первого Президента России

Премия Rossica учреждена фондом Academia Rossica в партнерстве с Фондом Первого Президента России Б. Н. Ельцина. Фонд был основан в Москве в 2000 году как независимая благотворительная организация. Его главная цель — развивать гуманитарное и культурное сотрудничество и открытый обмен идеями и информацией между Россией и западным миром.

'Ушла целая эпоха' — часто звучало в дни последовавшие за уходом из жизни первого Президента России. Это утверждение и банально, и ложно.

Эпоха Ельцина, по счастью, никуда не ушла. Она продолжается в заложенных им институтах гражданских прав и свобод, рыночной экономики, политической системы и общества.

Ценность наследия Ельцина заключается именно в этой институциональности, в открытости системы его взглядов на мир, в ее целостности и современности. Нужно принять это наследие как общественное достояние и суметь им правильно распорядиться. Например, хотя бы последовать его личному примеру и создать из собственной жизни модель того самого гражданского общества, в которое стремится Россия. И которое рождается не по команде, а из глубокого осознания личной ответственности перед страной и людьми, в мужественных актах самодеятельности и самоорганизации. Весь путь Б.Н.Ельцина состоял из бесконечной череды именно таких, гражданских поступков.

Легко сегодня предъявлять счета за девяностые годы. Сам первый президент уже не ответит. Да, впрочем, и при жизни он не слишком любил комментировать собственные президентские хроники. Он предоставлял разбираться в них времени и самим своим соотечественникам.

Тем более, что из его рук они получили безграничную волю открыто высказывать собственные суждения. Принципы свободы слова, свободный обмен идеями, открытое информационное пространство были для президента священны.

Фонд Ельцина пытается сохранить и приумножить его идейное наследие. Поэтому для нас столь важен опыт Премии Rossica в Англии, 'Русской премии' в странах СНГ, 'Русофонии' во Франции, премии за перевод с русского языка на испанский — в них воплотилась любовь Б.Н.Ельцина к русской культуре и родному языку и его вера в надмирность духовных ценностей.

Он сам был совершенно открыт миру при всей самобытности и колоритности своего настоящего русского характера. Осуществив прорыв в свободу, он доказал, что мы можем стать другой страной. Он верил, что Россия уже никогда не вернется в прошлое.

Теперь в это должна, наконец, поверить сама Россия.

Александр Дроздов
Исполнительный директор
Фонда Первого президента России Б.Н. Ельцина

Отчет жюри Премии Rossica 2007

Члены жюри рассмотрели 29 книг, вышедших в свет в 2005-2006 годах — для сравнения, в 2005 году на соискание премии были выдвинуты 37 изданий, опубликованных за четырехлетний период. Большинство книг поступило организаторам непосредственно от издательств, хотя некоторые были допущены к конкурсу по просьбе членов жюри (см. Раздел 4 Устава). Было решено, что понятие 'художественный перевод' следует трактовать достаточно широко, включая в него, помимо собственно художественной литературы, также и 'малые жанры', среди которых мемуары, письма и дневники.

Среди присланных на конкурс книг — тексты самого различного характера. Почти половину из них составили переводы русских классиков XIX-XX веков — Пушкина (три перевода), Достоевского (три перевода), Толстого (два перевода), Лермонтова, Гончарова, Чехова, а также Маяковского, Булгакова, Ильфа и Петрова. Литература последних лет представлена обширной группой текстов, разнообразных по своей жанровой принадлежности. Среди них мемуары и близкие им произведения (четыре перевода), современная поэзия (четыре перевода) и современная художественная проза (семь переводов). Последняя категория включает как экспериментальные работы, так и книги, в недавнем времени получившие коммерческое признание. При этом хочется отметить, что члены жюри были несколько разочарованы малым количеством ярких работ в жанре современного романа. Некоторые из переводчиков уже успели проявить себя в качестве авторитетных специалистов — в частности, одному из них принадлежит целых пять присланных на конкурс текстов. В случае, когда переводы ранее уже частично публиковались, их экспертная оценка членами жюри основывалась исключительно на новом материале.

В процессе отбора книг члены жюри естественно столкнулись с проблемой объективных критериев их оценки. Действительно, как можно сравнивать такие непохожие друг на друга тексты, как переводы 'Войны и мира', популярной детективной повести или, например, небольшого сборника стихов? Главным параметром оценки для нас было качество перевода. Перевод мог попасть в список номинантов только в том случае, если мы были уверены, что он обладает самодостаточной литературной ценностью и при этом максимально выявляет содержательные и стилевые нюансы оригинального текста (а они могут быть самые разные, в зависимости от конкретной книги). Таким образом, наш метод заключался в следующем: сперва мы читали текст английского перевода и только после этого сравнивали его с русским оригиналом, руководствуясь критериями содержательной точности, передачи индивидуальной авторской манеры и сохранения общей стилистики произведения.

Победителя было выбрать нелегко. Нас искренне обрадовало высокое качество всех книг, вошедших в список номинантов, а также ряда других, по разным причинам в него не попавших.

Работа в качестве членов жюри, требующая огромной ответственности, в то же время, явилась для нас прекрасным опытом. Она позволила вновь осознать неоценимую важность труда сравнительно небольшого количество издателей и переводчиков, сохраняющих передовые позиции русской литературы, как новой, так и старой, в культурном обиходе англоязычного мира. Мы выражаем свою признательность фонду Академия Rossica за учреждение этой важной премии. Надеемся, что наша Премия Rossica будет способствовать появлению все новых и новых переводов, особенно в области современной художественной прозы.

Жюри Премии Rossica 2007

Элэйн Файнстайн получила образование в Кембриджском университете, и в 1980 стала членом Королевского литературного общества. Она является автором четырнадцати романов, радиопьес, телевизионных спектаклей и пяти биографий. В 1990 она получила Поэтическую премию Cholmondeley и стала Почетным доктором литературы Лестерского университета. Элэйн приглашают читать свои произведения на международные фестивали по всему миру. Ее 'Собрание стихов и переводов' (2002) удостоено Особой рекомендации Общества поэтической книги (Poetry Book Society Special Commendation). В июле 2005 года вышла написанная ею биография Анны Ахматовой 'Anna of All the Russias'.

Питер Франс – почетный профессор Эдинбургского университета. Издал много работ по русской и французской литературе, включаю книгу 'Поэты современной России' (1982). Является редактором Оксфордского руководства по литературе в английском переводе (Oxford Guide to Literature in English Translation) и пятитомной Оксфордской истории английского литературного перевода (Oxford History of Literary Translation in English) (издается с 2005 года). Среди его переводов с русского сборники стихотворений Александра Блока и Бориса Пастернака (совместно с Йеном Стилворти) и несколько томов поэзии Геннадия Айги.

Катриона Келли – профессор Оксфордского университета (New College), исследователь русской литературы и истории культуры. Среди ее многочисленных публикаций: 'Очень короткое введение в русскую литературу' (OUP 2001) и 'Товарищ Павлик: Расцвет и падение юного советского героя' (Granta, 2005). Катриона была редактором книги 'Утопии: Русские модернистские тексты, 1905-1940' (Penguin, 1999) и 'Антологии произведений женщин-писателей России, 1777-1992' (OUP 1994). Оба эти сборника включают произведения, переведенные ей самой. Она также опубликовала множество других переводов русской поэзии и прозы, в том числе, Маяковского, Елены Шварц, Ольги Седаковой, Сергея Каледина, Леонида Бородина.

Профессор Питер Франс
Член Жюри Премии Rossica 2007 года

Я один из тех пяти тысяч счастливцев, кому выпало учить русский во время прохождения военной службы – в Блумсбери и Бодмин Муре. Мы зубрили язык каждый день сутки напролет в течение восемнадцати месяцев, и, в конце концов, довольно прилично им овладели. Мы даже знали, как будет по-русски 'осевой компрессор'. Однако подобный языковой курс, разрабатывавшийся в тылу Холодной войны, разумеется, не был рассчитан на внушение ученикам искренней любви к России и ее культуре. Если нам и давали читать русскую литературу (в том числе и достойные вещи, например, 'Повесть о настоящем человеке' Бориса Полевого), это делалось исключительно для того, чтобы выучить как можно больше незнакомой лексики. К счастью, среди наших преподавателей были и русские эмигранты, любившие своих писателей, и поэтому, приступив к изучению русского языка в Оксфорде, я уже обладал достаточной культурной подготовкой, чтобы с упоением погрузиться в мир Пушкина и Достоевского.

По окончании учебы в университете я стал специализироваться на французской литературе. Тем не менее, мой русский никуда не делся – наоборот, судьба вдохнула в него вторую жизнь, когда Джон Стэлворти предложил мне сотрудничество над переводами Блока и Пастернака. Таким образом, я продолжил изучение русской литературы уже в роли переводчика, а не в роли ученого или преподавателя. В основном я переводил поэзию, и моя переводческая деятельность заложила основу моей дружбы с русско-чувашским поэтом Генадием Айги. Я перевел несколько сборников его стихов и много раз приезжал к нему в Россию и Чувашию.

Впоследствии у меня появился русский зять, художник Генадий Гоголюк, и некоторые мои внуки были крещены в соответствии с православным обрядом. Все это тесно связывало меня с Россией, при том что я никогда не был профессиональным славистом. Мне было очень приятно, когда в этом году я получил приглашение выступить в качестве члена жюри премии Rossica. Чрезвычайно интересно было посмотреть на блестящую работу ряда переводчиков, сталкивающихся с труднопреодолимыми терниями интерпретации лучших текстов русской литературы. Несмотря на то, что поэзию Пушкина часто объявляют 'не поддающейся переводу' (хотя не можем ли мы сказать то же о любых текстах, если переводчик априори задает себе слишком высокую планку?), я восхищен профессионализмом двух его переводчиков, по разным причинам не попавших в список номинантов, — Энтони Вуда и Роджера Кларка. Надо сказать, что и современная проза представляет немало трудностей для качественного перевода, стремящегося к воссозданию интонационных нюансов и чистоты стиля оригинала. Наши номинанты великолепно справились со всеми этими трудностями. Вообще, так как мы занимались сравнением переводов с оригинальными текстами, я получил прекрасную возможность прочесть — или перечесть — несколько русских текстов и оценить их независимо от нашей работы. Так, вдохновленный популярным переводом Энтони Бриггса, я решил вновь пройтись по русскому тексту 'Войны и мира' — пока пишу эти строки, я стремительно приближаюсь к Бородинской битве.

Многие из рассмотренных нами книг — старые знакомые в новом обличье. Однако были и замечательные открытия, относящиеся к литературе последних восьмидесяти лет. Это и современная поэзия, и 'Одноэтажная Америка' Ильфа и Петрова 1935 года, это и Сигизмунд Кржижановский, великолепный писатель двадцатых-тридцатых годов, только сейчас по-настоящему открытый в России, — и Хамид Измаилов — автор причудливой и вместе с тем преисполненной глубокого лирического чувства эпопеи об узбекской жизни. Не менее интересными были автобиографические сочинения — в частности, военные дневники Василия Гросмана, а также 'Тихая степь' — волнующая история Мухамеда Шайахметова о его тяжелой жизни в Казахстане в сталинские годы. Единственное, о чем я сожалею, так это о том, что в отборе участвовало совсем мало работ известных на родине современных российских авторов. Я надеюсь, что благодаря премии Rossica наши издательства начнут публиковать больше замечательных произведений, которые появляются сегодня в России .

Элэйн Файнштайн
Член Жюри Премии Rossica 2007 года

Я участвовала в процессе отбора книг для настоящей премии в качестве автора, работающего на английском языке, а не как эксперт, имеющий возможность судить о точности перевода с русского. Я обладаю довольно большим опытом перевода с русского — в особенности много я работала с поэзией Марины Цветаевой. При этом обычно, хотя и не всегда, я сотрудничала с

профессиональным славистом, специализирующимся на русской литературе — таким образом, привнося в работу над текстом скорее навыки поэта, чем лингвиста. Я никогда не переводила прозу, хотя сама написала ряд романов.

Книги, которые нам предстояло рассмотреть для премии Rossica, существенно отличались по времени создания, объему и честолюбию авторского замысла. Наряду с переводами главных произведений Пушкина, Толстого, Достоевского, Гончарова и Чехова, были тексты двадцатого века, среди которых аллегорическая повесть Булгакова 'Собачье сердце', остроумные детективные истории Бориса Акунина, путевые журналы и исторические описания малоизвестных уголков Советского Союза. Было и несколько отличных современных писателей, чьи имена мне были совершенно незнакомы, — надеюсь, что благодаря премии Rossica повысится число издательств, берущихся публиковать современную русскую литературу такого уровня.

Среди этих авторов Хамид Измаилов, 'вновь открытый' Сигизмунд Кржижановский и Людмила Улицкая. 'Железная дорога' Измаилова, в чрезвычайно ясном переводе Роберта Чандлера, повествует о жизни маленького, забытого городка в советском Узбекистане, который автор населил множеством необычных персонажей. Возникающие на их пути жизненные ситуации и человеческие дилеммы и в наше время кажутся неожиданно актуальными. Переводчица Джоан Тернбулл избрала для себя еще более сложную задачу: истолковать на английском причудливые рассказы Кржижановского — писателя, художественный мир которого, подобно борхесовскому, преисполнен иррациональными образами, уносящими читателя прочь от рассудочной логики окружающей его действительности. Поразительнее всего даже не то, что Кржижановский 'известен тем, что был неизвестен', а то, что его гений смог пережить времена советского табу и спустя много лет после смерти писателя, наконец, заявить о себе во весь голос. В свою очередь, повесть 'Сонечка' Людмилы Улицкой открывает одноименный сборник тихих, трогающих за душу рассказов. Книга вышла в ясном и тонком переводе Арча Тэйта.

Обсуждение книг членами жюри проходило в дружеской атмосфере, однако прийти к единому мнению относительно списка номинантов оказалось непросто. Меня лично в особенности поразил великолепный свежий перевод 'Войны и мира' Энтони Бригса. С моей точки зрения, этот перевод откроет великий роман Толстого для целого поколения новых читателей. При этом выполненный Хью Эплином перевод 'Смерти Ивана Ильича' того же Толстого, произведения лаконичного и мрачного, оказался не менее достойным. Последними авторами, включенными нами в список, стали обаятельные сатирики Ильф и Петров, чьи американские записки, надо отметить, не содержат ничего такого, что читатель того времени мог бы назвать антисоветским.

Наконец, те, кто подобно мне искренне восхищаются той самоотверженностью, с которой Энтони Вуд посвятил себя переводу произведений Александра Пушкина, наверняка, будут разочарованы, не обнаружив его имени среди номинантов. Я думаю, что не ошибусь, если скажу, что самая острая полемика при отборе книг велась как раз вокруг его работы. Но, как известно, самый сложный выбор перед арбитром любой литературной премии ставят произведения наиболее прославленных писателей.

Истоки русской литературы
Святые Кирилл и Мефодий

Премия Rossica вручается 24 мая, в день памяти равноапостольных святых Кирилла и Мефодия, создателей славянского алфавита.

Создание славянского алфавита – величайший вклад Византии в русскую культуру. Двух братьев-греков, равноапостольных Кирилла и Мефодия, мы должны благодарить за это. Никогда в жизни не ступала их нога на русскую землю, они жили за век до Великого Князя Владимира Киевского, чьи люди приняли христианское вероисповедание, но создав славянский алфавит, они положили начало русской письменности и литературе последующих столетий и открыли славянам христианскую и эллинскую культуры. Кирилл и Мефодий – славянские первоучители, великие проповедники христианства, канонизированы не только православной, но и католической церковью

Рожденные в Салониках, Кирилл был младшим, а Мефодий – старшим из восьми сыновей знатного греческого военачальника. Мефодий (820-885) состоял на военной службе, десять лет был правителем одной из подчиненных Византии славянских областей, а затем удалился в монастырь Олимп в Малой Азии. Кирилл (827-869), одаренный, но болезненный мальчик, воспитывался при дворе, обучался вместе с малолетним императором Михаилом III. Обучаясь у лучших учителей своего времени, Кирилл изучал классическую литературу, риторику, грамматику, диалектику, астрономию, музыку, иврит, греческий, латинский, арабский, а также славянские языки, которые они с братом знали с детства. Среди его преподавателей был Фотий, будущий прославленный патриарх Константинопольский. Кирилл стал патриаршим

библиотекарем в соборе Святой Софии, а позднее преподавал в высшем учебном заведении Византии эллинскую и христианскую философию.

Около 860 года братья отправились в миссионерскую поездку к хазарам с целью обратить их в христианство. На пути они остановились в Херсонесе Таврическом, где обнаружили мощи Святого Климента, папы Римского. Обратив в христианство около двух сотен хазар, они вернулись в Византию. С собой они привезли мощи Святого Климента. В уединенном монастыре столицы они приступили к созданию алфавита для славян.

Среди ученых нет единого мнения о том, какой именно алфавит создали Кирилл и Мефодий. Была ли это кириллица, названная в честь младшего брата, алфавит, используемый примерно 60 народами? Или же это была глаголица – отличающаяся более сложным написанием букв, которые, как предполагается, произошли от иврита или арамейского языка? В X-XI веках оба алфавита использовались одновременно, а впоследствии кириллица вытеснила более сложную по написанию глаголицу. Двадцать пять букв, использовавшиеся тогда и сейчас в кириллическом письме, были заимствованы из греческого, тогда как другие восемнадцать были добавлены, чтобы передать звуки, существовавшие только в славянских языках.

С помощью своего брата Мефодия Кирилл сначала перевел на славянский язык Евангелие, Послания Апостолов и Псалтырь – тексты, важнейшие для церковной службы. В 863 году император отправил их в качестве помощников принцу Моравии (часть современной Чешской республики) Ростиславу. Епископ Баварии объявил территорию частью своей юрисдикции, немецкие принцы, руководимые Людвигом Немецким, мечтали завоевать и аннексировать земли Моравии. Разразилась война, подогреваемая враждебностью германского духовенства. Кирилл и Мефодий решили вернуться в Константинополь с моравскими новообращенными, но когда братья прибыли в Венецию, был созван совет местных епископов и братьев обвинили в нарушении церковных установлений, по которым богослужение могло отправляться только на трех языках: греческом, латыни и иврите.

С IX века было разрешено проповедовать на языке просвещаемого народа, но Кирилл и Мефодий были осуждены за перевод на славянский язык богослужебных книг. В конце этого же года они получают из Константинополя печальные вести: их покровитель император Михаил III был убит в ходе дворцового переворота, а патриарх Фотий, бывший учитель Кирилла, низложен. Братья решили обратиться за помощью к Папе Адриану III. Он устроил им торжественный прием в своем дворце, вероятно, потому что они привезли с собой останки его канонизированного предшественника Климента. Адриан одобрил их переводы библейских и литургических текстов на славянский язык, рукоположил некоторых последователей Кирилла и Мефодия в священники и разрешил отслужить славянскую литургию в соборе св. Петра. Однако вскоре Кирилл, который никогда не славился крепким здоровьем, скончался. Его останки были сначала похоронены в усыпальнице пап, а потом по просьбе брата перенесены в базилику св. Климента.

Кирилл умер 14 февраля 869 года, в конце этого же года Папа Адриан рукоположил Мефодия в епископы Моравии и Паннонии. В епархии нового епископа служба могла проводиться на славянском языке с условием, что Евангелие и Послание апостолов читались сначала на латыни, а затем на церковно-славянском. Однако этому новому порядку не суждено было прижиться. Мефодий вернулся в Паннонию, но в том же году был призван к архиепископу Зальцбургскому и обвинён в посягательстве на епархию последнего. Последовали три года сурового заточения, и только когда был провозглашён новый Папа Иоанн VIII, Мефодий был выпущен из тюрьмы и вернулся в Моравию, чтобы продолжить ведение службы на славянском языке.

После Великого Раскола 1054 года церковь разделилась на восточный и западный лагеря, христиане Моравии и других частей будущих Чехословакии и Хорватии отошли к христианскому миру Запада. Однако миссионерская и просветительская деятельность Кирилла и Мефодия имела огромное значение для последующего развития славянских народов, заложив основы их письменности и литературной традиции.

День памяти двух греческих братьев, живших в IX веке, Святых Кирилла и Мефодия, отцов русской письменности, отмечается каждый год 24 мая.

Sigizmund Krzhizhanovsky, 7 Stories
Moscow: GLAS/New Russian Writing, 2006
Перевод Джоанны Тернбулл

Сигизмунд Кржижановский, 'Семь историй'
Написанные в период между 1922 и 1939 гг., эти замечательные истории свидетельствуют о неисчерпаемой фантазии, чёрном юморе и умопомрачительной иронии Кржижановского. Человек потерялся в огромном чёрном ничто своей маленькой комнатки.

Прежние любовники женщины обречены на то, чтобы остаться в глубине её зрачков. Возмущённая рука известного пианиста спасается бегством через весь концертный зал во время выступления. А другой человек находит смысл жизни в попытках укусить свой локоть. Литературоведы считают, что он потерял собственное 'я' в новой Советской жизни. Учёный находит выход из энергетического кризиса в преобразовании человеческой злобы в энергию. Эйфелева башня сошла с ума и утопилась в озере Констанц.

Джоанн Тернбулл перевела ряд книг с русского языка, в том числе такие произведения, как 'Травяная улица' Асара Эппеля, 'Альбом с марками' Андрея Сергеева, авторский сборник Льва Рубинштейна 'Here I Am', 'Дневник советской школьницы: 1932-1937' Нины Луговской, 'Иван-дурак: очерк русской народной веры' Андрея Синявского, опубликованные в издательстве GLAS/ New Russian Writing. В данный момент работает над переводом нового сборника произведений Кржижановского, на этот раз для NYRB Classics. С 1987 года живёт в Москве.

Сигизмунд Кржижановский (1887-1950) родился в Киеве в семье польских католиков, был их единственным сыном и проявлял большие способности к музыке. Уже в подростковом возрасте он прочитал 'Критику чистого разума' Канта и это произвело на него неизгладимое впечатление: 'Раньше всё казалось таким простым: предметы отбрасывают тени, но если посмотреть с другой стороны, то кажется, что тени отбрасывают предметы, или вообще, предметов этих вовсе не существует'. Немного погодя, он открыл для себя Шекспира: 'Перевод был грубым и неточным, однако я почувствовал, что нашёл друга, который способен спасти меня от этих метафизических заблуждений'. Кржижановский закончил юридический факультет, параллельно изучал шесть языков и открывал для себя Европу. После революции и краткосрочной службы в Красной Армии, он начал читать лекции по психологии творчества, истории и теории театра, литературы и музыки в Киевском университете. Но именно переезд в Москву (лейтмотив многих его историй) в 1922 году дал импульс к началу собственного литературного творчества: философские 'новеллы' (как он их и называл) с фантастическими сюжетами. Многие герои Кржижановского буквально срывались с катушек в окружающем их алогичном мире: 'Я не понимаю', — говорит один из них. 'Понимание, — звучит ответ, — строго запрещено'. 'Вместо того, чтобы изобретать все эти запатентованные средства от зубной боли и простуды, — говорит другой, — науке следовало бы поискать лекарство от угрызений совести'. Неизменные отказы советских издателей, и, наконец, Горький самолично уговорил писателя-сатирика свифтовского уровня изменить хотя бы форму произведений в сторону более приемлемых для цензуры: драматургия 'Человека, который был четвергом' Честертона и 'Евгения Онегина' Пушкина; статьи о лаконичности и о психологическом романе в Большой Советской Энциклопедии; эссе о драматургии шахматной доски и искусстве ставить эпиграф на материале Шоу и Шекспира. Цензоры и тут были непреклонны. Даже запоздалое вступление Кржижановского в 1939 году в Союз Писателей не помогло ему, однако открыло доступ на полку Государственного Архива для его произведений, где они и были найдены четверть века спустя после смерти писателя. Еще четверть века спустя после этого события было опубликовано собрание трудов Кржижановского — он бы не поверил своим ушам, узнав о том, что его откроют и поймут только спустя полвека.

Об 'Автобиографии трупа' Сигизмунда Кржижановского
Джоанн Тернбулл

В своем знаменитом эссе против социалистического реализма (1959) Андрей Синявский мечтает о 'фантасмагорическом искусстве с гипотезами вместо намерения и гротеском вместо описания повседневной жизни'. Одному только надо научиться, по его мнению — это 'быть правдивым при помощи абсурдной фантазии'.

Синявский не знал, что был такой киевский автор (и не Булгаков), который писал именно так. Сигизмунд Кржижановский (1887-1950), 'экспериментальный реализм' которого пользовался гиперболой, иронией, парадоксом и фантасмагориями, медленно умирал, а его произведения были погребены (романы, истории, пьесы, эссе — большинство не опубликовано) в Государственном архиве. Среди них — 'Автобиография трупа'.

Трудно устоять против истории с таким названием. А Кржижановский подходил к выбору заглавия серьезно. Он считал сочинения заглавий искусством. В 34-страничной монографии на эту тему, 'Поэтика заглавий' (1931), он упрекает писателей за то, что они напяливают названия на текст 'неразборчиво и торопливо, как шляпу на чью-то голову'. Как книга есть квинтэссенция 'фразеологии жизни', так и название должно быть квинтэссенцией книги.

Действие 'Автобиографии трупа' начинается с прибытия в 1920 году провинциального журналиста по имени Штамм. Штамм полон решимости 'обменивать чернильные капли на рубли', несмотря на ужасающий дефицит жилых мест в столице. Внезапно гостеприимная удача приводит его в одну мрачную комнату с хорошим видом из окна, но без ключа. Ключ потерян. Как будто его никогда и не было. Штамм покупает висячий замок и отправляется на поиски работы. Проходит время, и однажды поздно вечером, подойдя к своей комнатке, он находит рукопись,

заткнутую в дверной проем. Ее автор, бывший хозяин квартиры, — самоубийца. И он постарался написать свою автобиографию перед тем, как покончил с собой. С этого момента речь в рассказе идет о жизни этого трупа.

В эссе с восхитительным названием 'Страны, которых нет', посвященном воображаемым попыткам человека расширить 'стены мира', Кржижановский обращается к одному из моментов из 'Путешествий Гулливера': 'Интересно, что в первой и во второй частях Свифт, как истинный художник, позволяет себе изменять реальность только в единственном случае — для того, чтобы уменьшать или увеличивать размеры тел людей, среди которых живет его герой. В иных случаях, он чрезвычайно точен и более нигде не отклоняется от реалистической манеры письма'. В этом и состоит изюминка индивидуально-авторского стиля Кржижановского, который мы называем 'экспериментальным реализмом'.

Как Штамм, Кржижановский приезжает в советскую Москву, уже будучи писателем, в надежде завоевать этот город. Это был 1922 год. Через друга друзей он находит кельеподобную комнатку на Арбате (дом 44, кв.5). Квартира принадлежала пожилому графу. Комнату Кржижановского, как и Штамма, до этого снимал умерший человек. Александр Нарышкин, до революции служивший вице-губернатором, жил в этой квартире, пока его не арестовали ночью 1919 г. Он умер в тюрьме 2 года спустя.

'Автобиография трупа' — история эрудированного библиофила, который в постреволюционное время находится в состоянии полной растерянности в алогичном советском порядке. Он не может преодолеть себя, чтобы заинтересоваться другим 'я'; и наконец, он не может определиться со своим 'я'. Чтобы описать свое затруднительное положение, он призывает на помощь 'символы математической логики'. 'Точка может быть отыскана в пространстве, говорят они, лишь при посредстве скрещения координат. Но ведь стоит координатам разомкнуться, и … пространство огромно, точка же не имеет никакой величины. Очевидно, мои координаты разомкнулись, и отыскать меня, психическую точку в беспредельности, оказалось невозможным'.

Эта ошеломляющая математическая метафора характерная для стиля Кржижановского. С одной стороны, мы видим его логику, его оригинальность, его простоту, его яркость. С другой стороны, мы видим обычную для него отсылку к нелитературным дисциплинам. Как повествователь 'Автобиографии Трупа', Кржижановский был библиофилом, чрезвычайным эрудитом и полиглотом. И как Свифт, он чрезвычайно точен в использовании терминов — будь они математическими, музыкальными, географическими, историческими, философскими, физическими, астрономическими или анатомическими. Когда, например, он упоминает (в другой истории) 'хаос звуков, данным кортиевым спиралям', он имеет ввиду 'спираль органа Корти' — этой особой части внутреннего уха, с помощью которой непосредственно воспринимается звук.

Другое наблюдение, которое может быть интересно

переводчикам Кржижановского, касается его привязанности к неологизмам, например, 'разбездушить' из 'Автобиографии трупа'. Для носителей русского языка значение абсолютно ясно; этот новоизобретенный глагол, со свежим натуральным звучанием, не подвергается переводческой дрессировке. Алгоритм действий переводчика таков: сначала разобрать по частям русское слово для того, чтобы затем сконструировать его по-английски: 'душить' (сдавливать горло, подавлять, удушать – to choke, stifle, suffocate), образованное от слова 'душа' ('soul'); '-без' ('-less, -free, -non, un-'); 'раз-' (вторая приставка, здесь – 'окончание действия', 'completion of action'). Моим окончательным переводом было 'to desoulerate' – слово, которое мне не совсем нравится, так как оно не звучит также четко, как русское 'разбездушить', и еще потому что оно выделяется.

Эти сделанные слова часто встречаются. На русском изобретения Кржижановского оживляют текст, даже если его не читать вслух. В английском – по-другому. Небольшой неологизм проходит долгий путь. Потому иногда я выбираю существующий английский эквивалент несуществующему русскому слову ('брезг' - 'glimmer' – 'мерцание, тусклый свет' англ.).

Другая ловушка для переводчиков Кржижановского заключается в его языковой игре. Самый яркий пример 'Якоби и Якоби', непереводимое название первого рассказа Кржижановского (1919), 'фантазия-диалог' между Якоби, немецким философом, и 'якобы' ('Supposedly') суть каждого человеческого предположения. Другой замечательный пример – из 'Автобиографии': 'Меж 'я' и 'мы' – ямы'. Буквально это переводится как 'between 'I' and 'we': pits'(or holes or hollows or depressions). Тонкая игра Кржижановского теряется в переводе: ''I' and 'we' are separated by gulfs' ('я' и 'мы' разделяет пропасть).

Конечно, пропасть разделяет Кржижановского и советский культурный истеблишмент, провозглашавший социалистический реализм. Из 3000 страниц, оставленных писателем, только 450 (в основном, его критические эссе) были напечатаны при его жизни. 'Всю мою тяжелую жизнь', – замечает он в одной из записных книжек, – 'я был литературным небытием, честно боровшимся за существование'.

Hamid Ismailov, The Railway
London: Harvill Secker, 2006
Перевод Роберта Чандлера

Роман 'Железная дорога', события которого, в основном, развиваются в Центральной Азии 1900-1980 гг., знакомит нас с обитателями небольшого города под Ташкентом: это узбеки, русские, персы, евреи, корейцы, татары и египтяне. Мы узнаем их истории – Мефодия-юриста, городского пьяницы-интеллектуала; отца Иоанна – русского священника; Кара-Мусаева Младшего, начальника полиции; Умарали Денежного Мешка, старого ростовщика, и других. В центре города и романа находится

железнодорожная станция. Захватывающая сложностью замысла и наивной причудливостью повествования, 'Железная дорога' отражает драматические перемены, постигшие Центральную Азию в XX веке.

Роберт Чандлер переводил поэзию Сафо и Гийома Аполлинера. С русского он перевел 'Жизнь и судьбу' Василия Гроссмана, 'Леди Макбет Мценского уезда' Лескова, 'Дубровского' и 'Капитанскую дочку' Пушкина. В сотрудничестве со своей женой Элизабет и другими переводчиками он перевел многие произведения Андрея Платонова. Его перевод повести Платонова 'Джан' (в английском переводе 'Soul') был признан Американской Ассоциацией Преподавателей Славянских и Восточноевропейских Языков 'лучшим переводом года', он также вошел в шорт-лист Премии Rossica 2005 года и Европейской Вайденфельдской Переводческой Премии (Rossica Translation Prize и Weidenfeld European Translation Prize). Роберт Чандлер преподает в Лондонском Университете Queen Mary.

Хамид Исмаилов родился в 1954 году. Он жил в Ташкенте, Москве, Париже, Бамберге, а также в Лондоне, где живет по сей день и возглавляет Центрально-Азиатский отдел ВВС. Он является автором большого количество сборников поэзии и прозы на русском и узбекском языках, а также романа 'Пленник небесных турок', изданного на английском языке ('Hostage to Celestial Turks'). Хамид Исмаилов был принудительно устранен с политической арены Узбекистана, и его произведения находятся в этой стране под запретом. Его последний роман 'Товарищ Ислам' (Comrade Islam) был издан в Великобритании, но эта работа выглядит слишком 'сомнительной', чтобы быть изданной в России и тем более в Узбекистане. В настоящее время роман переводится на английский язык.

Параллельные линии
Отрывок из разговора Хамида Исмаилова с переводчиком Робертом Чандлером и его женой и помощницей Элизабет.

Р.: 'Железная дорога' представляет огромную галерею характеров. Однажды Вы сказали мне, что город Гилас есть микромодель Советского Союза или даже всего мира в целом – Ноев ковчег, собравший в себя все человеческие типы.

Х.: Да, и так как этот Ноев ковчег был склеен с русской помощью – русскими концепциями в политике, русским коммунистическим жаргоном – имело смысл писать скорее на русском, чем на узбекском языке. Кстати, размышляя на эту тему, я понял, как мало все-таки по-настоящему советских романов. Сейчас мне кажется, что советская литература того времени была собранием особого рода 'тематических парков или искусственных заповедников': узбекская проза, где все характеры, кроме нескольких русских, узбекские; русская проза, где все персонажи русские, кроме нескольких евреев и грузин; грузинская проза; армянская проза и так далее... И все это довольно далеко от моего личного опыта жизни в Советском союзе. Но скажите мне, что в романе Вам было труднее всего перевести?

Р.: Воссоздание прозвищ персонажей. Мы с женой знали, что читатель потеряется среди огромного количества героев, если мы не найдем более или менее запоминающийся, информативный и убедительный перевод всех этих прозвищ. Это было тяжело, но увлекательно; обнаружение имен с правильным звучанием, ритмом, смыслом рождало чувство удовлетворения, как если бы это была удавшаяся стихотворная рифма. Часто подходящая версия имени приходила после тысячи попыток, проделываемых мною и Лиз в течение нескольких недель или даже месяцев. Мы всегда оставляли имя главного персонажа таким, как оно звучит в оригинале (по-узбекски); мы переводили только прозвище. И если у нас получалось, мы всегда это знали. Особенно нам запомнился Abubakir-Snuffsniffer (школьный сторож), Bakay-Croc (лишенный двух конечностей командир движения инвалидов), Bolta-Lightning (городской электрик), Mukum-Hunchback (владелец чайханы), Ortik-Picture-Reels (администратор в кинотеатре), Tolik-Nosetalk (рабочий-алкоголик), Osman-Anon (маскирующийся офицер КГБ, который меняет имя и паспорт каждый месяц), Rizo-Zero (инженер, ученик теней и предполагаемый зачинщик ужасного затмения) или Vera-Virgo (местная проститутка)... Я всегда хотел Вас спросить: эти имена Вами выдуманы, или Вы их взяли из реальной жизни?

Х.: Прозвища были обычным делом в советскую эпоху. Чуть ли не каждый в Узбекистане носил прозвище. Их возникновение имело разные предпосылки: характер человека или его происхождение, профессия или просто яркий эпизод из жизни... Часто прозвище, прилипшее еще в детстве, имело в жизни людей гораздо большее значение, нежели имя, данное при рождении; и так образом, их настоящие имена сохранялись от мясорубки повседневности, вульгарности жизни и от профанации. Я помню, как однажды, мне тогда было около 12 лет, мы с друзьями сидели в вагоне позади локомотива, и мой одноклассник Федька, который был куда остроумнее всех нас, выкрикнул: 'Кочегар, подкинь полено покривей, мы подъезжаем к повороту'. После этих слов он прослыл Федькой-Кочегаром. Несколько лет спустя, я узнал, что он стал пожарным и погиб. Может, стоит даже пытаться бороться с этими чарами прозвища... Я однажды провел небольшое исследование этого вопроса. До социализма, в XIX веке прозвища не были так популярны, как и в последние 15 лет после неожиданного обретения независимости. Это что-то вроде

характерной черты социалистического периода, времени, когда каждый человек вел две разных жизни – настоящую в сердце и в мечтах и фальшивую в реальном мире.

Лиз (читая расшифровку беседы): Прозвища не просто выдумка, они способны многое поведать о своих обладателях. Как Вы думаете, может быть, имена такого рода способны на нечто большее, чем просто характеризовать личность? Я представляю, что многие чувствовали себя шестеренками коммунистической машины. Что могло быть более важным в такой ситуации, чем их собственное имя – единственное, что у них было – или имя товарища или соседа, которого они могли любить или ненавидеть?

Х.: Да! Их имена очень узбекские, и очень, очень индивидуальные. Они настолько узбекские и настолько индивидуальные, что поначалу трудно было представить, что их возможно перевести на английский язык... Кстати, я часто размышлял над возможностью литературного перевода агрикультурных реалий. Вы знаете, единственное дерево, которое растет в наших жарких и пустынных краях, – саксаул. Возможно ли пересадить центрально-азиатский саксаул в английский сад? И как это сделать, не потеряв его 'саксаульность', и чтобы при этом он там крайне неуместен? В чем Ваше ноухау, Роберт?

Р.: Интересно, что Вы воспользовались этой садоводческой метафорой. Я плохой садовник, но вот Лиз тонкий и чувствительный знаток в этой области. Она много думает, много читает, но она никогда не забывает о том, что здесь нет четких правил. Каждый сад уникален. Каждый год и каждый месяц каждого года погода имеет свой собственный характер. Если Лиз будет искать место для Вашего саксаула, ее будет интересовать не только определенное количество света, качество воды и почвы, но и другие растения, способные создать антураж. Какие из соседей по грядке помогут саксаулу вырасти? Какие из соседей помогут ему выглядеть эффектно? Будет ли он лучше смотреться среди растений похожих или среди тех, чей внешний вид кардинально не совпадает с ним? Лучше ли оставить его в одиночестве, чтобы растение выделялось на фоне песка и камней? Или лучше окружить его растениями, характерными для той местности, если мы хотим, чтобы все выглядело как можно более натурально и естественно? И в этом случае наблюдатели согласятся с этим выбором и не станут задавать лишние вопросы.

Х.: Хорошо, но какое это имеет отношение к Вашей лингвистической работе?

Р.: Порой я провожу целый день в поиске синонима к определенному слову или в попытках воспроизвести ритмику определенного отрывка. И затем, потратив кучу времени, я вдруг понимаю, что суть проблемы отнюдь не там, где я предполагал вначале. Стоит изменить слово в предыдущей строке или предложении, и проблема исчезнет. Мне просто необходимо умение подобрать нужное растение, которое будет расти рядом с саксаулом. Но чем больше я думаю об этом, тем больше вопросов возникает. За этот год я, пожалуй, отправил Вам по электронной почте штук 500 вопросов. Мы много времени провели вместе, обсуждая буквально все: от пошлых шуток и политических слоганов до суфийской литературы. Скажите, Вам не хотелось меня убить за этот неостановимый поток вопросов? И как Вам нравится наблюдать со стороны, как труд Вашей жизни, основанный на воспоминаниях детства медлительно, с трудом вырывают из почвы, на которой он вырос, и пересаживают в почву для него чуждую?

Х.: Я провел много лет за переводами классической и современной литературы: с русского на узбекский, с узбекского на русский, с французского на узбекский, с узбекского на французский, с турецкого на русский, с английского на узбекский и т.п. Но я никогда не изучал текст так скрупулезно и внимательно, как Вы изучаете мой. Каждое отдельное слово 'рассматривается на просвет'. Порой писателем управляют его собственные ассоциации, необходимость ассонанса и аллитерации. В результате, он оставляет определенные 'темные места' в своем тексте. Вы же их открыли и подняли на поверхность. И это открыло мне глаза на более глубокие вещи, смыслы. Профессор в Ташкентской консерватории любил повторять нам с женой одну и ту же шутку: 'Я так часто объяснял эту концепцию моим студентам, что в конце концов сам ее понял'. И спасибо Роберту за его вопросы, которые помогли мне понять все, что я так наивно описал. И я абсолютно уверен, что Роберт понимает мой роман гораздо лучше, чем я.

Р.: Ну, я, конечно, не знаю, но Мы с Лиз почли за счастье работать с таким щедрым и великодушным писателем. Но, как я уже сказал в предисловии, 'Железная дорога' такая же щедрая книга, как и ее автор. Это открытая и толерантная книга, в ней есть место всему: истории и фантастике, ярости и нежности, сатире и почтительности.

Leo Tolstoy, War and Peace
London: Penguin Books, 2005
Перевод Энтони Бриггса

Роман 'Война и мир', часто называемый величайшим в мире, — непревзойденный образец сосуществования огромных просторов наряду с мельчайшими интимными деталями, и сочетания невероятного разнообразия и бесконечного единства. На фоне сменяющих друг друга войны и мира, Толстой разворачивает множество сюжетных линий: история трех аристократических родов и более чем пятисот отдельных персонажей. Эпические черты романа четко видны в описании наполеоновского вторжения в Россию в 1812 году, но большинство читателей гораздо более увлечены судьбами молодых героев, которые вырастают среди своих юношеских сомнений и прокладывают путь к зрелому пониманию жизни. О Наташе Ростовой говорят как о 'самой блистательно сделанной героине, которая подошла бы для любого романа'.

Профессор Энтони Бриггс учился в школе Короля Эдуарда VII в Шеффилде, имеет степень магистра в Кембриджском университете и звание доктора философии в университете Лондона. Он возглавлял кафедры русского языка и литературы в Бристольском и Эдинбургском университетах. Помимо многочисленных статей, он отредактировал и перевел более двадцати книг: пять книг об Александре Пушкине (он самый известный в стране специалист по творчеству поэта), а также шесть томов английской поэзии. В издательском доме 'Penguin' вскоре выйдет сборник 'Смерть Ивана Ильича и другие рассказы' под его редакцией. В настоящее время он работает над переводом романа Толстого 'Воскресение'.

Исправляя Льва Толстого
Энтони Бриггс

Льва Толстого трудно назвать поборником точности. Р.Ф. Кристиан напоминает нам: 'Правила его раздражали и утомляли, и студент вряд ли сочтет его прозу образцом грамматической правильности. Он попросту не знал, да и не хотел следовать официальной грамматике'. Он приводит многочисленные примеры грамматических ошибок и стилистических погрешностей Толстого, в особенности, его повторов. 'Война и мир' переполнена фактическими ошибками, например, Пьер видит комету в 1811 году, на самом деле пролетавшую в 1812; а сам Толстой то вспоминает, то забывает о том, что у Кутузова был один глаз.

Вопрос, что же делать со всеми этими неточностями, ставит переводчика в тупик. Исправлять каждую погрешность и стилистически выравнивать повествование – естественно, значит создавать ложное впечатление о стиле Толстого у читателя. С другой стороны, концепцию так называемого 'бесшумного исправления' можно оправдать лишь в отдельных случаях. К примеру, все семь переводчиков 'Войны и мир' разбивали длиннейшее толстовское предложение (из 230 слов) на более короткие. Итак, иногда улучшения, сделанные переводчиком, кажутся совершенно оправданными.

Но попадаются случаи, когда переводчик делает прямо противоположное: превращая и без того непростые фразы в еще более сложные. Вспомним описание Берга – 'assistant to the head of the staff of the assistant of the chief officer of the staff of the commander of the left flank of the infantry of the first army...' (III, 1, 16, выделение наше). В этой фразе несравненной Констанс Гарнетт удается даже превзойти и без того достаточно нескладную фразу Толстого. На самом деле, эту беду не так уж сложно исправить: Берг был 'assisting the Head of Staff commanding the First Army Infantry, left flank ...'

Но в романе есть одно немаловажное место, в котором Толстой не только грешит плохим стилем, но и допускает более серьезную ошибку. Это место на самом деле нуждается в исправлении, но пока никто из переводчиков этого не сделал. В томе третьем (часть первая, глава 19) Толстой описывает неловкие попытки Пьера связать свою судьбу с судьбой Наполеона, используя странную смесь библейских предсказаний и нумерологии. Рассказ Толстого о том, что делает Пьер, поистине сбивает с толку. Вот что пишет автор: 'Французские буквы, подобно еврейскому число-изображению, по которому первыми десятью буквами означаются единицы, а прочими десятки, имеют следующее значение: ...' Мало того, что употребить сочетание 'французские буквы' невозможно в принципе (хотя предыдущие переводчики так и перевели), так еще и в самом предложении, имеющем вполне конкретное значение, но которое при этом выражено неясно, автор допускает ошибку. Дело в том, что единицы могут быть представлены только первыми девятью буквами алфавита, потому что десятая буква означает первый десяток.

Из предыдущих переводчиков только Вейнер оставляет неправильное 'десять'; Бэлл, Доул, Гарнетт, Мод, Эдмонды и Даннигэн (некоторые копируют предшественников) молча исправляют ошибку. Итак, мы все согласны, что это исправление необходимо. Но переводчики не утруждают себя дальнейшими пояснениями. Например, совершенно бесполезное 'The French alphabet written out with same numerical values as the Hebrew ...'. Еврейское что? Еврейский алфавит? Еврейского алфавита нет. Большинство существующих версий предлагают этот перевод, который сбивает с толку еще больше. Гарнетт почти подходит к объяснению, но ее стиль неловок: 'the French alphabet is treated like the Hebrew system of enumeration ...'. Употребление слова 'нумерация' вполне уместно, но сочетание 'treated like' не проясняет ситуацию.

Этот пассаж действительно нуждается в исправлении. Буквы соотносятся с цифрами, и мы должны это упомянуть. Цифры – это цифры еврейские, но это ни о чем не говорит западному читателю. Другое дело – арабские цифры, что одно то же. Итак, в нашем переводе мы должны либо опустить 'еврейские', либо хотя бы упомянуть 'арабские'. Вот наша версия перевода:

'The French alphabet, laid out alongside the Hebrew (or Arabic) numerical system, with the first nine letters representing units, the next tens, and so on, gives the following values: ...'

В этом есть доля иронии. Сомнительно, чтобы кто-нибудь когда-нибудь замечал, какими малопонятными были предыдущие английские версии (и русский оригинал перед ними всеми) по одной единственной причине. Растянувшиеся на всю страницу 25 букв французского алфавита (i и j считаются за дну букву) с аккуратно расставленными внизу них арабскими цифрами. Они привлекают внимание, как только вы переворачиваете страницу, сразу понятно, что к чему: a = 1, b = 2 ... Система понятна до тех пор, пока автор не приступает к ее вербальному объяснению. Увлеченный читатель проскакивает неадекватный английский перевод, даже не задавая вопросов. Однако ж, пришло время кому-нибудь расставить все по местам. Будет ли кто-нибудь оставлять, будь то русский или английский текст в его первозданном виде?

Нелегко выбрать из возможных исправлений единственно верное. Это вопрос предпочтения и быстрого решения (Не можешь же ты звонить другу часто, когда тебе нужно расправиться с 600000 слов). Иногда встречаются такие ошибки, которые ни в коем случае исправлять нельзя. Когда Пьер говорит, делая грамматическую ошибку 'All I said was – we could make better sacrifices when we know what the needs are' (III, I, 23), он обеспокоен и смущен, было бы неправильным в данном случае исправлять его речь.

Подробное изучение языка Толстого профессором Кристианом было весьма полезным для разработки стратегии перевода всего творчества писателя. Один комментарий особенно ценен: 'Толстой думал вслух, переносил свои мысли на бумагу и иногда забывал, что он пишет, а не говорит'. Это разумное замечание не только предостерегает нас от чрезмерного вмешательства и исправлений, но также оправдывает использование разговорной речи не только в диалогах, но и в повествовании. Это не значит, что нужно пользоваться сленгом или неологизмами; все это значит лишь то, что нужно использовать простую, естественную речь, которая и является языком 'Войны и мира'.

Отрывок из романа 'Война и мир'
Том третий, часть первая, глава 19

С того дня, как Пьер, уезжая от Ростовых и вспоминая благодарный взгляд Наташи, смотрел на комету, стоявшую в небе, и почувствовал, что для него открылось что-то новое, — вечно мучивший его вопрос о тщете и безумности всего земного перестал представляться ему. Этот страшный вопрос: зачем? к чему? — который прежде представлялся ему в середине всякого занятия, теперь заменился для него не другим вопросом и не ответом на прежний вопрос, а представлением ее. Слышал ли он, и сам ли вел ничтожные разговоры, читал ли он, или узнавал про подлость и бессмысленность людскую, он не ужасался, как прежде; не спрашивал себя, из чего хлопочут люди, когда все так кратко и неизвестно, но вспоминал ее в том виде, в котором он видел ее в последний раз, и все сомнения его исчезали, не потому, что она отвечала на вопросы, которые представлялись ему, но потому, что представление о ней переносило его мгновенно в другую, светлую область душевной деятельности, в которой не могло быть правого или виноватого, в область красоты и любви, для которой стоило жить. Какая бы мерзость житейская ни представлялась ему, он говорил себе:

'— Ну и пускай такой-то обокрал государство и царя, а государство и царь воздают ему почести; а она вчера улыбнулась мне и просила приехать, и я люблю ее, и никто никогда не узнает этого', — думал он.

Пьер все так же ездил в общество, так же много пил и вел ту же праздную и рассеянную жизнь, потому что, кроме тех часов, которые он проводил у Ростовых, надо было проводить и остальное время, и привычки и знакомства, сделанные им в Москве, непреодолимо влекли его к той жизни, которая захватила его. Но в последнее время, когда с театра войны приходили все более и более тревожные слухи и когда здоровье Наташи стало поправляться и она перестала возбуждать в нем прежнее чувство бережливой жалости, им стало овладевать более и более непонятное для него беспокойство. Он чувствовал, что то положение, в котором он находился, не могло продолжаться долго, что наступает катастрофа, долженствующая изменить всю его жизнь, и с нетерпением отыскивал во всем признаки этой приближающейся катастрофы, Пьеру было открыто одним из братьев-масонов следующее, выведенное из Апокалипсиса Иоанна Богослова, пророчество относительно Наполеона.

В Апокалипсисе, главе тринадцатой, стихе восемнадцатом сказано: 'Зде мудрость есть; иже имать ум да почтет число зверино: число бо человеческо есть, и число его шестьсот шестьдесят шесть'.

И той же главы в стихе пятом: 'И даны быша ему уста глаголюща велика и хульна; и дана бысть ему область творити месяц четыре — десять два'.

Французские буквы, подобно еврейскому число-изображению, по которому первыми десятью буквами означаются единицы, а прочими десятки, имеют следующее значение:

a	b	c	d	e	f	g
1	2	3	4	5	6	7
h	i	k	l	m	n	o
8	9	10	20	30	40	50
p	q	r	s	t	u	v
60	70	80	90	100	110	120
w	x	y	z			
130	140	150	160			

Написав по этой азбуке цифрами слова L'empereur Napoléon, выходит, что сумма этих чисел равна 666-ти и что поэтому Наполеон есть тот зверь, о котором предсказано в Апокалипсисе. Кроме того, написав по этой же азбуке слова quarante deux, то есть предел, который был положен зверю глаголати велика и хульна, сумма этих чисел, изображающих quarante deux, опять равна 666-ти, из чего выходит, что предел власти Наполеона наступил в 1812-м году, в котором французскому императору минуло 42 года. Предсказание это очень поразило Пьера, и он часто задавал себе вопрос о том, что именно положит предел власти зверя, то есть Наполеона, и, на основании тех же изображений слов цифрами и вычислениями, старался найти ответ на занимавший его вопрос. Пьер написал в ответ на этот вопрос: L'empereur Alexandre? La nation Russe? Он счел буквы, но сумма цифр выходила гораздо больше или меньше 666-ти. Один раз, занимаясь этими вычислениями, он написал свое имя — Comte Pierre Besouhof; сумма цифр тоже далеко не вышла. Он, изменив орфографию, поставив z вместо s, прибавил de, прибавил article le и все не получал желаемого результата. Тогда ему пришло в голову, что ежели бы ответ на искомый вопрос и заключался в его имени, то в ответе непременно была бы названа его национальность. Он написал Le Russe Besuhof и, сочтя цифры, получил 671. Только 5 было лишних; 5 означает 'e', то самое 'e', которое было откинуто в article перед словом L'empereur. Откинув точно так же, хотя и неправильно, 'e', Пьер получил искомый ответ: l'Russe Besuhof, равное 666-ти. Открытие это взволновало его. Как, какой связью был он соединен с тем великим событием, которое было предсказано в Апокалипсисе, он не знал; но он ни на минуту не усумнился в этой связи. Его любовь к Ростовой, антихрист, нашествие Наполеона, комета, 666, l'empereur Napol on и l'Russe Besuhof — все это вместе должно было созреть, разразиться и вывести его из того заколдованного, ничтожного мира московских привычек, в которых он чувствовал себя плененным, и привести его к великому подвигу и великому счастию.

Leo Tolstoy, The Death of Ivan Ilich
London: Hesperus Press, 2005
Перевод Хью Аплина

Лев Николаевич Толстой не нуждается в представлении: его титул самого известного русского писателя в англоязычном мире могут оспаривать только Достоевский и Чехов. Будучи наиболее известным благодаря своим маститым романам, он также был мастером короткого рассказа или повести; и в 1880 году в результате растущего недовольства большой формой романа, который увековечил его в литературе, Толстой предпочел потратить свою творческую энергию на короткие произведения. В работах последних трех десятилетий прослеживаются следы его личной духовной борьбы, которые были представлены читателям с поразительным художественным эффектом.

Хью Эплин изучал русский язык в Школе Эммануэль в Лондоне и в университете Восточной Англии, студентом провел три года в Советском Союзе в Воронеже, Ленинграде и Москве. Он возглавлял факультет русского языка и литературы в Вестминстерской Школе почти два десятилетия, и побуждал десятки студентов продолжать изучение русского языка в университете. Его перевод романа Булгакова 'Роковые яйца' был выдвинут на Премию Переводов Rossica, которую в результате получил его бывший ученик. Среди его переводов 'Хаджи Мурат' Толстого, на основе которого была сделана радио-версия романа на БиБиСи, а также 'Фальшивый купон'.

Повесть 'Смерть Ивана Ильича' представлена в книге наряду с повестью 'Дьявол', а на их фоне собраны рассказы поздних 1880-х, которые обращены к двум важнейших повторяющимся темам творчества Толстого последних лет — любви и смерти. Но повесть 'Смерть Ивана Ильича' связана вероятно с главным вопросом для писателя: как человек должен прожить свою жизнь. Она имеет много общего с его религиозными эссе, начиная с 'Исповеди' и далее. Грандиозный исторический охват романа 'Война и мир' меркнет на фоне унылого, блеклого описания одной души, на грани умирания.

Сплетая ткань жизни
Хью Эплин

Повесть 'Смерть Ивана Ильича' начинается с описания событий, произошедших непосредственно после смерти человека в возрасте сорока пяти лет. Мы видим реакцию его коллег и его домашних; а во второй главе Толстой начинает разбирать жизнь, которая предшествовала этой смерти, жизнь, которую можно описать словами 'самая простая и обыкновенная, и самая ужасная'. Этот пассаж наиболее ярко выражает характер этого произведения — яркого, возможно, поучительного, и невероятно эффектного.

Точка зрения Толстого — это всеведущий, но отстраненный взгляд, который проходит красной нитью через все повествование, и потому переводчику не приходится бороться с разноголосицей различных персонажей. Даже диалог сведен к минимуму: хотя слуга крестьянского происхождения, Герасим, и является значимым персонажем в идейном построении произведения, его речь, которая отличается от речи образованных представителей среднего класса, безусловно преобладающих в романе, является характерным признаком лишь в некоторой степени; и нет необходимости наделить его речь индивидуальными интонациями.

Таким образом, главной целью переводчика здесь (наряду, разумеется, с точностью) вероятно, является передача характерного стиля толстовской прозы, который именно в этой повести, как мне кажется, идеально соответствует сюжету, что и объясняет несомненную силу произведения. Большая часть повествования написана, сложным язык, где длинные и синтаксически громоздкие предложения, состоящие из многочисленных придаточных оборотов, служат для того, чтобы показать язык судебной бюрократии, которая является фоном для происходящего. Этот же язык используется и для исследования психологии как отдельного человека, так и всего его окружения, раскрывая тягостную и извилистую реальность через подходящие витиеватые предложения. Если временами английский текст и кажется излишне громоздким, неуклюжим, то только из-за того, что чтение самого русского текста нельзя назвать 'легким и приятным' — фраза, которой Толстой дает определение тому духовному обнищанию, которое он описывает.

Определенные трудности встают на пути у любого, переводящего прозу такого типа, по той причине, что синтаксис английского языка построен совершенно по-другому. К примеру, Толстой использует огромное количество причастных оборотов, и если в оригинале окончание указывает на то, к какому слову относится причастие, в английском на первое место выходит порядок слов. Есть соблазн упростить стиль, разбив сложные предложения на более ясные и короткие, но приходится с этим бороться, чтобы передать стилистику толстовской прозы.

Другая черта толстовского стиля, которая искушает переводчика отклониться от оригинала, — это его пристрастие к повторам. Временами это кажется попросту небрежностью, когда слово не имеющее особой важности, повторяется по нескольку раз в одном предложении. Но даже в таких случаях, я считаю, что переводчик должен оставаться верным оригиналу и не пытаться редактировать текст. В повести 'Смерть Ивана Ильича' есть много подобных 'малозначительных' повторов. Взять, к примеру, союзные слова, повторяющиеся более одного раза в коротком абзаце. Они — неотъемлемая часть толстовского стиля. Более 'значительные' повторы вызывают и более значительные проблемы: есть много слов и фраз, которые Толстой намеренно снова и снова употребляет в рамках одного предложения, или абзаца, или произведения в целом — такие как, например, 'легкий и приятный' упоминавшиеся выше.

Особенно важны в рассказе понятия благопристойности,

внешних приличий, светских манер, которых придерживается Иван Ильич в попытках управлять своей жизнью вплоть до самой болезни. Это хорошо видно на примере выбранной мною цитаты. Здесь мы сталкиваемся с использованием более десятка слов, означающих благопристойность, правила приличия и пр. Они практически всегда образованы от русского существительного 'приличие'. Возможно, в английском языке следует выбрать единственный вариант перевода и употреблять его на протяжении всего отрывка, например слово 'decorum', и далее использовать производные от него: 'decorous', 'decorously', 'indecorous', 'indecorously', и 'indecorum' или 'indecorousness'. Последние два слова кажутся, однако, слишком неясными в сравнении со стандартным русским 'неприличие', на удивление они не помещены в русско-английский словарь. Похожие проблемы с альтернативным переводом слова 'приличие' и его производными в конце концов заставили меня принять решение использовать не одно слово, но, где это возможно, синонимичные слова. Везде, где повторение этого лейтмотива необходимо, я пытался использовать одно английское слово и его производные. В других работах, где повтор значимых слов и фраз случается гораздо реже, этот прием искусно используется, чтобы, например, связать персонажей или события, которые явно между собой не связаны, в этом случае отстаивать наш подход было бы гораздо сложнее.

Особенности русской жизни могут представлять проблему для переводчика – лучше ли приблизительный эквивалент чем более точное, но громоздкое описание или сноска транслитерированного слова, когда речь идет, например, о деталях одежды? Однако, если говорить о юридических терминах, встречающихся нам в повести, чем непонятнее для читателя они звучат, тем лучше. Так как Толстой хотел, чтобы род деятельности Ивана Ильича выглядел как бы оторванным от того, чем должна быть жизнь, любые колебания по поводу точной разницы между 'допрашивающим судьей' и 'заместителем прокурора' и их функций, или другие подобные детали, могут быть даже на руку, так как они наоборот подчеркивают оторванность от реальности, с которой Иван Ильич был вынужден столкнуться за пределами своей уютной службы. Именно универсальность главнейших у Толстого тем жизни и смерти делает этот рассказ захватывающим и важным чтением на любом языке.

Ilya Ilf and Evgeny Petrov, Ilf and Petrov's American road trip: The 1935 travelogue of two Soviet writers New York: Princeton Architectural Press & Cabinet Books, 2006
Перевод Анны О. Фишер

Илья Ильф (1897-1937) и **Евгений Петров** (1903-1942) родились и выросли в Одессе, плавильном котле культур, в известном и по сей день оживленном центре русского и еврейского юмора. Несмотря на то, что большинство русскоговорящих людей сейчас считают Ильфа и Петрова

нераздельной единицей (дочь Ильфа, Александру Ильф, шутливо называют дочерью Ильфа и Петрова), они встретились только1925 году, когда начали работать журналистами в Москве. Старший брат Петрова, известный писатель Валентин Катаев, познакомил их и посоветовал работать вместе, и даже предложил сюжет для их первого, совместно написанного романа '12 стульев' (1928). Плутовская сатира на поздний период НЭПа дала толчок карьере Ильфа и Петрова во многом благодаря обаянию главного героя, Остапа Бендера, чье остроумие выдавало одесское чувство языка его создателей. Остроты Бендера немедленно вошли в повседневную речь. Ильф и Петров написали продолжение – 'Золотой телёнок' (1931), но в 1932 их отговорили писать третий роман о ставшем теперь неугодным Бендере. К тому времени, однако, они отошли от журналистики и занялись написанием рецензий, сценариев, рассказов, и стали штатными авторами газет 'Правда' и 'Литературная газета'. Но многообещающие карьеры внезапно оборвались: Ильф скончался от туберкулёза в 1937 году, а Петров погиб в авиакатастрофе, когда он освещал события Второй мировой войны.

Анн О. Фишер изучала русский язык в школе в Оклахоме, чтобы внести в собственную жизнь немного экзотики. В течение одного года она училась в России, где впервые прочла роман Ильфа и Петрова '12 стульев'. С тех пор она написала докторскую диссертацию в университете штата Мичиган, посвящённую этой книге и ее продолжению, утверждая, что эти популярные книги и их авторы олицетворяют специфически советскую культуру чтения романов, их написания и издательства.

Серьёзный взгляд на Америку самых веселых советских писателей
Анн О. Фишер

Зимой 1935-1936 по заданию газеты 'Правда' Ильф и Петров съездили в командировку по Америке дабы высказать свою точку зрения в непрекращающейся советской дискуссии об Америке. В отличие от других советских писателей, посетивших Америку, они провели в стране четыре месяца, два из них – путешествуя через всю страну на машине. Ильф сделал по дороге более тысячи любительских снимков. Вернувшись в СССР, писатели напечатали фото-эссе о своей поездке, отличающееся проницательной критикой американской жизни и глубоким взглядом на американский народ, религию и популярные развлечения эпохи Великой Депрессии.

Илья Ильф и Евгений Петров издали 'Американские фотографии', серию из одиннадцати эссе, посвященных их четырехмесячному путешествию по Америке в журнале 'Огонёк'. С тех пор 'Американские фотографии' были изданы только один раз, в 1947 году, хотя книга Ильфа и Петрова 'Одноэтажная Америка', вышедшая без фотографий спустя год после их поездки хорошо знакома русским читателям. Так, взгляд двух писателей на Америку с идеально дополняющими друг друга текстом и фотографиями, был забыт и заменен голым текстом, который подвергся с тех пор нескольким редактурам.

Многое уже не вернуть. Историк искусства Эрика Вулф наткнулась на 'Американские фотографии', изучая работы советского фотографа и теоретика Александра Родченко; она осознала ценность фото-эссе Ильфа и Петрова и решила вернуть их из забвения, а меня пригласила перевести текст книги на английский язык. Эрика Вулф потратила немало времени и усилий на то, чтобы проследить историю фотографий и негативов, но в результате убедилась, что негативы утрачены, а может быть, и уничтожены, а уцелевшие фотографии пребывают в ветхом состоянии. Однако, по ее словам, 'Путешествие Ильфа и Петрова по дорогам Америки' 'возвращает к жизни значительную часть истории советской художественной культуры и истории документальных снимков США'.

Правильно! Правильно! Как переводчик, я могу добавить, стоит восстановить также и сам текст 'Американских фотографий', ради увлекательного и яркого повествования Ильфа и Петрова. Этот текст примечателен еще и характерным юмором, а также его сочетанием с американским английским, попадавшимся писателям особенно часто на рекламных плакатах. Писатели относятся к ним как к американским двойникам советской политической риторики, над которой они незабываемо смеялись в романах об Остапе Бендере. Этот перевод интересовал меня как американку, и потому, что требовалось не просто перевести русский текст обратно на американский английский образца 30-х годов, но и передать откровенное веселье, с которым иностранные путешественники слушали и записывали этот английский язык.

Наличие фотографий Ильфа меняет саму природу повествования, позволяя читателям стоять у авторов за спиной и вместе с ними наблюдать за разворачивающейся вокруг них жизнью. Ильф полушутя называл себя зевакой, но искусство соавторов строится как раз на наблюдении и оценке ситуации, и через фотографии они дают нам возможность поучаствовать в их творческом процессе. Так, писательские убеждения, наблюдения и замечания передаются нам, как, например, когда они жалуются на рекламу 'Крестовых походов', эпопеи Сесилии Б. Демиль: 'Товарищи и братья, продолжим путь! Господь им судья, этим Сесилиям!' Эта непосредственность, этот совместный взгляд на американцев подразумевают, что читатели согласятся с субъективной оценкой Ильфа и Петрова, и создают некую общность между рассказчиком и рассказанной историей, подчеркивая важность точного воспроизведения их неформального стиля повествования.

Невозможно обсуждать Ильфа и Петрова, не упомянув их знаменитое остроумие. Значительная часть зависит от структуры и контраста, как, например, их любимый прием: когда заключительный элемент списка вообще не соответствует предыдущим. Этот пример, описание первого знакомства писателей с буррито в Санта-Фе, построен на преувеличениях: 'Судя по вкусу, это оказались длинные аппетитные блинчики, начиненные красным перцем, тонко нарезанным артиллерийским порохом. Решительно, сесть за такой обед без пожарной каски на голове — невозможно. Огонь горел во рту три дня'. Другой прием, который они используют для создания юмористического контраста — это параллельные конструкции. Они описывали свои первые впечатления от Нью-Йорка, когда корабль вошел в порт, 'два предмета обратили на себя наше внимание. Один был маленький, зеленоватый — статуя Свободы. А другой — громадный и нахальный — рекламный щит, пропагандирующий 'Чуингам Ригли' — жевательную резинку'. Ильф и Петров часто меняют тон повествования для создания комического эффекта. Иногда они используют нечто вроде ложного наивного сарказма, как в эпизоде, когда они заявляют, что если бы в Америке не было рекламы, 'жизнь усложнилась бы до невероятия. Над каждым своим жизненным шагом приходилось бы думать самому. Нет, с рекламой значительно легче'. Зачастую они невозмутимо сыпали замечаниями, например, описывая 'вульгарную голливудскую привычку завладевать кинозвездами', 'И это называют триумфом цивилизации!'. Что касается их излюбленного юмористического приема — ироническая цитата или использование официозного языка, с этим им не повезло: только Петров владел английским языком. Тем не менее, они не переставали обращать пристальное внимание на другие типы дискурсов, два из них, наиболее часто попадавшиеся во время путешествия: дорожные знаки, чрезвычайно им нравившиеся, и рекламные плакаты, которые они безжалостно высмеивают в одноименной главе.

Изображение американской речи Ильфом и Петровым, я подозреваю, тоже было не слишком честным и серьезным. Вот пример, в котором сопровождающий Ильфа и Петрова спрашивает у прохожего дорогу:

— Боже ты мой! Дорогу на Кливлэнд! — говорил он горячо. — Да ведь я родился в Кливлэнде. Уж я-то знаю дорогу на Кливлэнд. Еще бы! На меня вы можете смело положиться. Ай-яй-яй! Дорогу на Кливлэнд! Нет, вам положительно повезло, что вы напали на меня.

'Oh my goodness! The way to Cleveland!' he was saying excitedly. 'After all, I was born in Cleveland. If anybody knows the way to Cleveland, it's me. I'd say so! You can count on me for sure. Oh, my, yes. The way to Cleveland! Yep, you really got lucky when you ran into me.'

Понятно, что им понравилось как само слово 'Кливленд', так и желание деревенского парня угодить. И признаю, мне было удивительно слышать междометье 'Ай-яй-яй' от коренного жителя Среднего Запада.

Некоторые истории Ильфа и Петрова безнадежно устарели или потеряли свою остроту в процессе позднейшего редактирования, но многие по прежнему звучат свежо и искренне. Книга 'Путешествие Ильфа и Петрова по дорогам Америки' сохранила объективный портрет Америки, и мы можем не просто созерцать, какими мы показались им семьдесят лет назад, но и поразмышлять над тем, какими мы будем казаться любознательным иностранным гостям через следующие семьдесят лет.

Ludmila Ulitskaya, Sonechka: a novella and stories
New York: Schocken Books, 2005
Перевод Арча Тэйта

Арч Тэйт учил русский язык в Школе Латимер (Лондон), Тринити колледже (Кэмбридж) и Московском государственном университете. Получил степень доктора философии в Кэмбриджском университете, всерьез занялся литературным переводом в 1986 году после знакомства с Валентиной Жак, в то время редактором журнала 'Советская литература'. В 1993-2003 работал британским редактором книжной серии английских переводов современной русской прозы 'Glas New Russian Writing', главным редактором которой является преемница Валентины Жак, Наташа Перова. К настоящему времени перевел 14 романов, 30 рассказов и 25 статей большинства ведущих современных российских авторов. Его перевод книги Анны Политковской 'Русский дневник' вышел в апреле 2007 года в издательстве Harvill Secker.

За время с 1993 года я перевел один роман, одну повесть и одиннадцать рассказов Людмилы Улицкой, и мне всегда было приятно работать с ее текстами. В 2001 году Улицкая получила Русскую Букеровскую премию; ее произведения переведены на двадцать пять иностранных языков, и она является лауреатом Премии Москва-Пенне (Италия, 1997 и 2006), Премии Медичи (Франция, 1998), Премии 'Иванушка' (Россия, 2004, в номинациях 'Роман года' и 'Лучший писатель года'), Национальной литературной премии (Китай, 2005) и Премии 'Олимпия'

Российской Академии Бизнеса и Предпринимательства (2007).

Героинями (а в некоторых случаях героями) Людмилы Улицкой становятся люди, в СССР являвшиеся маргиналами, совсем не советские по своему мироощущению. Как правило, они преодолевают даже самые, казалось бы, безнадежные жизненные обстоятельства: девочка-подросток влюбляется в мужчину за шестьдесят и рожает ему нескольких здоровых сыновей, в то время как ее соседи ломают голову — как это она вообще может забеременеть; непримечательная провинциальная библиотекарша выходит замуж за ссыльного художника и, когда, уже постарев, тот вдруг увлекается более молодой женщиной, оборачивает свое несчастье в триумф; узбекская медсестра переживает уход мужа после рождения их умственно-отсталой дочери, смертельно заболевает, но все же находит способ позаботиться о будущем ребенка; наконец, черноморская гречанка, одна из последних оставшихся в Крыму, не попадает в сталинские депортационные списки благодаря полученной в замужестве фамилии Мендез и изобретает различные способы каждый год собирать у себя дома всю свою многочисленную родню.

Говорят, что в историях Улицкой жизнь и любовь героев протекают под пристальным контролем 'радара угнетения'. 'Если личное счастье в жизни — лучшая месть, — то персонажей Людмилы Улицкой, пользующихся необыкновенной благосклонностью судьбы, — можно считать скромными героями повседневности, — пишет Лесли Чемберлейн. — Свежий, утонченно чувственный мир Улицкой, наполненный простыми человеческими радостями и ошибками, бесконечно далек от унылых, коренящихся в чувстве страха дум об участи личности, раздавленной советским режимом...Улицкая вновь привнесла в русскую литературу успокаивающее ощущение какой-то универсальной, общечеловеческой нормальности'. Зиновий Зиник отметил, что 'В мудрых историях Улицкой человеческое достоинство, преодолевая любые препятствия, всегда одерживает победу над страданием и притеснением'.

В художественном мире Улицкой мы встречаем и злодеев, по большей части испорченных воспалившим их тщеславие фальшивым благополучием советской системы. Среди них роковая женщина, подобно вампиру с наслаждением высасывающая жизненные соки из своей семьи; пожилой профессор-педофил, женившийся на уборщице с красивым молодым сыном; интеллектуально заносчивая молодая пара, чье честолюбие приводит к тому, что советская действительность не дает им возможности создать семью, и школьная учительница, охмурившая швейцарского бизнесмена на международной конференции, ставшая в итоге богатой, однако бесконечно опустошенной.

Авторская манера Людмилы Улицкой обладает подлинной литературной глубиной. Встречающиеся подчас в ее произведениях отсылки к медицине и физике могут заставить читателя задуматься над их скрытым смыслом, отдельные ее фразы длинны и извилисты. Один критик, оценивший всю сложность моей задачи, написал: 'Перевод Арча Тэйта достоверно воссоздает тщательно продуманный разговорный стиль Улицкой'. В ее текстах почти всегда ощущается 'присутствие автора', и тот моральный посыл, который его голос имплицитно доносит до читателя, преодолевая конкретное место и время, гласит: пренебрежение мудростью древних ведет к бездне бессмысленности. Принцип этот в каком-то смысле сообразует иудейскую мораль с законами кармы. На фоне все отчетливее проявляющих себя в последнее время тенденций к возрождению наиболее порочных черт советской системы, книги Людмилы Улицкой предостерегают нас о том, что возведение песочных замков неизбежно обречено на горькую неудачу.

Ценность и ценности литературного перевода

Аманда Хопкинсон

Я получила совершенно обычное для своего времени литературное образование. Мама рассказывала мне сказки Ганса Христиана Андерсена, Лафонтена и Перро, а папа, имевший за плечами классическую школу, зачитывал мне Эзопа и Гомера. Во Франции я проводила каникулы в компании Астерикса и Тантана, в Австрии моими спутниками были братья Гримм, а в Италии меня веселил Пиноккио. Я влюблялась в Юного Вертера, в поэзию Сефериса, Ахматовой, Вийона и Овидия, боролась с бессонницей при помощи '1001 ночи' или, когда настроение было невеселым, – 'Ада' Данте. Наконец, я хихикала над эротическими проказами, которые вытворяли персонажи Рабле и 'Баллады об эскимоске Нелл'. Я внимательно читала Чосера, ставшего писателем после того, как он перевел 'Роман о розе', и Шекспира, укравшего не только сонеты, но и большую часть сюжетов для своих комедий у Петрарки. Я поняла, что хотя 'Дон Кихот' и был первым романом, еще почти два столетия должно было миновать до появления Большого романа – жанра, прославленного такими именами, как Шиллер и Гете, Манцони и Эка де Кейрос, Кнут Гамсун и Ги де Мопассан, Золя и Бальзак, Толстой, Достоевский и Пастернак.

Одним словом, все было вполне предсказуемо, и ровным счетом ничто мне не говорило, что читала я 'иностранную' литературу (кроме, пожалуй, малопонятного выговора Братца Кролика из 'Сказок дядюшки Римуса', характерного для жителей южных американских штатов). И вдруг меня поразило одно открытие. Когда я перешла в среднюю школу, на одном из обязательных уроков Слова Божьего я обнаружила, что все другие ученики в классе пребывали в полной уверенности, что Библия с самого начала была написана на английском. Сегодня мы бы могли отреагировать на это примерно так: 'Не кажется ли вам, что

это похоже на слова того американского республиканца, который считал, что если 'английский устраивал Иисуса, то он вполне устроит и меня'?'. В тот момент я поняла, что и представления не имею о том, сколько нужно было сделать переводов с разных языков для того, чтобы на свет могло появиться одно из величайших произведений англоязычной литературной традиции – Библия короля Иакова. Мне вдруг стало ясно, что я не знаю, откуда пришел арабский язык Корана и совершенно не понимаю, на каком же языке были написаны недавно еще популярные философские тексты вроде Бхагавад-гиты или эпоса о Гильгамеше. По крайней мере, с латинскими эпитетами Марка Аврелия было проще – они хоть были короткими.

Именно тогда я поняла, насколько трудная задача стоит перед переводчиком. Преодолевая пространство и время, он должен донести до школьников, сидящих в обычном классе в лондонском Кемден-тауне, не только текст произведения, но и его контекст, порой целую систему всевозможных ценностей и убеждений. При этом я совершенно не думала о том, что понять язык Псалмов может быть, по существу, труднее, чем понять настолько же высокопарный язык 'Книги общественного богослужения'; а плутовские выходки Лазарильо де Тормеса или Тиля Уленшпигеля кому-то могут показаться более странными, чем подобные шалости, творимые персонажами 'Кентерберийских рассказов' или 'Рыцарей круглого стола'. Несомненно, взятая современными поэтами мода на перевод классики среднеанглийской литературы (например, 'Беовульф' в переводе Симуса Хини или 'Сэр Гавейн и Зеленый Рыцарь' в переводе У.С. Мервина и Саймона Эрмитажа) воссоединяет новое поколение читателей с произведениями, которые в противном случае были бы им совершенно недоступны. Однако полагать, что эти тексты являются 'естественно понятными' британцам просто по факту их принадлежности к их национальной литературе было бы так же наивно, как думать, что 'Метроленд' Джулиана Барнса, 'Амстердам' Яна МакЭвана или, предположим, 'Юг' Кольма Тойбина или 'Будапешт' Чико Буарке на самом деле – про точки на карте мира.

Дело в том, что мир воображения намного шире и причудливее, чем мир, разделенный государственными границами. Тем не менее, как минимум до 1980-х годов в британском обществе существовало весьма выраженное предубеждение против писателей со 'смешными именами' – особенно со стороны сетевых розничных магазинов, заявлявших, по совершенно неясным причинам, что для таких книг сложно находить полки. Спустя некоторое время, с расцветом постколониального романа, Великобританию неожиданно наводнили бестселлеры таких авторов, как Салман Рушди, Бен Окри, Юнг Шан, Арундати Рой, В.С. Найпол, Чинуа Ашебе, Воле Соинка и Бенджамин Зефания. Книги эти были написаны на английском, а их авторы, в основном, имели британское гражданство. Вскоре началось возрождение региональной литературы Соединенного королевства: взволнованная шотландская романтика Вальтера Скотта у Ирвина Уэлша сменилась на неистовство совершенно иного характера, а место валлийских пасторалей Р.С. Томаса заняли урбанистические пустыри Ниалла Гриффитса. Английские поэты-метафизики семнадцатого века грезили о поиске 'единичного в универсальном' — теперь же эта максима приобрела новое значение, противоположное по смыслу. То, что некогда считалось универсальным, теперь отходило на задний план — на первый же выходила проблематика конкретного, локального места действия.

Такой литературный плюрализм был тесно связан с весьма противоречивыми общественными сдвигами. По мере культурной диверсификации послевоенной Великобритании в результате постоянных реформ системы образования самим британцам был закрыт доступ к огромной части их языкового наследия. За время смены одного поколения древние языки перестали играть основополагающую роль в учебных планах государственных образовательных учреждений. Прошло еще одно поколение, и та же участь постигла новые языки. Тем временем Лондон превратился в мировую столицу этнолингвистического многообразия — сегодня в начальных школах города звучит речь на более чем 340 различных языках. По распространенности за английским следуют португальский и йоруба. В наши дни многоязычными вырастают те дети, родители которых, будучи иммигрантами в первом или втором поколении, сохраняют и передают им свою национальную культуру.

Ввиду того, что иммигрировавшие в Великобританию семьи сохраняют в этой стране статус аутсайдеров, отношение общества к понятию 'иностранный язык' в корне меняет свое застывшее каноническое значение. В 2001 году под совместной редакцией поэтов и переводчиков Дэниэла Вайсборта и Стивена Уоттса вышел специальный номер довольно интересного ежеквартального журнала 'Современная поэзия в переводе'. Озаглавленный 'Родной язык', этот номер содержал поэзию, сочиненную носителями самых разных языков — от сомали до чешского, от пенджаби до русского, от арабского до болгарского. В основе проекта лежал принцип межнационального сотрудничества, и работы многих поэтов были переведены на английский их британскими коллегами, среди которых Энтони Рудольф, Клайв Уилмер, Джордж Сиртес, Джонатан Гриффин и Кит Босли. Не менее примечателен был также и объединивший обе группы поэтов тур, профинансированный Советом по искусствам Великобритании. В качестве его координатора выступила Сиан Уильямс. Там, где родной язык какого-либо поэта был наиболее распространен (урду в Лидсе, пенджаби в Бирмингеме, турецкий в Северном Лондоне), стихи на нем декламировались как автором, так и поэтом-переводчиком. На чтении, которое я посетила в Британской библиотеке, отдельные члены аудитории вставали (некоторые даже на стулья) в ответ на слова 'своих' поэтов, в то время как более приличные (и в то же время более пассивные, что свойственно британцам) слушатели просто сидели и завороженно слушали выступления: на языке оригинала и в переводе.

По некоторым данным Великобритания является страной, в которой лишь около 2-3% из 160,000 публикуемых ежегодно книг составляют произведения художественного перевода. Для сравнения, в Венгрии и Франции эта цифра составляет 14%, в Испании и Голландии 40%. Если посмотреть на отдельные литературные жанры — к примеру, на современный или исторический роман, — можно констатировать, что значительно больше половины их продаж в Италии или Германии — это переводы, причем, по большей части с английского. И напротив, переводные книги, которые продаются здесь лучше других, можно отнести к более специфическим жанровым нишам: это остросюжетный 'еврокрайм' — подборка наиболее показательных книг в этом жанре составлена рядом независимых издательств — или 'женское порно', недавняя мода на которое, внезапно вспыхнувшая, похоже начинает выветриваться.

Традиционная реакция на то, что британцы обделены хорошими, современными художественными переводами, примерно такая: 'Мы же можем читать о том, что происходит в мире, по-английски, так зачем беспокоиться и читать что-то во вторичной обработке?'. Вывод таков: переводы мыслятся не просто как продукты 'вторичной обработки', а как нечто в принципе второсортное. В декабре 2006 года именно это, по сути, высказал Джеймс Фентон в интервью Кристине Паттерсон для газеты Independent. Объясняя, какими принципами он руководствовался при отборе стихотворений для нового издания 'Книги любовной лирики' издательства Faber & Faber, он сказал, что решил не включать в издание переводы, 'по той причине, что все-таки по качеству они чаще всего уступают оригинальным работам'. Если такие серьезные предрассудки существуют у тех, кто по идее должен хорошо, если не безупречно, разбираться в этом вопросе, можно утверждать, что художественным переводчикам предстоит еще много работать, чтобы даже понимающие люди смогли оценить их труд по достоинству.

При этом мы должны быть рады, что, по крайней мере, предпринимаются маленькие шаги для повышения общественно-культурного статуса художественного перевода, а также самих художественных переводчиков. Семь лет назад при поддержке Совета по искусствам Великобритании была восстановлена Премия в области независимой зарубежной художественной литературы (Independent Foreign Fiction Prize). Это единственная премия, на равных правах присуждаемая как авторам, так и переводчикам. В то же время, именно благодаря этой премии возникла инициатива расширения ряда Переводческих премий (Translation Prizes), ежегодно вручаемых Ассоциацией переводчиков совместно с Центром художественного перевода Великобритании (British Centre for Literary Translation). Среди новых Переводческих премий следует отметить Премию Порджеса (иврит), Премию Банипала (арабский) и вручаемую с 2005 года Премию Rossica (русский). Вскоре их пополнит еще одна премия, проект которой в настоящее время рассматривается Польским институтом книги. Проходящие в рамках церемоний награждения чтения с каждым годом привлекают все больше людей и активно освещаются средствами массовой информации.

Переводчики, являющиеся членами Общества писателей Великобритании, имеют статус полноправных авторов. Таким же статусом обладают переводчики Школы писательского мастерства при Университете Восточной Англии — научно-образовательного института, в структуру которого входит Центр литературного перевода Великобритании. Арч Тэйт, в прошлом номинированный на Премию Rossica, отмечает, что еще в 1976 году на Генеральной конференции ЮНЕСКО было объявлено о том, что 'статус переводчиков должен приравниваться к статусу авторов'. Он также указывает, что принятый в 1988 году Закон о защите авторских и патентных прав, а также прав в области конструкторских изобретений, признает за переводчиком статус создателя литературного произведения. 'Но все же, — подводит итог Тэйт, — перевод воспринимается как что-то качественно отличное от сочинения текста, существенно менее оригинальное. Не ясно, является ли перевод по-настоящему творческим, самодостаточным литературным произведением, или же он представляет собой лишь набор механических лингвистических операций?'.

Должна признаться, меня этот вопрос ввел в заблуждение. Не имея достаточного воображения для самостоятельного сочинения поэзии или художественной прозы, я, тем не менее, всегда активно и много писала. Среди моих работ тексты для популярных радиостанций, печатных СМИ, академические рецензии, исторические биографии и интервью, а также статьи для многочисленных каталогов, монографий, специальных публикаций о литературе и фотографии. Я также выступала куратором, по меньшей мере, дюжины выставок. В каждом случае я чувствовала, что занимаюсь чем-то сродни переводу. Другими словами, все мои 'оригинальные' работы в какой-то мере выполняют функцию 'проводников' для произведений других авторов. Несмотря на это, мне одинаково важен результат любой моей работы, будь то перевод или выставка, рассказ о чьей-то жизни или же повествование о целой эпохе.

Переводчики работают с уже существующим текстом, однако это не делает их работу сугубо механической по определению. Мы все прекрасно знаем, какой получится нелепый результат, если пропустить отрывок даже самого элементарного прозаического текста через компьютерную программу-переводчик. Поэтому те английские слова, которые публикуются в результате моей переводческой работы — это мои слова, а не слова автора оригинального текста. И у него и у меня свои собственные задачи, и пускай они разные, они равноправны. Ведь мне не нужно прожить чью-то жизнь, чтобы написать биографию этого человека — подобным же образом, мне не нужно быть автором испанской или португальской версии текста, чтобы написать английскую. И все же, поскольку любой перевод является актом воссоздания, бывает так, что автор заслуживает своего переводчика. Отсюда такое большое количество современных поэтов, занятых работой

над переводом своих и чужих произведений — например, Киаран Карсон, Дэвид Константин, Джордж Сиртес, Гвинет Льюис, Джо Балмер. А иногда автор заслуживает ни кого-то, а самого себя: что может быть остроумнее, чем переводы собственных работ, выполненные Беккетом или Набоковым?

Сьюзен Зонтаг однажды написала: 'Переводы подобны зданиям. Если они хорошие, время делает их еще лучше: Монтень в переводе Флорио, Плутарх в переводе Норта, Рабле в переводе Мотто... (Кто—то ведь сказал — 'Величайший русский писатель столетия Констанс Гарнет'). Самые прославленные и долговечные переводы — не самые точные'. На самом деле, Констанс Гарнет обвиняли в том, что она самая викторианская из русских писательниц: ошибка вдвойне, поскольку Гарнет фигура все-таки исключительно позднеэдвардианская. Несмотря на это, Констанс Гарнет сумела занять почетное место в истории как единственный художественный переводчик, удостоившийся отдельной биографии, — а в наше время красноречивым свидетельством ее высокой оценки профессиональным сообществом является тот факт, что ей посвящено больше страниц в Интернете, чем любому другому переводчику. Все это она заслужила, посвятив свою долгую жизнь тому, что знакомила англоязычных читателей с произведениями Пушкина, Тургенева, Толстого, Достоевского, Чехова, Горького и Пастернака.

Ни один современный переводчик не может себе позволить проигнорировать Констанс Гарнет. Так, Энтони Бриггс, чьи новые переводы 'Войны и мира' и 'Воскресения' вышли, соответственно, в 2005 и 2006 годах, отдает ей необходимую дань уважения. Оскар Уайлд встретил ранние переводы Гарнет превосходным афоризмом, сказав, что русскую литературу делает великой 'то сострадание, которой она преисполнена'. Орландо Фиджес в своем 'Послесловии' к 'Войне и миру' в переводе Бриггса так характеризует роман Толстого: 'Из 'Войны и мира' английский читатель узнает о русских больше, чем, пожалуй, из любой другой книги. Но главное, этот роман дает ему повод задуматься о жизни и своем месте в этом мире. Поскольку 'Война и мир' — общечеловеческое произведение...плоть от плоти русской традиции, оно функционирует как необъятная поэтическая конструкция, сталкивающая нас с фундаментальными вопросами бытия'.

Похожим образом (по крайней мере, столь же многословно) высказалось огромное количество слушателей британской радиопрограммы 'На необитаемом острове'. Они выбрали 'Войну и мир' в качестве той единственной книги, без которой не обошлись бы, потерпи они кораблекрушение. Вероятно, объясняется это тем, что Толстой вложил в роман не только то, что считал самым главным, а именно свою философию, результат многолетних размышлений и судьбоносных поступков, но и то, чего превыше всего жаждет читатель — эпическую историю. В этой истории неистовый накал страстей на поле брани сменяет не менее напряженное действие, разворачивающееся за закрытыми дверями частной жизни героев. В этой параллели есть что—то близкое каждому читателю. Если непреходящая ценность литературного произведения каким—то образом выражается в количестве его переводов, то 'Война и мир', как и 'Мадам Бовари' Флобера, с одной стороны, подтверждает это предположение, а с другой, — из раза в раз ставит перед переводчиком непростую задачу, во многом, в связи со своим громадным объемом.

У всех нас есть свои личные библиотеки: отчасти хранящиеся дома на полках, отчасти – в недрах нашего индивидуального сознания, и пускай в моей библиотеке переводов больше, чем у других, едва ли найдется хотя бы один человек, у которого их не будет вовсе. Дело в том, что читатель сам является первым переводчиком книги. Он считает текст со страницы и видоизменяет его в своем уме, следуя за своим воображением. Тысячелетия назад, до того, как книги были изобретены, и столетия назад, когда они были редкими и дорогостоящими артефактами, мы получали предания и легенды только лишь из уст избранных. Эти посредники были носителями устной фольклорной традиции. Благодаря им землю словно окутали мифы, каждый из которых, хотя и имел свои локальные разновидности, в основе своей восходил к предвечной теме человека и его природы.

Подобно рассказчикам-мудрецам, художественные переводчики заменяют одни слова другими, в точности рассчитывая степень требуемого семантического и эмоционального воздействия этих новых слов, тщательно оценивая их значение для читателей. Ведь, исключая те случаи, когда переводчик не обладает достаточным профессионализмом (не понимает текст источника или не может грамотно и точно писать на требуемом языке), все согласятся с тем, что он, по крайней мере, не менее компетентный истолкователь текста, чем простой читатель.

Пионеры русских переводов
Питер Франс

Перевод русской литературы пользуется сейчас большим успехом. К Премии Rossica в этом году были представлены около 30 наименований, от новой версии 'Войны и мира' до тонких двуязычных изданий малоизвестных поэтов. Однако так было не всегда. Перенеситесь на двести лет назад – к 1807 году не больше полдюжины произведений русской литературы было опубликовано на английском языке.

Девятнадцатый век прорубил великолепное окно в русскую литературу и культуру – настолько, что Дональд Дэйви однажды написал, что 'пробуждение англо—саксонского народа к русской литературе' был 'переломным моментом, не менее определяющим, чем открытие итальянской литературы поколениями английского ренессанса'. Великий период этого пробуждения начался в конце девятнадцатого века, но дорога уже была расчищена пионерами разнообразных жизненных путей. Их переводы варьировались от традиционных народных сказок и былин до новой литературы Пушкина, или Толстого.

Первым из пионеров был Джон (позднее сэр Джон) Боуринг (1792–1872), который в 1820 году выпустил первый из его двух томов 'Образцов русских поэтов' (Specimens of the Russian Poets). Как переводчик с русского он был опережен анонимным переводчиком 'Ивана царевича, или о том, как роза без шипов не колется' ('Ivan Czarowicz, or, The Rose without Prickles that Stings not') Екатерины великой, опубликованного в эдинбургском журнале 'Пчела' (The Bee) в 1790х, и Дэйном А. А. Фелдборгом, который перевел несколько историй и путешествий Николая Карамзина с немецкого. Однако именно Боуринг привлек внимание английских литераторов к русским работам, что было наглядно продемонстрировано многочисленными рецензиями на его антологию, включающую в себя, общим числом, 400 страниц.

Родившись в Экзетере, он начал путешествовать и изучать языки достаточно рано, в качестве торговца вином и сельдью. Несмотря на то, что перевод помог начать его карьеру, это была лишь малая часть очень наполненной жизни этого высокопринципиального, но колкого и тщеславного человека. В политическом плане он был последователем философа Джереми Бентама, который в 1824 году сделал его политическим редактором нового радикального ежеквартального издания the Westminster Review, для которого он писал многочисленные статьи. Позже он путешествовал за границей с общественной службой, совершал набеги на мир индустрии, дважды был членом Парламента и в 1848 году стал британским консулом в Кантоне и позднее губернатором Гонконга.

Боуринг провел несколько месяцев в Петербурге с 1819–20, в течение которых он якобы встречался с Карамзиным и баснописцем Иваном Крыловым, а также слышал народные песни, поющиеся в 'деревянных избах крестьян'. Он составил второй том своей русской антологии, когда был в тюрьме во Франции в 1822 году по подозрению в шпионаже и саботажных действиях. Это была первой из серии антологий, которые позднее включили в себя поэзию Сербии, Богемии, Венгрии, Голландии и Испании. Словарь национальных биографий (The Dictionary of National Biography) отмечает, что у Боуринга имелись планы по 'написанию истории и предоставлению переведенных примеров популярной поэзии как западного, так и восточного миров'. Он сам считал свою миссию 'благожелательной', говоря, что он никогда не покидал родную землю без 'желания вернуться, неся с собой свежие оливковые ветви мира и свежие венки поэзии'. Перевод был особенно необходимым упражнением во взаимном понимании, поскольку было слишком легко 'презирать то, что не понимаешь'.

Учитывая количество языков, с которых он переводил, притязания Боуринга на понимание были действительно широки и иногда становились предметом насмешек. Джордж Борроу, в каком—то смысле похожая фигура, с которым Боуринг работал вместе над скандинавским проектом до того как рассорился с ним, заявил в своем едком литературном портрете 'Старого радикала' ('The Old Radical') в The Romany Rye, что он был 'поверхностно знаком с четырьмя, или пятью более легкими европейскими диалектами'. Что касается русского, он признал, что получал помощь от Фридриха Аделунга, который снабдил его немецкими и английскими прозаическими шпаргалками. Однако он знал русский достаточно хорошо, чтобы цитировать русские оригиналы в своей дискуссии о поэтических формах и он настаивает на подлинности своего предприятия, цитируя пять строк поэта Батюшкова написанных кириллицей на его титульном листе. Его антология содержит стихи 23 поэтов, а также 50 страниц народных песен. Его добросовестно рифмованные версии не были так уж хороши, однако достаточно, чтобы их включил в свою антологию русской литературы американец Лео Винер в начале двадцатого века. Вот несколько строк из его перевода Батюшкова 'Тень друга' ('Shade of a Friend'):

Вечерний ветр, валов плесканье,
Однообразный шум, и трепет парусов,
И кормчего на палубе взыванье
Ко страже, дремлющей под говором валов,—
Все сладкую задумчивость питало.

The dancing surge, the evening breezes falling,
And through the sails and shrouds those breezes whistling shrill,
And to the watch the active helmsman calling,
The watch, who, midst the roar, sleeps tranquilly and still.
All seemed to rock itself to gentle thought.

Более интересным для нас, теперь, пожалуй, является то, что Боуринг говорит в своем введении. Он видит современную ему Россию, появляющуюся 'как будто в миг, из ночи невежества'. Сторонник радикальных взглядов, он считает возмутительным продолжающийся в России деспотизм, отчаянную пропасть между привилегированными классами и крестьянством, но подтверждает, что 'фундамент теперь заложен, на котором гордое строение цивилизации будет возведено'. Даже если большая часть нации еще погружена в свое старое варварство, 'значительное политическое влияние, которое Россия приобрела [вследствие войн с Наполеоном], и, кажется, будет поддерживать, будет менее ужасным, по крайней мере, к моралисту, если не к государственному деятелю, чем если бы было совершенно лишено духа литературы'. А поскольку поэзия выражает в чем-то национальный характер, то политическим деятелям стоило бы 'изучить тенденцию и характер того фонтана, чьи воды простираются над поколениями людей и над широчайшей империей в мире'. Потребность более глубоких познаний о великане на Востоке окажется часто повторяющейся темой в истории перевода, вплоть до наших дней; всего через тридцать лет

после антологии Боуринга 'Крымская война чудесным образом повлияла на судьбу Тургенева в Британии, как прочем и на других, также принадлежащих к русской культуре '.

Пушкин появился на сцене позднее и не был включен в тома Боуринга. Одним из его первых переводчиков оказался соперник Боуринга, блистательный Джордж Борроу, который провел два года, работая на английское Общество Библии в России, и выпустил два тома переводов со многих языков, Targum и The Talisman, в Санкт-Петербурге в 1835. Вследствие трудности перевода поэзия Пушкина не была столь известна и важна для представлений британцев девятнадцатого века о русской литературе, в то время как существовало много переводов таких текстов как 'Пиковая дама' и 'Капитанская дочка'. Был только один перевод Евгения Онегина, который на самом деле намного лучше, чем представляется из едких комментариев Набокова. Это была работа подполковника Х.Спалдинга, притягательной и малопонятной фигуры, который, должно быть, жил в русскоговорящем окружении и переводил напрямую с русского. (Как мы уже видели в случае Боуринга, переводить с русского через французский, или немецкий языки было – и долго оставалось – обычным делом.)

Есть, однако, еще один пионер переводов Пушкина, который заслуживает упоминания: Томас Бад Шо (1813–62). В отличие от Боуринга и Борроу, Шо сделал карьеру в России и описывается Патриком Ваддингтоном в Оксфордском словаре национальной биографии (the Oxford Dictionary of National Biography), как человек, обладавший уникальной способностью интерпретировать британскую культуру для русских и русскую культуру для британцев. Сын знаменитого архитектора, он уехал в Россию, чтобы избежать бедности и где зарабатывал в качестве личного преподавателя великих князей, как учитель английского в пушкинском лицее в Царском селе и, наконец, как профессор английского языка в Санкт-Петербурге. Он написал учебники по английской литературе, а также статью о Санкт-Петербурге для Энциклопедии Британика (Encyclopedia Britannica). Его переводы включали русские популярные романы, Гоголя и Лермонтова. А в 1845 он опубликовал три статьи под названием 'Пушкин, русский поэт' ('Pushkin, the Russian Poet') в журнале Blackwood's Edinburgh Magazine. Статьи основаны на воспоминаниях еще живущих друзей поэта и дополнены основательно подобранными стихотворениями, прилежно исполненными в размере, близком к оригиналу, и в более приглаженном переводе, чем мы видим у Боуринга и Борроу.

Настоящей звездой русской литературы в англо–говорящем мире, во всяком случае, до драматического появления Толстого в 1880–х, был Иван Тургенев, которого высоко ценил Генри Джеймс и американцы и которого некоторые британские критики считали лучшим новеллистом, чем писателем. А через Тургенева мы имеем возможность познакомиться с еще тремя пионерами русского перевода, В. Р. С. Ральстоном (1828–1889), Изабель Хапгуд (1850–1928), и Констанцией Гарнетт (1861–1946). В отличие от уже упомянутых переводчиков, Ральстон изучал русский в Лондоне и стал специалистом по русской культуре во время долгих лет работы в Британском Музее. Он также часто ездил в Россию и был избран член-корреспондентом Императорской Академии наук в Санкт-Петербурге в 1886. Он был в дружеских отношениях с Тургеневым, поддерживая его имя в глазах общественности, атакуя плохих переводчиков его работ (включая те, что были сделаны через французский язык), строя так и неосуществившиеся планы по написанию совместного политического романа и выпустив один из лучших переводов его романа 'Лиза', варианта 'Дворянского гнезда' (A Nest of Gentlefolk).

Ральстон писал для литературных периодических изданий и был, по мнению окружающих, остроумным собеседником и одаренным рассказчиком. Он, также как и многие из его современников, глубоко интересовался фольклорным искусством, публикующимися коллекциями тибетских сказок, 'песнями русского народа' и русскими народными сказками. Когда молодой Артур Рэнсом искал вдохновение для своего собственного сказительства, он наткнулся на Ральстона: 'В Лондонской библиотеке я нашел 'Русские народные сказки' (Russian Folk Tales) Ральстона и несмотря на то, что мне не понравилась его кажущаяся неприемлемой 'литературная' проза, которой они были написаны, я увидел, какой богатый это был материал'. Так Рэнсом отправился в Россию, выучил русский язык, работал журналистом (и возможно шпионом), женился на секретарше Троцкого и (среди всего остального) написал замечательные 'Русские сказки старого Питера' (Old Peter's Russian Tales), переработка сказок для детей.

В то время как Ральстон перевел лишь один роман Тургенева, две выдающиеся переводчицы позднего девятнадцатого века, Изабель Хапгуд из США и Констанция Гарнетт из Англии, обе выпустили полные издания его романов и рассказов — помимо многого другого. Имя Хапгуд теперь не так известно, но ее производительность была почти такой же впечатляющей, как и Гарнетт, и в те дни ее имя было хорошо знакомо читателям. Она переводила с французского и немецкого, также как и с русского и по данным 'Нации' (The Nation), ее работа определяла 'новый стандарт точности перевода'. В дополнение к полному Тургеневу, она перевела также произведения Гоголя и Толстого. Ее переводы 'Мертвых душ' (Dead Souls) и 'Тараса Бульбы' (Taras Bulba) были немедленно перевезены в пиратском варианте по эту сторону Атлантики издателем Генри Визетелли; они появились в слегка измененной форме в его серии 'Русские романы' ('Russian novels'), которая также включала первые британские переводы Достоевского — с названием на титульном листе: 'русский реалистический роман'.

Хапгуд родилась в Бостоне, учила французский и латынь в школе, затем сама изучила польский, русский и церковно-славянский, перед тем, как начать карьеру литературного переводчика. Одним из первых переводов был ее новаторский сборник 'Эпические песни России' (Epic Songs of Russia) (1885), литературное изложение в прозе русских былин, таких как

'Садко', сюжет которого лег в основу оперы Римского–Корсакого. Несмотря на то, что они сначала не пользовались большим успехом, они предназначались для широкой публики, в надежде рассеять 'непроницаемое невежество' в отношении России, которое царило на Западе. Она сама посетила Россию вместе со своей матерью в 1887. Ее 'Русские прогулки' (Russian Rambles) 1895 года описывают, насколько реальность России оказалась отличной от идей, полученных из ее 'от первого знакомства с русским языком'. Описывая свои встречи с поэтами и писателями, включая Толстого, чья слава находилась тогда в зените, она производит впечатление интересного и очень остроумного человека. Позже она выпустила 'Обзор русской литературы' (a Survey of Russian Literature) (1902) и молитвенник для Православной церкви, а также совершила еще одно путешествие в Россию с тем, чтобы собрать церковную музыку.

Изабель Хапгуд была значительной фигурой того времени, однако для британцев доминирующим персонажем в переводе с русского была Констанция Гарнетт — а ее история переносит нас в двадцатый век. Из-за общего невнимания к переводам, вы едва ли найдете сноску на ее имя в большинстве трудов по истории английской литературы. Однако ее многочисленные переводы оставили намного более глубокий след в развитии британской и американской литературы, чем большинство литературных работ, не считая нескольких 'оригинальных' писателей. Ее достижения были отмечены лучшими английскими писателями — так Джозеф Конрад писал в мае 1917: 'Тургенев для меня — это Констанция Гарнетт, а Констанция Гарнетт — Тургенев. Она прекрасно смогла поместить его работы в английскую литературу, и там я ее вижу, а точнее чувствую.'

Констанция Блэк родилась в Брайтоне. Дочь адвоката и внучка человека, который сделал проект парохода для российского правительства, но умер, доставив его в Кронштадт. После детства омраченного болезнью и семейным несчастьем, она изучала классиков в Кэмбридже и работала частным преподавателем и библиотекарем до того, как вышла замуж за ученого, Эдварда Гарнетта. Она выучила русский благодаря знакомству с русскими революционерами, жившими в Англии. Один из них, Сергей Степняк, стал ее литературным сотрудником, договорившись в 1893 о том, что он будет редактировать ее переводы за 20 процентов от ее гонораров — однако, он умер два года спустя. Она продолжала консультироваться с русскими в течение долгих лет, несмотря на то, что ее знание русского, конечно же, улучшалось со временем, особенно после визита в Россию в 1893, включавшего непременный визит к Толстому.

Можно сказать, что она училась по ходу работы, взяв для разминки 'Обычную историю' Гончарова (A Common Story). Однако эта разминка привела к великим свершениям: 15 томов Тургенева, 6 – Гоголя, 6 –Толстого, 6 –Герцена, 15 –Чехова (рассказы и пьесы) и конечно же (в смысле влияния) 12 –Достоевского, все за период в 40 лет, производя почти по два тома в год. Можно себе представить, что она работала быстро и напряженно, она повредила зрение и, в конечном счете, ей пришлось прибегнуть к помощи секретаря, которому она могла диктовать. Когда она была в расцвете своих творческих сил, Д. Х. Лоуренс зачарованно наблюдал, как она писала страницу за страницей, кидая их одну за другой на пол.

Таким образом, за исключением Лескова, она преподнесла английской литературе почти полную когорту русских писателей прозаиков XIX века, и всю первую половину XX века. Классические русские романы, которые читала английская публика, прошли почти все через осмысление и язык Констанции Гарнетт. Однако ее почти полная монополия, какой бы благотворной она не была, не могла длиться вечно. Иногда ее переводы перерабатывались (процесс продолжающийся и по сей день), а со временем столо выходить все больше и больше новых переводов, поскольку каждая популярная серия (Penguin, Signet, World's Classics, etc) хотела иметь свою версии знакомых текстов.

В то же время переводы Гарнетт стали критиковать за неточность (что случалось редко) и за старомодность (что, вероятно, справедливо, хотя вопрос понятия стиля в переводе остается открытым). В частности, и, с некоторой долей достоверности, ее укоряли в том, что она 'сглаживала' часто идеосинкретичный язык своих оригиналов, в особенности Достоевского. Но даже если современные переводчики могут теперь делать переводы с большей внимательностью к фактуре всегда трудных, но интересных романов, их работа не может умалить огромного достижения этой хрупкой женщины, сделавшей русскую литературу значительной частью нашего культурного багажа. Когда ее 'Братья Карамазовы' достигли Лондона в 1912, критик Миддлтон Мюррей писал, что это было 'самым удачным переводом в истории английской литературы'. Возможно, он думал о шоковом эффекте таких сцен, как та, что в конце романа, где Грушенька сталкивается с Катей:

Катя стремительно шагнула к дверям, но, поравнявшись с Грушенькой, вдруг остановилась, побелела как мел, и тихо, почти шепотом, простонала:

— Простите меня!

Та посмотрела на нее в упор и, переждав мгновение, ядовитым, отравленным злобой голосом ответила:

— Злы мы, мать, с тобой! Обе злы! Где уж нам простить, тебе да мне? Вот спаси его, и всю жизнь молиться на тебя буду.

Katya moved swiftly to the door, but when she reached Grushenka she stopped suddenly, turned as white as chalk and moaned softly, almost in a whisper:

'Forgive me!'

Grushenka stared at her and, pausing for an instant, in a vindictive, venomous voice, answered:

'We are full of hatred, my girl, you and I! We are both full of hatred! As though we could forgive one another! Save him, and I'll worship you all my life.

Были и другие пионеры, но среди них нельзя не упомянуть Луизу Шэнкс. В отличие от предыдущих переводчиков, о которых мы писали, Луиза Шэнкс родилась в самой России – в Москве в 1855, в семье квакеров, занятых в торговле ювелирными изделиями. В 1884, она вышла замуж за Айлмера Мода, который был на три года ее младше и жил в Москве с шестнадцати лет. Вместе они составили долголетнюю супружескую команду, знаменитую, прежде всего, благодаря их переводам Толстого, которые завершились выпуском столетнего издания издательства Оксфордского университета (Oxford University Press,1928–37, 21 том), которое доминировало на рынке англоязычных изданий Толстова в середине XX века. Моды познакомились с Толстым в 1888, стали друзьями и учениками, которым великий писатель доверял переводить свои тексты. По возвращению в Англию в 1897, они жили некоторое время в коммуне Толстого, и Айлмер посетил Канаду, сопровождая группу духоборов, которую поддерживал Толстой (хотя он признался, что ехал в кабине первого класса). Позже они участвовали в Обществе Фабиан, а также поддерживали кампанию за контрацепцию Марии Стоуп.

Во время перевода, Айлмер концентрировался на философии, Луиза на беллетристике (оба были равно важны для раннего влияния Толстова в Британии). Первым переводом Луизы было 'Воскресение' (Resurrection), которое, с разрешения автора и благодаря его сотрудничеству, было издано одновременно на русском и английском в 1899–1900. Английский вариант вышел в лейбористском журнале 'Клэрион' (Clarion) и в тринадцати 'карманных частях' по цене одного пенни каждый и выпущенные издательской компанией Братства Толстова (Tolstoyan Brotherhood Publishing Company) (далекий отзвук прямолинейного коммерческого мира, для которого работала Констанция Гарнетт). Оно было очень удачным и часто переиздавалось. Луиза пожертвовала £150 из своего авторского гонорара для помощи духоборам в Америке, но когда духоборы обнаружили, какие страшные дела описываются в романе, они вернули деньги.

В течении века после Изабель Хапгуд, Констанции Гарнетт и Луизы Мод было много поразительных переводчиков русской литературы, и в годы после перестройки ни их количество, ни их качество не ухудшились. Переводы пионеров постепенно оходят в прошлое; теперь только ученые заглядывают в Боуринга и даже классические работы Гарнетт не являются автоматически первыми, куда заглянут те, кто хочет читать Тургенева, или Достоевского. Однако, все современные переводчики остаются в неоплатном долгу перед этими подвижниками, которые, каждый по–своему, стремились сблизить наши культуры и чей труд, полный любви, заставил снежный ком русских литературных переводов сдвинуться с места и покатиться.

Bonhams
1793

The Russian Sale
Thursday 31 May at 2pm
New Bond Street

Viewing
Friday 25 May 9am to 4.30pm
Sunday 27 May 11am to 3pm
Tuesday 29 May 9am to 4.30pm
Wednesday 30 May 9am to 4.30pm
Thursday 31 May 9am to 11am

Enquiries
Sophie Hamilton
+44 (0) 20 7468 8334
sophie.hamilton@bonhams.com

Catalogue
+44 (0) 1666 502 200
subscriptions@bonhams.com

1 Natalia Sergeevna Goncharova
(Russian, 1881-1962)
Companions: a poster design
56.5 x 43.5cm (21½ x 16¼in).
Estimate: £26,000 - 28,000

2 Alexei Alexeevich Harlamoff
(Russian, 1840-1925)
Portrait of a young girl
48 x 36cm (19 x 14¼in).
Estimate: £100,000 - 150,000

3 Alexei Alexeevich Harlamoff
(Russian, 1840-1925)
Study of a girl
44.5 x 32cm (17½ x 12½in).
Estimate: £100,000 - 150,000

4 Alexander Konstantinovich Bogomazov
(Ukrainian, 1880-1930)
Portrait of an actor
57.5 x 57.5cm (22¾ x 22¾in).
Estimate: £200,000 - 300,000

5 Konstantin Alexeevich Korovin
(Russian, 1861-1939)
Still life with brightly-coloured roses
46 x 55cm (18 x 21½in).
Estimate: £100,000 - 150,000

6 A silver-gilt and cloisonné enamel salt
throne, Khlebnikov, St. Petersburg, 1908-1917
height: 14.5cm (5¾in).
Estimate: £4,000 - 6,000

7 A pair of Fabergé silver groups,
Julius Rappoport, St. Petersburg, 1908-1917
height of each: 12.5cm (5in)(2).
Estimate: £12,000 - 18,000

8 A serving plate from the Kremlin Service,
Imperial Porcelain Manufactory, St. Petersburg,
period of Nicholas I (1825-55)
diameter: 32.5cm (12¾in).
Estimate: £3,000 - 5,000

9 A Fabergé gold, enamel and diamond
magnifying glass, workmaster Henrik
Wigstrom, St. Petersburg, 1908-1917
length: 10cm (4in).
Estimate: £17,000 - 19,000

Bonhams
101 New Bond Street
London W1S 1SR
+44 (0) 20 7447 7447
+44 (0) 20 7447 7400 fax
www.bonhams.com/russian

FOURTEEN LITTLE RED HUTS

Robert Chandler

[1] This was written in 1932. Platonov revised the first act in 1936, probably intending it to stand on its own. The play was never produced in Platonov's lifetime; it was first published in the journal *Volga*, 1988, no. 1.

Academia Rossica in collaboration with Robert Chandler organised the staging of parts of a production of Fourteen Little Red Huts, a play by Andrey Platonov. Apart from his translation of this play, Robert is well known for many other renditions of Platonov's work in English. His translation of Soul was short-listed for the 2005 Rossica Translation Prize. This article represents Robert's introductory comments prior to the performance on 26 June 2006 at the London Review Bookshop.

At Queen Mary College, where I teach part-time, we stage a Russian play, in Russian, once a year. This year I offered to direct a play I had translated five years before: Andrey Platonov's The Fourteen Little Red Huts.[1] Other members of staff tried to persuade me to choose something 'more straightforward', 'less harrowing', 'more stageable'; I replied that, since I had never directed before, I wanted at least to choose a play that I knew well and loved.

The Fourteen Little Red Huts has seldom been

[2] 'Чехов присутствовал.'

staged. I have heard only of two productions: in Saratov in the late 1980s and in Paris in 2000. Platonov wrote several plays, as well as film scripts, but Russian theatre directors seem to prefer to put on adaptations of his novels. Why they ignore the plays I do not know. Perhaps there really is a problem and it is only my blindness that enabled me to 'step in where angels fear to tread'. Or it may be that Russian directors are simply slow to seek out new repertoire; Russian publishers are equally slow to bring out accessible editions of recently discovered stories by Platonov.

After the college production of *Uncle Vanya* the previous year, a Russian colleague, Boris Ravdin, said to me, 'Chekhov was present';[2] I knew what he meant; it had not been a faultless production, but it had embodied something of Chekhov. Katya Grigoruk, the director, had not placed any barriers between Chekhov and the audience – something that even the most prestigious directors do surprisingly often. My hope was that the audience for *The Fourteen Little Red Huts* should respond as Boris had done, that people should feel afterwards that something of Platonov 'had been present'. I wanted to allow Platonov to speak; he had, after all, already suffered more than enough from interfering editors and censors. I wanted to impose as little as possible of my own, to allow the spirit of the production to emerge from the text itself. I know that Platonov used to read his work out loud in a neutral, inexpressive voice. I know that Beckett,

Photos by Evgeny Kazannik

[3] We also decided to stencil a more complex red black and white Malevich design on the backs of the T-shirts. It was the art historian, Igor Golomstock, who first drew my attention to similarities between Malevich and some aspects of Platonov. The four volumes of Platonov I have co-translated for Harvill all bear reproductions of figurative paintings by Malevich on their front covers; Golomstock's thoughts about Platonov and Malevich are summarized in my preface to *The Foundation Pit*.

[4] Классовый враг нам тоже необходим: превратим его в друга, а друга во врага — лишь бы *шахматная* игра не кончилась.

whose work *The Fourteen Little Red Huts* in many ways anticipates, constantly enjoined his actors 'not to act'. I knew that the worst mistake I could make would be to lose faith in this brilliant but somewhat plotless play and slip into trying to add something extra to make it more 'audience-friendly'.

On the other hand, I had to work with little time, little money, and a small, almost all-female cast with no understudies; whatever ideas I might have, I had to accept that chance would play an important role. Platonov himself can be seen as a collage artist, someone who cobbled together works of remarkable philosophical and psychological subtlety out of whatever materials were nearest to hand: Soviet songs and slogans, articles from *Pravda*, speeches by Stalin, the language of bewildered – though often perceptive – workers and peasants. Throughout the rehearsals I tried to keep his example in mind. In the end, chance was generous to us, transforming the aspect of the production about which I felt least certain of all: the visual aspect.

Malevich's most famous work, his 'Black Square', seems to have been intended as an expression of revolutionary optimism; it is difficult, however, not to see it as an expression of despair. Three of the four acts of *The Fourteen Little Red*

Huts are set in a collective farm where there is nothing to eat, nothing to fill the workers' mouths except Communist slogans. Thinking that Malevich's black futurist icon encapsulates the mood of the play, we decided that the workers on the collective farm should wear white T-shirts with a Malevich-style black square on the front.[3] I then learned that a black and white chequerboard floor was being laid down for a history department play to be staged a week before *The Fourteen Little Red Huts*. Chance's gifts can be oddly hard to recognize; we talked about repainting this floor, but I realized in time that we could use it to good effect. As well as harmonizing with the costumes, the chequerboard provided a striking symbol for the Soviet Union in the 1930s, a black and white world in which everyone was seen as either a loyal supporter of Stalin or a Trotskyist saboteur. And it was not difficult to make the floor seem part of Platonov's original vision. The phrase 'bely svet' (literally 'the white world', although I would usually translate it as 'the wide world' or 'the whole wide world') occurs several times in the play. The addition of the words 'chernaya byl'' (black reality) to one passage, immediately after 'bely svet', made Platonov's text and our floor appear to reflect one another perfectly. I also added the words 'of chess'

[5] In most cases I came up with English equivalents for the characters' often expressive names. In this article I shall be using my English versions of the names; when I mention a character for the first time, I shall also include the original name, after the English.

to the following sentence and asked the actor to look down at the floor as she spoke it: 'The class enemy is also essential: we must make foe into friend, and friend into foe – so the game *of chess* can continue.'[4] This proved a powerful moment in the production.

My main task was to provide an 'empty space' – as Peter Brook entitled his first book about the theatre; inside this empty space, with luck, a coherent production might take shape. I gave little specific advice to the actors; for the main part, they arrived at their own interpretations of their roles. Not all of these were what I expected, but all were convincing. An empty space, however, can exist only inside defining boundaries; it was essential that I keep the boundary walls in place. During one rehearsal, a reunion scene between Futilla/Suenita,[5] the collective farm chairman, and her husband Garmalov seemed to be turning into a jolly romp that could have been titled 'Carry on up the Collective Farm!' I had to remind the cast that Futilla, like all the collective farm workers, was close to death from starvation; the play is a farce, but it is the blackest of black farces – Platonov's response to the famine brought about by Stalin's policies of forced collectivisation and the compulsory requisitioning of grain. There is, of course, a certain absurdity in a privileged teacher having to insist to privileged students on the reality of death from starvation, but it is remarkable how seldom I felt the need to say things like this; for the main part, Platonov's vivid

language – and there is not a sentence in which you cannot sense the rhythms and intonations of living speech – told the actors all they needed to know.

The history department had provided us with an eloquent floor; I myself had to provide a protective roof for our 'empty space'. I had to prevent minor irritations turning into dangerous flare-ups, to acknowledge the reality of problems while professing confidence that they could be solved. Two things kept me going through the inevitable difficulties. One was an underlying sense of good will from the cast; I treated them with respect and they responded in kind. The other was that I never ceased to be enthralled by the dialogue. No doubt I often said and did too little during rehearsals, listening intently but failing – sometimes simply from exhaustion – to come up with new thoughts of my own. There are times, however, when an interested listener is what an actor needs most of all.

The central role in the play is that of Bos/ Khoz. This 101-year-old man seems to be intended as a generic Western intellectual; it is likely, however, that he is based on a specific figure – that of George Bernard Shaw. Shaw celebrated his seventy-fifth birthday in the Soviet Union in 1931, and he asserted afterwards that the world's only hope lay in the success of Stalin's five-year plan. On one occasion he ridiculed the idea that there might be famine in the Soviet Union, saying he had 'never dined so well or so sumptuously' as during his travels there. Platonov's Bos is sometimes wise, sometimes silly, sometimes caring, sometimes brutal. He survives on a diet of chemical powders and milk, as if he has either outworn his humanity or never fully entered into it. In the first act he says wearily, 'Boys and girls, children, make me a stick from a graveyard cross, so I can walk to the wretched beyond!' Soon afterwards he says with real or pretend optimism, 'We want to gauge the candle-power of the dawn you claim to have lit.'

This demanding role was played by Josefine Olsen, a 25-year-old student from Sweden. At first, Josefine seemed simply competent and diligent, learning her lines with impressive efficiency. Gradually, however, her performance grew subtler and more multi-layered – like the text itself. We agreed that, rather than being embarrassed by any difficulties she might have with pronunciation, she should incorporate them into her part; she was, after all, playing a man whose first names are Edward-Louis-Johann and whose knowledge of Russian is imperfect. When she found long Russian words hard to pronounce, I encouraged her to separate them out into their component syllables: 'bu-shu-yu-schi-ye pust-yak-ki (raging piffle); 'Ne ras-psikh-ov-yv-ai-tye men-ya! (Stop trying to drive me crazy!). This not only made it easier for both Josefine and the audience; it also enabled us to emphasize that Bos is himself a student, a foreigner struggling to adapt to alien patterns of speech and behaviour. I also suggested that when Bos is talking to himself, which he does quite often, he should occasionally revert to English; Josefine added yet another layer of linguistic complexity by choosing to speak these lines in a German accent. As for the question of sex, Katya Grigoruk, who played Khoz's young girl friend, has written to me that Josefine was so convincing as a man that she herself felt inspired 'to be more feminine and flirty'. I initially assigned the role of Bos to Josefine simply because she volunteered for it and because I had already learned – as her teacher – to respect her intelligence and commitment. I find it difficult, however, to imagine a mature Russian man bringing so many layers of feeling and meaning into the role as this young Swedish female polyglot. Josefine was both young *and* old, both male *and* female; Bos, in her interpretation, was not only an extraordinary and impossible figure but also a representative of humanity as a whole, beyond age, sex or nationality.

The Russian word for 'palate' *(nyobo)* is cognate with the Russian word for 'sky' *(nyebo)*; a tongue is a language, words mirror the world, the dome of the mouth mirrors the dome of the heavens – and struggling with unfamiliar sounds can help an actor to adopt another persona and enter an alien world. There were memorable performances by at least two other non-Russians – by Wolfgang Matt, an Austrian MA student, and by Paulina Wojnar, a young Polish girl who has

[6] Geoffrey Hosking, 'The yawning gap', TLS (London: Dec 6, 1996).

[7] See Natalya Kornienko in *Zdes' i teper'*, Moscow, 1993, 173

[8] А они побираться по морю пошли — мертвую рыбу по берегу искать, а Антошка даже лопух приступал жарить и лепешки печет из овечьего желудочного добра. Нам харчиться нечем стало

[9] Нет, я живу от сознания, разве у нас от пищи проживешь?

unusual difficulty with Russian pronunciation. During much of the rehearsal period I worried that I had made a serious mistake in casting her as Anton Endov, a fanatically Stalinist collective farm worker who acts and speaks, according to Platonov, 'with faultless precision'. Since there was no one appropriate for the role, I had thought it best to choose someone obviously inappropriate; a blatant incongruity between actor and role can, after all, generate considerable power. In the end my hope was borne out; Paulina's vulnerability as she struggled with the verbal and physical demands of her part revealed the desperation that typically underlies the blind optimism of a fanatical believer. More than any other actor, she managed to embody what Geoffrey Hosking, writing about Platonov's short novel, *The Foundation Pit,* once referred to as 'the strange and tormented mixture of hope and despair by which many ordinary people must have lived during Stalin's revolution from above'.[6]

Platonov knew more than most writers about the sufferings of the Russian peasantry; in August 1931 he had been sent to report on the progress of collectivisation in the central Volga and Northern Caucasus regions. The following entry from his notebooks is only one of many, all equally direct: 'State Farm no. 22 "The Swineherd". Building work - 25% of the plan has been carried out. There are no nails, iron, timber (...) milkmaids have been running away, men

have been sent after them on horseback and the women have been forced back to work. This has led to cases of suicide... Loss of livestock - 89-90%''[7] Few people would have dared write such things at this time. As I have said, *The Fourteen Little Red Huts* is Platonov's response to this tragedy, an artistic representation both of the famine itself and of official attempts to deny what was happening. When Bos and Futilla arrive from Moscow, one of the workers tells them that everyone has 'gone begging by the sea - looking for dead fish on the shore. Anton's even started frying burdock and making little cakes from what's been through sheeps' stomachs. There's no food for us to eat'.[8] Later, this same collective farm worker, Topov/Vershkov, says, 'No, what keeps me alive is consciousness. You can't stay alive here from food, can you?'[9]

Platonov's satire is at least as sharp as that of Brecht at his sharpest. There are, however, many other dimensions to *The Fourteen Little Red Huts*; like much of the work of this almost certainly atheist writer, it is surprisingly full of Christian symbolism, of references to sheep and shepherds, to bread and fish, to enlightenment and salvation. Futilla is Christ-like; she is not only a shepherd but also a sacrificial lamb, offering her own body — her milk, her lymph, her blood, her bones — as food for the starving people. And the lost boat, bearing the sheep, the grain and the children that have been stolen and carried out to sea by mysterious enemies, is called 'Distant Light', a phrase as

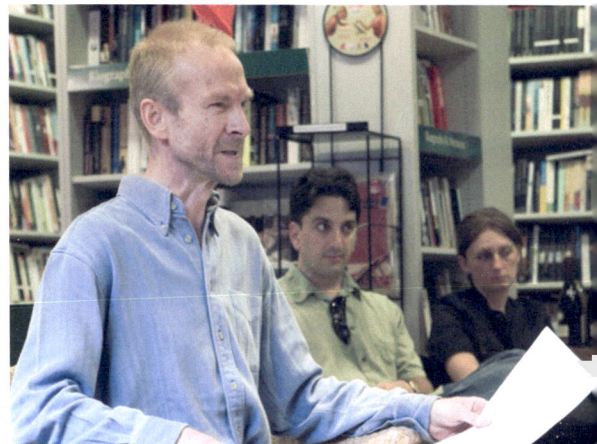

Christian as it is Communist.

In Platonov's novel, *Chevengur,* a recalcitrant peasant complains to one of the Bolsheviks, 'Very clever. You've given us the land, but you take away our every last grain of wheat. Well I hope you choke on our land. All us peasants have got left of it is the horizon. Who do you think you're fooling?' Platonov's peasants are orphans; both Mother and Father, both earth and heaven, have been taken away from them. They are at sea in the world; all they have left is a receding line of distant light and the webs of delusion that can be spun from words. Near the end of the last act of *The Fourteen Little Red Huts,* Anton Endov collapses, stands up again, says, 'It's nothing, my reason is alive, my ideology is fully intact. Hunger has nested only inside my body – and nowhere else! I shall rise again and charge forward to victory! Long live...'[10] He loses consciousness in mid-sentence but recovers a few minutes later to pronounce what is both his and the play's final word, 'Forward!!!'.[11] He then collapses once more.

For all the uniqueness of his style, Platonov is in many respects a deeply impersonal writer; the tragedy he voices is that of a nation. Brodsky has pointed out that his 'philosophy of the absurd' is all the more convincing for being voiced not by 'egocentric individualists' but by 'the traditionally inanimate masses'.[12] In the second act, for example, the oldest of the collective farm workers, Carbinov/Berdanshchik, unexpectedly refers to himself as a class enemy. Bos responds, 'Go to

the district centre and tell them to arrest you. It's time you learnt consciousness.' Carbinov's reply is disarmingly straightforward: 'I've already been. Twice now I've asked them to arrest me. But they're not interested. No social indicators, they say – you're one of the poor. They authorise some bread for me to eat on the way home – and off I go.'[13] It is not necessary to have studied Soviet history to appreciate the wit and power of these lines, but here is a weight of surreal and terrible reality behind them.

The Terror Famine of 1931-33 resulted in several million deaths. Platonov wrote of it while it was happening; few writers after him have dared to write about it at all. *The Fourteen Little Red Huts* modulates between farce and tragedy, between the realistic and the surreal, between resigned alienation and furious satire. This linguistic and structural dislocation serves a purpose; it is probably the only way to evoke catastrophes of this order without simply numbing the reader or listener. There is something strengthening, even inspiring, in Platonov's fierce wit and his determination to confront matters most of us are afraid even to think about. In the words of John Berger, the poet, novelist and critic who is one of Platonov's most passionate admirers, 'His stories do not add to the grief being lived; they save something'.[14]

[10] Мудреное дело: землю отдали, а хлеб до последнего зерна отбираете. Да подавись ты сам такой землей! Мужику от земли один горизонт остается. Кого вы обманываете- то?

[11] Вперед!!!

[12] Joseph Brodsky, *Less than One,* (New York: Farrar Strauss Giroux, 1986), p. 288. Translation as published.

[13] **Хоз**. ... Ступай в район и скажи, чтоб тебя арестовали. Пора бы уже сознанию научиться. **Берданщик**. Ходил уж. Дважды просился под арест. Не берут никак — признаков нету, говорят, нищий человек. Краюшку хлеба на обратную дорогу выписывают по карточке и пускают ко двору.

[14] John Berger, *A Season in London 2005* (London: Artevents, 2005), p. 87

Keeping Faith as Worlds Collide

Reflections on a Cumberland Lodge Conference

Daniel Washburn

King George VI Fellow at Cumberland Lodge

Religious Tradition and Innovation in the post-Soviet World: a case of revival or rejection? took place in cooperation with ACADEMIA ROSSICA, whose support granted a number of interesting speakers and excellent photography by Mark Polyakov. The photographs can be viewed at www.academia-rossica.org

From 31 January to 2 February 2007, Cumberland Lodge convened a conference on the theme of Religious Tradition and Innovation in the post-Soviet World: a case of revival or rejection? The conference took a broad approach to this theme, and considered not only the question of religious freedom, but also the intersections between religion and many other areas of contemporary life. It was also wide in its geographical coverage – whilst Russia was its main focus, the expertise of the speakers spanned Europe and Central Asia. The conference was also enriched by its eclectic mix of delegates: diplomats and lawyers, artists and musicians, historians and theologians, academics and students.

Throughout the last decades there has been much talk about how globalisation will transform the cultural landscape of the world. In post-Soviet Russia the globalisation debate is encountered everyday when people make choices between Russian or foreign products, including films, fashion, and arts. The pattern is the same the world over. In fact, often the process of consumption goes unquestioned – Nestlé chocolate on the store shelf simply becomes another choice, a potential preference. It loses the exotic appeal of otherness.

However, such acquiescence is rare once we move from the shop to the church. A foreign church is a receptacle of unfamiliar values, it is

not a silent object – it can actively challenge the idea of Nation and transform every aspect of a person. A foreign church presents its own vision of truth, which can disturb traditional understanding. Ultimately, when a nation subscribes to the ideal of religious freedom, and thus begins to court the presence of foreign churches, it acknowledges that the idea of its own nationhood may be challenged.

One idea that surfaced in many forms during the conference, and is related to the phenomenon of globalisation, had to do with the 'collision of worlds.' In the post-Soviet world, physical, political, and spiritual realms have been challenged by close contact with the religious 'Other' in the form of new, and non-traditional, groups. On one level are found the physical manifestations of collision, such as publications by Russian Orthodox Church leaders expressing concern about the behaviour of proselytising missions on what is understood to be canonical lands, occasional legal injunctions to halt the construction of non-Orthodox church buildings, and reactionary articles in the media that scrutinise the ongoing attempts by foreign and native 'new religious movements' to attract followers. These manifestations can massage nationalist sentiment or influence xenophobia. In short, they form a popular impetus for political decision-making.

On another level however, it is possible to talk of the cultural and psychological collision of worlds. In a classic late night discussion at

Cumberland Lodge is a former royal house in the middle of Windsor Great Park which acts as a forum for concepts and perspectives on contemporary issues of national and international significance. It is an independent educational organisation with a broadly Christian ethos, aiming to promote cross-sector cooperation and a balanced understanding of social issues, including consideration of significant ethical or moral questions. Its stately presence combined with neo-gothic fantasy, its long history encapsulated in royal portraits and glorious tapestries, and its tranquil surroundings of crown parkland, all come together to awaken the imagination.

the Lodge, several profound thinkers, including Orthodox delegates from Russia and Protestant delegates from Britain, compared their two religious traditions in an effort to tease out subtle, but key, differences in worldview. As the conference was held under the Chatham House rules, I am obliged not to reveal the names of the delegates. The following is an abridged version of their lengthy conversation.

The theology of many western Christians is what Vladimir Lossky might call cataphatic or positive theology, the practice of defining God according to scriptural revelation. 'Cataphatic' is derived from a Greek preposition meaning 'down from' or 'down into' — as in the scriptural revelation that has come down to humanity. Within the cataphatic tradition it is possible to state what God is. In the Eastern Church, by contrast, one may encounter apophatic, or negative theology, in which it is not possible to define God with words, in the belief that the divine cannot be captured by finite concepts. To this end, it can be difficult for Eastern and Western Christians to find common ground. This theological divide serves as a constant reminder of historic differences, such as the concept of Filioque — a Latin word meaning 'and the Son' which is used in the Nicene Creed of the Roman Catholic Church to indicate that the Holy Spirit proceeded from the Father and the Son. The Nicene Creed in the Eastern Church does

not include the Filioque, because it believes that the Holy Spirit came only from the Father. Although the schism between the Western and Eastern Church was a gradual process, involving substantial cultural and political shifts over centuries, in popular lore the adoption of the Filioque in the Nicene Creed was partially responsible for the 'Great Schism' of 1054. The altered Creed was adopted by the Roman Catholic Church without convening an ecumenical council of all the bishops. This, needless to say, offended the patriarchs and bishops of the Church in the East, who also considered it to be an invalid change as the Third Ecumenical Council in 431 had forbade and anathematised any additions to the Creed. This divide, according to the conference discussion, is still felt today, and, for many Orthodox believers, is only exasperated by the constant foreign demand for religious freedom.

This line of thought was expanded upon at other times during the conference, albeit in different terms. Almost every major facet of intra- and inter- faith misunderstanding in the post-Soviet world was discussed. Of specific interest were the tensions that these misunderstandings create, such as anxiety, nationalism, and xenophobia — in short, the observable symptoms in the clash between 'tradition' and 'innovation'. Many delegates, perhaps as a result of intensely focused discussion, also expressed their concern that the 'collision of worlds' observed in Russian

Overleaf:
Daniel Washburn,
Rafael Ibrahimov,
Ravil Bukharaev,
Svetlana Adjoubei,
Jonathan Luxmoore,
Alexei Lidov

Photos of participants
of the conference:
Ravil Bukharaev
Bettina Weichert
Jan Bank
Jonathan Sutton
Alexei Lidov
Stella Rock
Irina Kirillova
Panel discussion
Mark Polyakov &
Daniel Washburn

[1] For reference, the delegate quotes from Andrew Newberg, MD and Mark Robert Waldman, *Why we believe what we believe* (Free Press, 2006

and post-Soviet religious life, is merely a microcosm reflecting larger, irresolvable, cultural conflicts that plague the earth. As it was written in the conference materials, 'faith knows no borders, and yet it often becomes a principle factor dividing groups, nations and religions,' so it was vocalised on several occasions. And yet it proved very difficult to explain the primary roots of these religious and cultural clashes.

To summarise the general trend of thought that has grown out of the conference, regarding the nexus of belief and conflict, I should like to mention one delegate, who put it to me in a letter that we are born to believe because we have no other alternative. Our lives, whether we are religious or not, consist of a series of beliefs – everything from whom to trust and whom to avoid to the manner in which we pray, dine, and vote[1]. The contemporary world tests our ability to abandon, transform, or maintain our beliefs. While some people talk of a clash of civilisations, it is also useful to see a clash of Civilisation – the innovations of our world, including the religious ones, demand that we adapt to changing circumstances, but the traditions of our past ask that we have faith in immutable facts. This disjuncture is what brings forth conflict, whether it is with an individual, a society, or a long established religious institution. In one way or another no one likes to be told that his or her beliefs are wrong.

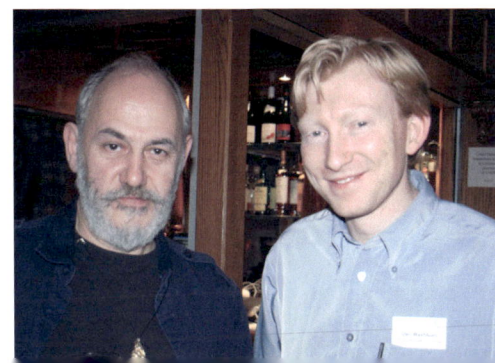

THE WALLACE COLLECTION AND
ANATOLE DEMIDOFF

Within the famous family collection, accumulated over five generations at Hertford House, lies an important, often overlooked, contribution by a flamboyant and enormously wealthy Russian collector. Anatole Demidoff (1812-1870) lived most of his life either in Paris or at the magnificent villa near Florence after which he took his title, Prince of San Donato. When he decided to auction off the works of art he had acquired over several decades, many found a new and lasting home in the London collection of the Marquesses of Hertford.

In presenting the 2007 Rossica Translation Prize at the Wallace Collection, Academia Rossica is delighted to uncover yet another page in the long history of contacts and cultural exchange, between Russia and Britain.

For many people the Wallace Collection is their favourite place in London. Although it is, like some of the capital's grandest institutions, a national museum, its particular charm lies in its intimacy. Here works of art are displayed in a sumptuous, yet unintimidating home and the tastes of one extraordinary family remain preserved in a single building. 'This palace of genius, fancy and taste': the description entered in the visitors' book in 1878 by Benjamin Disraeli perfectly captures its magic. To walk into the Wallace Collection is like stepping back into a leisured, more graceful age than our own; an age where time seems to have moved at a gentler pace and where beauty was enjoyed without the slightest trace of shame or embarrassment.

This superb collection was assembled in the 18th and 19th centuries by five generations of one remarkable family – the first four Marquesses of Hertford and Sir Richard Wallace, the illegitimate son of the 4th Marquess. The 5,470 objects in the Collection include an extraordinary array of 18th-century French art: furniture, porcelain and gold snuffboxes of the finest quality, together with French painting at its most elegant and sensuous in the works of Watteau, Boucher and Fragonard. Complementing these are masterpieces by some of the greatest names of European art, such as Titian, Rembrandt, Hals and Velázquez; the finest collection of princely arms and armour in Britain; and superb Medieval and Renaissance objects including Limoges enamels, maiolica, glass and bronzes. In each of the twenty-nine galleries there are works of the highest, international importance.

The history of the Wallace Collection begins in the mid-18th century when the 1st Marquess of Hertford, Francis Seymour Conway, bought six paintings by Canaletto (and Canaletto's studio) and two portraits by Reynolds. His son, the 2nd Marquess, added three further English portraits, by Reynolds, Romney and Gainsborough and a few pieces of French furniture and Sèvres porcelain. He began the family's occupation of Hertford House in 1797 and it was there that his wife, the Marchioness, was rumoured to have had liaisons with the future George IV.

It was only in the early 19th century, however, that a collector in any committed sense emerged within the family. The 3rd Marquess was a charismatic and disreputable personality and it is to him that the Collection owes, among other things, many of its finest Italianate bronzes, much of its Sèvres porcelain, twenty-seven seventeenth-century Dutch and Flemish paintings, along with Titian's celebrated *Perseus and Andromeda*. Greedy and clever, the Marquess's importance to the history of the Collection resides not only in the objects he acquired but in the extra wealth which he brought to the family from his marriage in 1798 to Maria Fagnani, the illegitimate daughter of a former dancer. It was this marriage that elevated the family to one of the very richest in England and ultimately ensured the wealth that enabled his descendants to build and maintain the collection.

It was the 4th Marquess, more than any of his immediate forbears, who set the tone of the collection by indulging his taste for artworks with a strong decorative appeal. He was as much French as English, at least in his taste and sympathies, and his purchases were so lavish and extensive that accumulation was clearly of as much importance to him as display and private enjoyment. The arts of 18th-century France were most in harmony with his distinct sensibility. At the same time, the 4th Marquess was, like his father, also especially fond of Dutch paintings and his purchases included grand gallery pictures such as Rubens's *The Rainbow Landscape*, Rembrandt's *Titus* and Hals's *Laughing Cavalier*.

When he died in 1870, the 4th Marquess left all his unentailed property to his illegitimate son

Karl Briullov, *The Last Day of Pompeii* (detail), 1833, oil on canvas, 456.5 x 651. State Russian Museum, St Petersburg
On Demidoff's commission Briullov also painted one of the most famous Russian paintings, *The Last Day of Pompeii*. It was exhibited to great acclaim in Paris and St Petersburg, and was then presented by Demidoff to the Tsar. 'Demidoff's need to please the Tsar was very pressing. Nicholas I strongly disapproved of this extravagant upstart who spent so much of his life abroad, ... and on number of occasions he seems to have threatened to confiscate Demidoff's Russian estates (and, hence, the source of his wealth). This was doubtless the reason for Demidoff's extended visit to St Petersburg in 1834, his gift of *The Last Day of Pompeii*, and his foundation in the Russian capital of various charitable institutions as well as a well-endowed literary prize to be administered by the Academy.' (Francis Haskell, 'Anatole Demidoff and the Wallace Collection', in *Anatole Demidoff, Prince of San Donato (1812-70)*, London, p.16)

Ary Scheffer, Francesca
da Rimini, 1835, oil on
canvas, 166.5 x 234

Richard Wallace. Shortly after his father's death Wallace began a short but vigorous campaign of buying works of art which transformed the character of the collection, greatly extending its variety and chronological range. This intense period of collecting was not sustained by Wallace in his later years, probably because his properties were full to bursting. He died in 1890 without an heir and after his death his widow Lady Wallace bequeathed the Collection to the British nation in 1897.

In the context of this rich family history it is perhaps easy to overlook the contribution of other connoisseurs, outside the family, to the character of the Wallace Collection. In the matrix of 19th-century collecting items frequently passed from hand to hand. Acknowledging the diversity and tracing the course of these patterns of acquisition and dispersal are fascinating tasks, and crucial to an understanding of the provenance of objects in the collection. One key figure worthy of study is Anatole Demidoff, Prince of San Donato.

Born in St Petersburg, Demidoff was immensely wealthy and lived on the proceeds of an industrial empire based in the Urals. His tastes, however, were very European and he lived most of his life in Paris and Florence. He was a flamboyant character and, in addition to his works of art, he kept a zoo as well as a magnificent collection of orchids in his enormous garden at the villa of San Donato, near Florence. He married Princesse Mathilde, cousin of Napoleon III and niece of the great Emperor Napoleon, but the marriage was not a success. In 1846 Tsar Nicholas I arranged the terms of their separation and Princesse Mathilde settled in Paris with her lover, the comte de Nieuwerke (whose collection of art, by coincidence, was also later acquired by Sir Richard Wallace)

Like his father in the 1820s, Demidoff caused a stir on the Parisian art market at a young age and soon he was acknowledged as one of the greatest collectors in Paris or, perhaps, in Europe. A key competitor of the 4th Marquess, Lord Hertford, there are many similarities in their taste. They shared a number of key enthusiasms: arms and armour, the decorative arts of 18th-century France, Old Dutch Masters and contemporary paintings. Like Lord Hertford, Demidoff had a great fondness for paintings with romantic historical

Interiors at Hertford House

Anatole Demidoff on horseback
A life-size equestrian portrait by Karl Briullov (begun c.1828, unfinished), oil on canvas, 314 x 227.
Palazzo Pittii, Florence
Commissioned by Demidoff in 1828, immediately after his father's death when Anatole himself was only sixteen, this enormous and ambitious work was never completed by the artist. 'Such a pose – and such a scale – would have been unusual for any patron other than a member of a royal family or an outstanding military commander. For a youth less than twenty it argues a degree of audacity that is breathtaking.' (Francis Haskell, 'Anatole Demidoff and the Wallace Collection', in *Anatole Demidoff, Prince of San Donato (1812-70)*, London, p.15

Illustrations for this article are reproduced by kind permission of the Trustees of the Wallace Collection

Jean-Honoré Fragonard, The Fountain of Love, c.1785, oil on canvas, 63.5 x 50.7

subjects and exotic, Oriental themes.

From 1861 to the year of his death in 1870, Anatole Demidoff, ravaged by syphilis and tired of life, began selling off his collection in a series of auctions. It is not surprising that Lord Hertford took this opportunity and made extensive purchases, al though he himself, ironically, would also die the same year. Among his acquisitions are some of the most celebrated works now in the Wallace Collection. The highlights include Ary Scheffer's *Francesca da Rimini*, showing the tragic lovers Paolo and Francesca being watched in Hell by Dante and Virgil, a poignant and sensuous picture which was hugely admired in the 19th century; many Dutch paintings; and Fragonard's *Fountain of Love*. Also purchased then were many pieces of furniture, including some beautiful mantel clocks, gold boxes and Sévres porcelain. The acquisitions from Demidoff's sales laid the foundations of the arms and armour collection,

later assembled by Sir Richard Wallace, with trophies of European and Oriental swords and even a grand Mazzaroli cannon.

In all, almost eighty works of art now in the Wallace Collection were once owned by Demidoff who thus made a remarkable if indirect contribution to the foundation of the collection. There were also striking similarities, between both the personalities and the fanatical collecting habits of Anatole Demidoff and the 4th Marquess of Hertford. As the art historian Francis Haskell wrote 'The Hertford-Demidoff' archetype of taste was eclectic: their appreciation of beauty was inextricably linked with luxury and the display of wealth. Pioneers of opulent taste, these men shaped a collection of extravagance, and today their ideal of beauty remains preserved in the rooms and galleries of Hertford House.

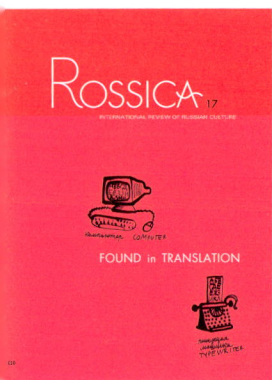

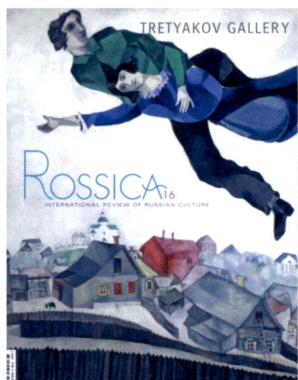

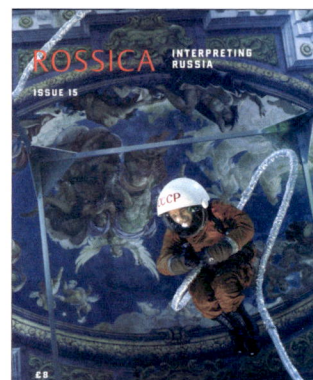

Found in Translation

Special issue devoted to the Rossica
Translation Prize.
Articles by shortlisted translators.
The Value and Values of Literary
Translation – by Amanda Hopkinson.
Vladimir Nabokov on the translator's
craft. Pioneers of Russian Translations
– by Peter France.
Borrow in Russia: A Writer in the
Making – by John Crowfoot

ROSSICA 17   £10
ISBN 978-1-905345-03-8

Tretyakov Gallery

Tireless Devotion: pages from the
history of Pavel Tretyakov's collection
– by Tatyana yudenkova. The Icon
Collection at the Tretyakov – by Lev
Lifshits. Rethinking Russia's Twentieth
Century Avant-Garde – by Svetlana
Adjoubei & Natalia Sidlina. The
Tsaritsino Collection: Contemporary
Art at the Tretyakov – by Tatyana
volkova

ROSSICA 16   £10
ISBN 978-1-905345-02-01

Interpreting Russia

Special issue devoted to the Rossica
Translation Prize.
Articles by shortlisted translators:
Oliver Ready (Winner), Robert
Chandler, Hugh Aplin, Andrew
Bromfield, Arch Tait, Michael Molnar.
Exhibitions: RUSSIA!, Circling the
Square, The House of Dreams by Ilya
Kabakov

ROSSICA 15   £8
ISBN 978-1-905345-01-4

Please note that all issues of Rossica are priced individually
Please add postage & packing – £2 for the U.K. and £3 for overseas orders

Redefining Identities
in Russian Contemporary Art

From Russian underground art to
Post-Soviet experiments
Art and Power – by Alexander
Borovsky
Uniform Pluralism – by Boris Groys
The Aesthetics of the Green Square
– by Ekaterina Degot
Exhibitions: Berlin-Moscow;
Oleg Prokofiev: Compositions

ROSSICA 9 £6

Dionisy & Kandinsky:
Revelations in Colour

Visions in Colour: Dionisy's Frescoes
at the Ferapontov Monastery (16th C.)
– by Irina Danilova & Lev Lifshits
Kandinsky and the Russian Romantic
Tradition
'The Scars Heal. The Colours Come to
Life' – by Alexander Rappaport
The History of the Walpole collection

ROSSICA 7/8 £14

The Seductions of Europe

Arkhangelskoe, the estate of Prince
Nikolai B. Yusupov, became a
sanctuary of Russian Enlightenment.
Prince Yusupov's collection rivalled
that of Catherine the Great.
Russian grand travellers in 18th-
century Europe – by Anthony Cross
Dmitry Prigov's Phantom Installations

ROSSICA 5 £6

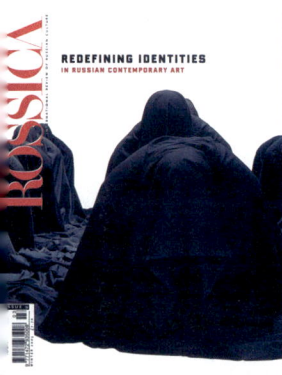

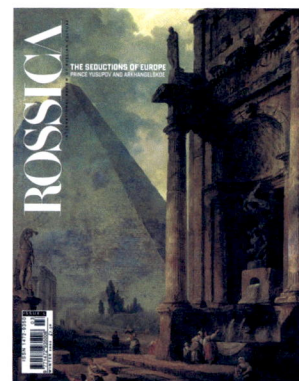

Russian Summer in London

Tamara de Lempicka: Art Deco Icon
The Sky in the Russian Landscape
by Alexander Pappaport
The Space of Russianness
by Ekaterina Degot

ROSSICA 14 £8

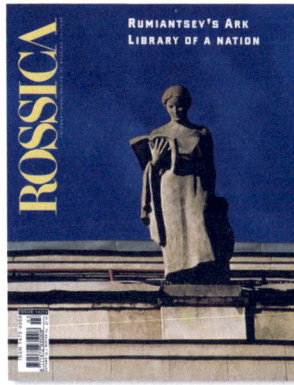

Rumiantsev's Ark:
Library of a Nation

Rumiantsev's Ark: Creation of the
National Russian Library
Nikolai Fedorov: the Philosopher-
Librarian
The Stalinist Leninka
Tributes: Metropolitan Anthony of
Sourozh; John Stuart; Catherine Cooke

ROSSICA 12/13 £8

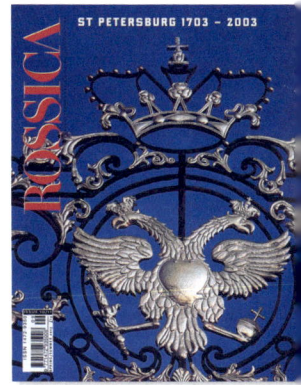

St Petersburg 1703–2003

Peter the Great and St Petersburg:
Between Heaven and Hell – by Lindsey
Hughes
Decoding St Petersburg – by
Alexander Ivanitsky
The Alexander Column: Myth of Empire
– by Grigory Sternin
Jerusalem on the Neva – by Grigory
Kaganov

ROSSICA 10/11 £14

COMPLETE YOUR ROSSICA LIBRARY

Moscow: the Third Rome,
Stalin's Capital, Global City

The Throne of Monomakh
Moscow – New Jerusalem: Myth as
Reality
A Vision of Paradise: Stalin's Moscow
Moscow as a Global City – by
Catherine Cooke

ROSSICA 4 £6

Imperial Russian Ballet

Oranienbaum: Chinoiserie a la Russe
Petipa and the Creation of Russian
Imperial Ballet
Swan Lake: Lake of Tears
The Chinese Palace at Oranienbaum,
Catherine the Great's Dacha

ROSSICA 3 £6

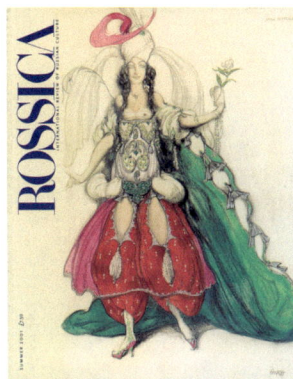

Creation of the Bolshoi
Moscow in the 1920s

The Beginning of the Bolshoi – Theatre
of Michael Maddox
The Chimes of Communism
Moscow in the 1920s: Architecture as
a Stage Set for the New Life –
by Catherine Cooke
In the Company of Saints:
Christian Relics in the Moscow Kremlin

ROSSICA 2 £6

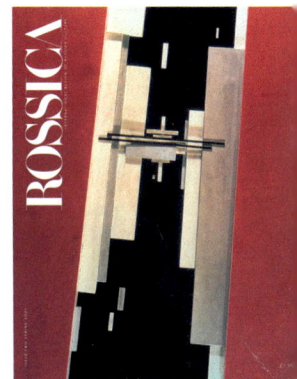

SUBSCRIBE TO ROSSICA

AN INTERNATIONAL REVIEW OF RUSSIAN CULTURE

ISSN 1472-9350

Rossica is a series of publications devoted to the many facets of Russian culture, past, present and future.

Rossica is published by Academia Rossica, a non-profit organisation (UK Registered Charity no 1091022) created in 2000 with the aim of promoting a deeper international understanding of Russian culture.

UK subscription:
1 year (4 issues) – £40
2 years (8 issues) – £75

Overseas subscription:
1 year (4 issues) – £50
2 years (8 issues) – £90

Institutional subscription:
1 year – £75 (world-wide)

I would like to subscribe to Rossica and/or order back issues

Your name :

Address :

Postcode :   Telephone :   Email :

Payment Details
Please debit £   from my Visa / MasterCard / Switch   Card No

Security Code   Expiry date   /   Issue No (Switch only)

I enclose a cheque for £   payable to Academia Rossica

Gift Aid

If you are a UK tax-payer, please help us by giving your consent to reclaim tax on your subscription, increasing the value of your contribution by 28% at no extra cost to you.

I consent to Academia Rossica claiming Gift Aid on my contributions from 6 April 2000 until further notice.

Your signature:

Please send the completed form and payment to:
Academia Rossica, 151 Kensington High Street, London W8 6SU
Tel/fax: 020 7937 5001   Email: subscription@academia-rossica.org